LITERARY
MASTERS

ISSN 1526-1530

LITERARY MASTERS

Volume **5**

Gabriel García Márquez

Joan Mellen

A MANLY, INC. BOOK

GALE GROUP

Detroit
San Francisco
London
Boston
Woodbridge, CT

GABRIEL GARCÍA MÁRQUEZ

Matthew J. Bruccoli and Richard Layman, *Editorial Directors*

ISBN 0-7876-3970-2

ISSN 1526-1530

Printed in the United States of America

10 9 8 7 6 5 4 3 2 1

TABLE OF CONTENTS

A Note to the Reader
 by Alvin Kernan vii

Acknowledgments . . . . *x*

GABRIEL GARCÍA MÁRQUEZ

CHRONOLOGY OF EVENTS IN GABRIEL GARCÍA MÁRQUEZ'S LIFE 1

ABOUT GABRIEL GARCÍA MÁRQUEZ 7
 Personal Data 7
 His Childhood and Biographical Glimpses 10
 Awards and Recognition 20

GARCÍA MÁRQUEZ AT WORK 24
 Getting Established 24
 Techniques 28
 Subject To Revision 46
 Critical Reception 49

GARCÍA MÁRQUEZ'S ERA 60
 García Márquez's Country 60
 García Márquez's Era and Time in History 65
 Lifestyle and Culture 76

GARCÍA MÁRQUEZ'S WORKS 83
 Books 83
 Scripts and Screenplays 103

Critical Summary 106

Art Imitating Life 108

The Works' Place In History 114

Adaptations 114

Public Response 117

GARCÍA MÁRQUEZ ON GARCÍA MÁRQUEZ 120
Gabriel García Márquez's Nobel Prize Lecture 120

Interview with García Márquez 125

GARCÍA MÁRQUEZ AS STUDIED 135
Other Authors Frequently Studied with García Márquez 135

Gabriel García Márquez and the Invention of America 139

RESOURCES FOR GARCÍA MÁRQUEZ STUDY 157
Study Questions 157

Glossary of Terms 161

Bibliography 163

MASTER INDEX 169

A NOTE TO THE READER

THE TELLER IN THE TALE

by Alvin Kernan,
Senior Advisor in
the Humanities,
The Andrew W.
Mellon Foundation

A few years ago it was fashionable to speak of "the death of the author" and to argue that "language writes, not the man." These post-modernist views were part of a philosophy that discounted the individuality of the writer in favor of a world of impersonal texts and systems, such as language, which furnish a "scriptor" with the only conceptions of reality he or she can have. In this view of things the author disappeared into a "mere grammatical subject"; the time and place were doing the writing, not the author.

This vast, gray, impersonal view has not prevailed, however, because it goes against the grain of what we all know and feel to be the actual case. Historically, our literature is not just a set of coded texts but living writings intertwined with the names of the men and women who wrote them. We cannot think of *The Canterbury Tales* without thinking of the sly but somewhat bumbling Geoffrey Chaucer, good-natured but sharply ironic, who introduces himself as one of the pilgrims in his own poem. And we try our best to see William Shakespeare, always a somewhat mysterious fellow, in the figure of the magician Prospero on his magic island in *The Tempest*. Charles Dickens, as a frightened boy sent to work in the blacking factory in industrialized London, hangs about his novels in the same way that Ernest Hemingway in his macho pose and his death by suicide is always present when we turn the pages of *A Farewell to Arms* or the "Up in Michigan" stories. As in the last example, the lives of the poets often throw dark shadows back on their works. The alcoholic F. Scott Fitzgerald ends his life trying desperately to write another novel as good as his early *The Great Gatsby*. Flannery O'Connor sits in her small house in Georgia, suffering from a disease—lupus—that ravages her immune system, and records experiences of Americans who are as vulnerable to the world as is her own body.

The tellers not only write the tale, but, in doing so, he or she becomes a part of it; and our sense of the tale is not complete until the teller's presence is evoked. This is one reason why biographies and vignettes, collections of biographical information, and memories of the type found in these volumes about our writers are so interesting and so useful. More than useful, really. We have not fully read the tale until we can see the teller in it, who will, if we come to know him or her well enough, sensitize us to how the tale is told and what is likely to be in it. Every tale-teller has a distinctive way of telling—the style—and a particular subject matter. To know who is writing is, therefore, to know to look for things that would otherwise escape us. Theodore Dreiser, the American novelist, was a moody man, pessimistic about the possibilities of life, convinced that our fates are woven from a host of small details, the need for a winter coat in *Sister Carrie* or the bright attractiveness of an upper-middle-class parlor in *An American Tragedy*. These ordinary details can in their bulk bore us and turn us away from the story if we are not aware that this is the Dreiserian signature, the way in which he renders the flatness of ordinary life and points to the fate that lies concealed in it.

Every author differs from every other in how and what he or she writes, but in the end they combine, if we see and know them well enough, to create a scene that is close to the center of literature, to its place and role in the world. Some writing careers portray this scene more powerfully than others do. Samuel Johnson, for example, was a personality so titanic as nearly to overwhelm his writings, physically grotesque, frequently nearly mad with depression, an impoverished hack most of his life, endlessly talking for victory and heroically facing the hard facts of human life. In Johnson's life, writing his great dictionary of the English language or his *Lives of the Poets* was his defense against the madness of emptiness and meaninglessness. That is to say, he wrote to preserve his sanity by giving order and meaning to the world and to the language through which we approach it.

Every teller of tales, when we come to know him or her, is engaged in something like this Johnsonian struggle to order and make sense of the world of random facts and experiences, to preserve some sense of things, people, and times that would otherwise be forgotten and lost forever in the past. Consider another writer, our own Southern novelist William Faulkner, a struggler who is not as successful as Johnson in his authorial task of imposing order on a messy and painful sense of the confusions of life. Faulkner's story is that of a mythical Mississippi county, Yoknapatawpha County, that he creates in an attempt to locate and order in time and space the confused and confusing memories of the Southern past, such as the Civil War and slavery and primitive wilderness, with modern-day consciousness that cannot forget the past but also cannot reconcile it with its own immediate interests and thoughts. The strain shows in Faulkner's stories, in the absence of clear chronology, in the tangled syntax of his long sentences, in his frequent descent into stream-of-consciousness writing.

To include the tellers with their tales, which is what this series of the Gale Study Guides is designed to make possible for the common reader, is to see the heroic scene of literature itself, throughout the world, where men and women writers make and have made the most skillful use of the word-hoard of language and the freedom of fiction to preserve our collective past and to make sense out of things that in their multitude are always threatening to fly apart into chaos.

ACKNOWLEDGMENTS

This book was produced by Bruccoli Clark Layman, Inc. R. Bland Lawson is the series editor and Jan Peter F. van Rosevelt is the in-house editor.

Production manager is Philip B. Dematteis.

Copyediting supervisor is Phyllis A. Avant. Senior copyeditor is Thom Harman. The copyediting staff includes Brenda Carol Blanton, James Denton, Worthy B. Evans, Melissa D. Hinton, William Tobias Mathes, and Jennifer S. Reid.

Indexing was done by Cory McNair and Alex Snead.

Layout and graphics supervisor is Janet E. Hill. Graphics staff includes Karla Corley Brown and Zoe R. Cook.

Photography editors are Charles Mims, Scott Nemzek, Alison Smith, and Paul Talbot. Digital photographic copy work was performed by Joseph M. Bruccoli.

Systems manager is Marie L. Parker.

Typesetting supervisor is Kathleen M. Flanagan. The typesetting staff includes Mark J. McEwan, Kimberly Kelly, and Patricia Flanagan Salisbury.

Gabriel García Márquez. From his Nobel Prize Lecture. 8 December 1982. Reproduced by permission.

New York Times Book Review, 5 December 1982; 7 April 1985; 21 February 1988; 11 April 1988. Copyright © 1982, 1985, 1988 by The New York Times Company. All reproduced by permission.

PHOTOGRAPHS AND ILLUSTRATIONS APPEARING IN *Literary Masters, Volume 5: Gabriel García Márquez* WERE RECEIVED FROM THE FOLLOWING SOURCES:

Simón Bolívar, portrait. From *El maestro del Libertador.* By Fabio Lozano y Lozano. P. Ollendorff, 1913.

Casa de la Finca Macondo, photograph. From *García Márquez El viaje a la semilla.* Alfaguara, 1997. Reproduced by permission.

Fabio Vásquez Cástaño, Víctor Medina Móron, Father Camilo Torres Restrepo, photograph. Joan Mellen.

Corrected proof for *El Otoño del Patriarca.* By Gabriel García Márquez. Reprinted from *Writers at Work: The Paris Review Interviews,* sixth series. Viking, 1984.

Cover of *Chronicle of a Death Foretold.* By Gabriel García Márquez. Alfred A. Knopf, 1983. Reproduced by permission of Alfred A. Knopf, Inc.

Cover of *Cien Años de Soledad.* By Gabriel García Márquez. Editorial Sudamericana. Reproduced by permission.

Cover of *El Otoño del Patriarca.* By Gabriel García Márquez. Editorial Sudamericana, 1975. Reproduced by permission.

Cover of *In Evil Hour.* By Gabriel García Márquez. Harper & Row, 1979. Reproduced by permission of HarperCollins Publishers.

Cover of *Innocent Eréndira and Other Stories.* By Gabriel García Márquez. Harper & Row, 1978. Reproduced by permission of HarperCollins Publishers.

Cover of *Love in the Time of Cholera.* By Gabriel García Márquez. Alfred A. Knopf, 1988. Reproduced by permission of Alfred A. Knopf, Inc.

Cover of *The Autumn of The Patriarch.* By Gabriel García Márquez. Harper & Row, 1976. Reproduced by permission of HarperCollins Publishers.

Cover of *The General in His Labyrinth*. By Gabriel García Márquez. Alfred A. Knopf, 1990. Reproduced by permission of Alfred A. Knopf, Inc.

Gabriel García Márquez, advertisement for *El amor en los tiempos del cólera*. From *Gabriel García Márquez*. By Waleri Semskow. Historia del Arte Colombiano Barcelona/ Bogotá. 1991.

Gabriel García Márquez and Fidel Castro, photograph. From *The Fragrance of Guava*. Verso, 1983. By Gabriel García Márquez and Plinio Apuleyo Mendoza. © Fina Torres. Reproduced by permission.

Gabriel García Márquez and Joan Mellen, photograph.

Gabriel García Márquez and Plinio Apuleyo Mendoza, photograph. From *The Fragrance of Guava. Verso,* 1983. By Plinio Apuleyo Mendoza. Reproduced by permission.

Gabriel García Márquez and Teodoro Petkoff, photograph. *From El olor de la guayaba: conversaciones con Plinio Apuleyo Mendoza.* By Gabriel García Márquez and Plinio Apuleyo Mendoza. Bruguera, 1982. Reproduced by permission.

Gabriel García Márquez as a child, photograph. From *El olor de la guayaba: conversaciones con Plinio Apuleyo Mendoza*. By Gabriel García Márquez and Plinio Apuleyo Mendoza. Bruguera, 1982. Reproduced by permission.

Gabriel García Márquez, at a Latin American press conference, photograph. From *Gabriel García Márquez*. By Waleri Semskow. Prensa Latina, La Habana, Cuba.

Gabriel García Márquez, at the Nobel Prize ceremony in Stockholm, 1982, photograph. From *Gran Enciclopedia de Espana y America. Volume III*. Archivo de Espasa Calpe y Gela. Reproduced by permission.

Gabriel García Márquez, Mario Vargas Llosa, Julio Cortazar, and Carlos Barral. From *El olor de la guayaba: conversaciones con Plinio Apuleyo Mendoza*. By Gabriel García Márquez and Plinio Apuleyo Mendoza. Bruguera, 1982. © César Malet, 1982. Reproduced by permission.

Gabriel García Márquez, photograph by Rita Guibert. From *Seven Voices: Seven Latin American Writers Talk to Rita Guibert*. Alfred A. Knopf, 1973. Reproduced by permission of Alfred A. Knopf, Inc.

Gabriel García Márquez, photograph by Sara Facio-Alicia D'Amico. From *Seven Voices: Seven Latin American Writers Talk to Rita*

Guibert. Alfred A. Knopf, 1973. Reproduced by permission of Alfred A. Knopf, Inc.

Gabriel García Márquez, photograph. From *Gabriel García Márquez*. By Miguel Fernandez-Braso. Editorial Azur, 1969. Reproduced by permission.

Gabriel García Márquez signing books, photograph. From *Gabriel García Márquez*. By Waleri Semskow. Prensa Latina, La Habana, Cuba.

Irene Papas, in the motion picture *Eréndira*, photograph. From *Gabriel García Márquez*. By Waleri Semskow. Ardriv Film und Fernseheu, Berlin.

CHRONOLOGY

1928: Gabriel José García Márquez is born 6 March in Aracataca, Colombia, a tiny coastal town between Barranquilla and Santa Marta controlled by the Liberal Party, to Gabriel Eligio García and Luisa Santiago Márquez Iguarán. His father will later contend that the year of his birth was actually 1927.

1928–1936: García Márquez lives in the house of his maternal grandparents, Colonel Nicolás Ricardo Márquez Mejia and Tranquilina Iguaran.

1936–1940: When he is eight years old, García Márquez's grandfather dies, and he goes to live with his parents in Sucre, where his father is working as a pharmacist. He is sent to study at a boarding school in Barranquilla.

1940: At the age of twelve, García Márquez receives a scholarship to a secondary school run by Jesuits, the Liceo Nacional in Zipaquirá.

1946: García Márquez earns his *bachillerato* (high-school diploma).

1947: Enrolled as a law student at the Universidad Nacional in Bogotá, García Márquez publishes his first story, "La tercera resignación," in the newspaper *El Espectador* (Bogotá). The editor hails him as "the new genius of Colombian letters!"

1948–1949: Following the assassination of the Liberal senator Julio Eliécer Gaitán on 9 April 1948 and the subsequent rioting (called El Bogotázo), the National University is closed. García Márquez transfers to the Universidad de Cartagena, where he studies law while writing a column for *El Universal* (Cartagena).

1950–1952: García Márquez writes for *El Heraldo* and *El Nacional* in Barranquilla. He joins a literary circle called "el grupo de Barranquilla" and reads the works of Ernest Hemingway, James Joyce, Virginia Woolf, and William Faulkner.

1953: Quitting journalism temporarily, García Márquez travels around Colombia working at various jobs, including a stint selling encyclopedias in La Guajira. He becomes formally engaged to Mercedes Barcha Pardo.

1954: García Márquez moves back to Bogotá and joins the staff of *El Espectador* as a reporter and movie reviewer.

1955: García Márquez wins the Colombian Association of Writers and Artists Award for the story "Un día despues del sábado." *El Espectador* sends García Márquez to Italy to cover the death of Pope Pius XII, believed to be imminent. Back in Colombia, García Márquez's friends discover in his desk drawer the manuscript of a novel he had finished and take it to a publisher; his first novella, *La hojarasca,* is published in Bogotá. The Rojas Pinilla dictatorship closes down *El Espectador,* and García Márquez remains in Europe, where he studies in Rome at the Centro Sperimentale Cinematografico.

1956: A freelance journalist in Paris, García Márquez also works on the manuscripts for *La mala hora* and *El coronel no tiene quien escriba.*

1957: García Márquez and his friend Plinio Apuleyo Mendoza travel through the countries of the Communist Eastern Bloc; he then lives in London for two months. Late in the year, García Márquez goes to Venezuela and begins working for the newspaper *Momento* (Caracas).

1958: In March, García Márquez marries Mercedes in Barranquilla, Colombia. The couple returns to Venezuela. The novella *El coronel no tiene quien escriba* is published in *Mito* (Bogotá) magazine.

1959: García Márquez's son Rodrigo is born. García Márquez helps set up the Bogotá bureau of the Cuban news agency Prensa Latina, and works at the main office in Havana, Cuba. In 1960 the family moves to New York City, where García Márquez supervises the North American branch of Prensa Latina.

1961: García Márquez resigns from Prensa Latina and moves to Mexico City, traveling by bus across the United States. In Mexico

City, García Márquez is an editor for the magazines *Sucesos* and *La Familia*. He wins the Colombian Esso Prize for *La mala hora*.

1962: García Márquez's second son, Gonzalo, is born. *Los funerales de la Mamá Grande* is published in Mexico. *La mala hora* is published in Spain; García Márquez repudiates the book after the publisher removes "objectionable passages" and all Latin American idiom.

1963: García Márquez moves to a house in the San Angel Inn section of Mexico City. *El coronel no tiene quien escriba* is published (in book form) in Medellin, Colombia. He works for the Mexican branch of the J. Walter Thompson advertising agency and cowrites his first screenplay with Carlos Fuentes.

1965: In January, García Márquez begins writing *Cien años de soledad*.

1966: The authorized edition of *La mala hora* is published in Mexico.

1967: In June *Cien años de soledad* is published in Buenos Aires. Within a week all eight thousand copies are sold. *Isabel viendo llover en Macondo*, a novella, is published in Buenos Aires. In October, García Márquez moves to Barcelona, where he meets Mario Vargas Llosa, the Peruvian novelist.

1968: *No One Writes to the Colonel and Other Stories* is published in New York. García Márquez and Vargas Llosa publish *La novela en América Latina: Diálogo*.

1970: *One Hundred Years of Solitude* is published in New York and is chosen as one of the twelve best books of the year by U.S. critics. *Relato de un naufrago* is published in Barcelona.

1971: García Márquez receives an honorary Doctorate of Letters (LL.D.) from Columbia University in New York City. Vargas Llosa publishes the first book-length study of García Márquez's writing, *García Márquez: Historia de un deicidio*.

1972: *La increíble y triste historia de la candida Eréndira y su abuela desalmada* is published in Barcelona. Unauthorized publications of *Ojos de perro azul* in Argentina and of "Nabo, el negro que hizo esperar a los ángeles" in Uruguay appear. *Leaf Storm and Other Stories* is published in New York.

1973: García Márquez travels in Spain, France, and Mexico. A collection of early journalism, *Cuando era feliz e indocumentado,* is published in Venezuela.

1974: García Márquez founds *Alternativa,* a leftist magazine, in Bogotá.

1975: *El Otoño del patriarca* and *Todos los cuentos* are published in Barcelona. García Márquez leaves Spain and alternately resides in Bogotá and Cuernevaca, Mexico.

1976: *The Autumn of the Patriarch* is published in New York.

1977: *Operación Carlota,* a nonfiction account of Cuban participation in the Angolan Revolution, is published in Peru.

1978: *Innocent Eréndira and Other Stories* is published in New York. *De viaje por los paises socialistas: 90 dias en la "Cortina de Hierro,"* a collection of pieces García Márquez wrote about his 1957 trip through Eastern Europe, is published in Colombia. Two collections of journalistic pieces, *Crónicas y reportajes* and *Periodismo militante,* are published in Bogotá.

1980–1983: García Márquez writes a weekly column syndicated in Hispanic newspapers and magazines on subjects ranging from Johann Sebastian Bach to the "disappearances" of writers under the Argentine military regime.

1981: García Márquez is awarded the French Legion of Honor Medal and attends the inauguration of President François Mitterand. When he returns to Colombia from Cuba, the Conservative government accuses him of financing M–19, a guerrilla group. He flees Colombia and seeks political asylum in Mexico. *Crónica de una muerta anunciada* is published simultaneously in Colombia, Argentina, Mexico, and Spain.

1981–1983: *Obra periodistica,* four volumes of García Márquez's journalistic pieces, edited by Jacques Gilard, is published.

1982: García Márquez wins the Nobel Prize in literature. *El olor de la guayaba,* conversations with his friend Plinio Apuleyo Mendoza, is published in Buenos Aires. García Márquez writes *Viva Sandino,* an unproduced screenplay about the Nicaraguan Revolution, which is published in Nicaragua. *El rastro detu sangra en la* *nieve: El verano feliz de la señora Forbes* is published in Bogotá, as is *Chronicle of a Death Foretold* in London.

1983: García Márquez returns to Colombia from his exile in Mexico. *Chronicle of a Death Foretold* is published in New York and is nominated for the *Los Angeles Times* Book Prize. The motion picture *Eréndira,* with a screenplay adapted from García Márquez's novella *La increíble ye triste historia de la candida Erédira y su abuela desalmada,* is released by Les Films du Triangle. *The Fragrance of Guava* is published in London.

1984: García Márquez and Guillermo Nolasco-Juarez collaborate on *Persecución y muerte de minorias: dos perspectivas,* published in Buenos Aires. *Collected Stories* is published in New York.

1985: *El amor en los tiempos del colera* is published in Argentina, Colombia, Cuba, and Spain. García Márquez founds the New Latin American Cinema Foundation in Havana, of which he is president. *Tiempo de morir,* a motion picture based on a screenplay by García Márquez and Fuentes, is released in Mexico.

1986: García Márquez addresses the inaugural ceremony of the Ixtapa Summit in Mexico, attended by the presidents of Argentina, Mexico, and Tanzania and the prime ministers of Greece, India, and Sweden; his speech is later published as *El cataclismo de Damocles* in Bogotá. *The Story of a Shipwrecked Sailor* is published in New York and *La aventura de Miguel Littin, clandestino en Chile: un reportage* is published in Madrid.

1987: *Clandestine in Chile: The Adventures of Miguel Littin* is published in New York.

1988: *Love in the Time of Cholera* is published in New York. García Márquez's play *Diatriba de amor contra un hombre sentado: monologo en un acto* is produced at Cervantes Theater, Buenos Aires.

1989: The historical novel *El general en su labertino* is published simultaneously in Argentina, Colombia, Mexico, and Spain.

1990: *The General in His Labyrinth* and *Collected Novellas* are published in New York, as is *Primeros reportajes* in Caracas. A stage adaptation of the novel *Crónica de una muerte anunciada* is performed at the Public Theater in New York.

1991: A collection of journalism, *Notas de prensa, 1980–1984,* is published in Madrid.

1992: *Doce cuentos peregrinos* is published simultaneously in Argentina, Colombia, Mexico, and Spain; and *Elogio de la utopia: Una entrevista de Nahuel Maciel* is published in Buenos Aires.

1993: *Strange Pilgrims: Twelve Stories* is published in New York as are *The Handsomest Drowned Man in the World: A Tale for Children,* in Minnesota; the play *Diatriba de amor contra un hombre sentado,* in Bogotá; and the novel *Del amor y otros demonios,* in Barcelona.

1995: *Of Love and Other Demons* is published in New York.

1997: *News of a Kidnapping* is published in New York. It is reported that a motion-picture adaptation of *Autumn of the Patriarch* will be made, with Marlon Brando in the title role and Sean Penn as director.

1998: García Márquez is a guest of Fidel Castro during the historic visit of Pope John Paul II to Cuba.

1999: García Márquez purchases *Cambio,* a Colombian newsmagazine, and begins writing for it. In June he is hospitalized in Bogotá for fatigue; in September it is announced that he is in Los Angeles undergoing treatment for lymphatic cancer.

ABOUT GABRIEL GARCÍA MÁRQUEZ

Born: 6 March 1928 in Aracataca, Colombia

Married: Mercedes Barcha, March 1958

Education: Attended Universidad Nacional de Colombia, 1947–1948, and Universidad de Cartagena, 1948–1949

Gabriel García Márquez is the most widely read novelist writing in Spanish and the most critically acclaimed in his native Colombia, in Latin America, and, some have argued, in the world. His best-known novel, *Cien años de soledad* (1967; translated as *One Hundred Years of Solitude,* 1970), introduced readers to the technique of "magic realism," the mixture of fantasy and actuality for which this author has become known. In the magic realism of García Márquez, nature defies reason and logic, but always in the service of his profoundly humane worldview. He calls himself a "realist," adding that "reality is not restricted to the price of tomatoes."[1]

When *One Hundred Years of Solitude* was applauded as, at last, "the great American novel," García Márquez modestly demurred. "The great American novel," he argued, "was written by Herman Melville."[2] He was referring, of course, to *Moby-Dick; or, The Whale* (1851). "I am a writer through timidity," he has remarked, minimizing his storytelling mastery, "my real vocation is that of a conjurer."[3]

Tne Hundred Years of Solitude was followed by a series of master works, *El otoño del patriarca* (1975; translated as *The Autumn of the Patriarch,* 1976), which García Márquez considers his most personal book, his most artful and most complex; *Crónica de una muerte anunciada* (1982; translated as *Chronicle Of A Death Foretold,* 1982), a novella-length work that provides a microcosm of Colombian society; and *El amor en los tiempos del cólera* (1985; translated as *Love in the Time of Cholera,* 1988), an elegiac hymn to the love between his parents. Meanwhile, García Márquez

Gabriel García Márquez in the early 1970s

continued to practice the craft with which he began, that of the journalist. He honed his craft on American models rather than from the local examples, which he has said were "very heavy then, academic, classic, very Spanish."⁴ His themes have included the loneliness of solitude, its selfishness and its solace, the need for human solidarity, and the dangerous temptation of nostalgia. Those who are spiritually defeated in his novels, such as the Buendía clan in *One Hundred Years of Solitude* and Simon Bolívar in the historical novel, *El general en su laberinto* (1989; translated as *The General in His Labyrinth,* 1990), have sacrificed selflessness and connection to the community for their own desires, dreams, and ambitions.

Yet, solitude can be a comfort, as it is for the alter ego of García Márquez, Colonel Aureliano Buendía, hero of *One Hundred Years of Solitude,* who makes an appearance in several of his books. The Colonel, who haunts the fiction of García Márquez, in retirement from the civil wars between the Liberals and Conservatives that have revealed to him only the futility of the quest for power, fashions tiny fishes out of gold. Only in his laboratory does Colonel Aureliano Buendía discover a refuge from war, madness, and pain.

García Márquez has been a political man, a socialist, and man of the Left, as much as he has been a writer; however, he has never joined a political party. Instead he has called himself an "anti-colonial Latin American."⁵ In the late 1970s he refused an invitation to run for the presidency of Colombia (unlike his fellow novelist and biographer, Mario Vargas Llosa, who ran for the presidency of Peru and lost). García Márquez has also refused ambassadorships.

"I am an emergency politician," he has declared. "If I were not a Latin American, I would not be in politics. But how can the intellectual enjoy the luxury of debating the destiny of the soul when the problems are of physical survival, health, education, ignorance and so on?"⁶ Having lived in New York City as a correspondent for the Cuban news agency Prensa Latina in 1960, he has remarked that the people of the United States "will be the ones to create a great socialist revolution, and a good one too."[7] He has called New York "the greatest phenomenon of our time."[8]

He has been an international man, and by the time he was forty-three years old he had lived for three years in Spain, for one in Rome, for two or three in Paris, and for seven or eight in Mexico. He continues to believe that "it's very important for a Latin American writer to view Latin America from Europe at some given moment." Nor has it mattered to him where he lives. He has always found people who interested him, "whether in Barranquilla, Rome, Paris or Barcelona."[9]

He considers himself a man of imagination. "Anyone who doesn't contradict himself is a dogmatist," he has said. "And every dogmatist is a reactionary."[10] He has, however, taken many political stands. He was active in the campaign of President Omar Torrijos to persuade the United States to grant Panama sovereignty over the canal; he helped the Sandinistas of Nicaragua by serving as an intermediary for them with other governments; he has "conspired," as he put it, to promote peace talks between warring factions in El Salvador; and he has been an intermediary between the Colombian government and the guerrilla movements.

As were other Latin American artists, he was dismayed when in 1971 Fidel Castro jailed poet Herberto Padilla for his views. Padilla was forced to make a Stalinist-style confession before he was released. Other novelists broke with Cuba, but García Márquez termed Castro's action a "mistake" and vowed to combat such evils "from the inside." He noted that it was "only when there were problems with intellectuals in Cuba that intellectuals began to break with Cuba, and I think this is politically immature."[11]

He has also observed that since "intellectuals consider themselves the moral conscience of society," their perspective generally follows "moral rather than political channels." He distinguishes himself from such writers. "I think I am the most politicized of them all," he has said. Of his personal views, he has said he believes "the world ought to be socialist, that it will be, and that we should help this to happen as quickly as possible." As for the socialism practiced in the former Soviet Union, he was adamant: "that isn't socialism."[12]

In 1974 he helped found a magazine in Bogotá called *Alternativa,* to which he contributed political journalism, including articles on the liberation of Angola and the last days of President Salvador Allende of Chile, overthrown and killed in a military coup in 1973.

The magazine folded in 1980, partly because it refused to accept advertising; that a bomb had exploded in the offices was also a decided setback. Over the years García Márquez has continued to write journalism, arguing that there is no essential difference between one form of writing and another. In the early 1980s, however, he requested political asylum from Mexico. The guerrillas of the populist faction M-19 (Movimiento 19 de Abril; 19th of April Movement) had boasted that he was financing their activities and his name had been marked for arrest by the government of Colombia.

In 1982 he was awarded the Nobel Prize in literature. The previous year he had told the *Paris Review* that winning the Nobel would be "an absolute catastrophe. I would certainly be interested in deserving it, but to receive it would be terrible. It would just complicate even more the problems of fame." He went on to remark, "The only thing I really regret in life is not having a daughter."[13]

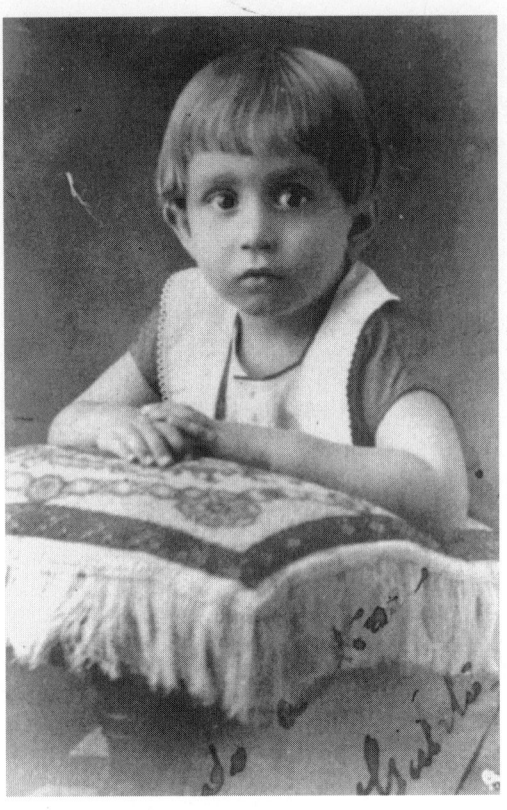

García Márquez at the age of two

HIS CHILDHOOD AND BIOGRAPHICAL GLIMPSES

Gabriel García Márquez was born on 6 March 1928 in Aracataca, a dusty Caribbean village between Barranquilla and Santa Marta in what was once the banana zone; it was settled by people who had fled the civil wars that beset Colombia for a century. The town had been built by the United Fruit Company with wooden shacks and roofs made of zinc and tin. His father, Gabriel Eligio García, however, later contended that his eldest son, the first of sixteen children, was in fact born in 1927. García Márquez has remarked, "no one knows for sure."[14]

His father was a telegraph operator. His mother, Luisa Santiago Márquez Iguaran, was of a higher social status; her father, who had been a colonel in the civil wars, opposed the marriage because Gabriel Eligio Garciá was a Conservative, was illegitimate, and was known to have been with many women. They would be married for sixty years.

Just prior to Gabriel's birth, his mother came home to Aracataca from Riohacha, where she and her husband had settled. "Come have the baby in our house," her parents pleaded. Then they added, "Leave Gabriel with us to raise."[15]

It was a commonplace practice of the Caribbean for grandparents to raise a child when the parents were poor. He was left to be raised by his grandparents and aunts in a large rambling house in the hot dusty town of Aracataca, the model for the town of Macondo in *One Hundred Years of Solitude*.

His maternal grandfather, Colonel Nicolas Márquez, had fathered more than a dozen illegitimate children and had served in the civil wars. He was, García Márquez has said, "the person I've gotten along with best and had the best communication with ever."[16] His grandfather took him to the circus and to the cinema and, he has said, "was my umbilical cord with history and reality."[17] "The guardian angel of my infancy was an old man— my grandfather."[18] Yet, he knew his grandfather had killed a man. Once, taking his grandson Gabriel to the circus, the colonel had stopped to exclaim: "Oh! You don't know how much a dead man weighs."[19]

His maternal grandmother, Tranquilina Iguaran, was addicted to telling fables and family legends and organizing his life according to the messages she received in her dreams. Her stories did not distinguish between the living and the dead. She was his "source of the magical, superstitious and supernatural view of reality."[20] Growing up among adults, he drew comic strips and cartoons before he could even write. His earliest recollection was of drawing these comics, which illustrated the stories his grandmother told him.

Once, when his mother came to visit, he walked into a room where many women were sitting. He did not know which one was his mother. "She wore a dress from the twenties with a low waistline and a straw hat," he remembered later. "Then she embraced me and I became very frightened because I felt I didn't love her."[21] It seemed evil to the boy not to love his mother.

ON HIS GRANDPARENTS

"They had an enormous house, full of ghosts. They were very superstitious and impressionable people. In every corner there were skeletons and memories, and after six in the evening you didn't dare leave your room. It was a world of fantastic terrors. There were coded conversations."

García Márquez

From Luis Harss and Barbara Dohmann, "Gabriel García Márquez, or the Lost Chord," *Into the Mainstream: Conversations with Latin-American Writers* (New York: Harper & Row, 1967), p. 319.

His grandfather died when he was eight years old; García Márquez later remarked, "Desde entonces no me ha pasado nada interesante" (Since then nothing interesting has happened to me).[22] He left the Montessori School in Aracataca in 1936 and returned to the house of his parents, who were now living in Sucre. He did not remain for long.

"I was living in a house where a new child was born every year," he later recalled. By the time he was thirteen years old, he must have had "about eight brothers."[23] He decided then that the only solution for him was to leave, both for his own survival and to lighten the daily burden of his family. He went as a boarding student to the Colegio de San José in Barranquilla. He was already a studious boy who shunned athletics and had been writing poetry from the age of ten. When he transferred to the "Colegio de Jesuitas," he was so serious that he became known as "the Old Man."

In 1940 he left Barranquilla to go to Bogotá to take the examinations for a scholarship. He studied at the Liceo Nacional in Zipaquirá, a high school for the gifted near Bogotá. At once he hated living in the interior, with its cold weather and the repressive culture.

He was shocked by Bogotá, where he found the men all dressed in black, wearing hats, and where there were no women in the streets. All his life he would consider it his great "good fortune" to have been born on the Caribbean coast rather than in Bogotá where, he says wryly in *Love in the Time of Cholera,* it has been drizzling since the year one. The cold offended him.

García Márquez writes in his coda to *The General in His Labyrinth* that as a student returning home on school vacations and holidays, he "sailed the [Magdalena] river eleven times in both directions, traveling on steamboats that came out of the shipyards of the Mississippi already condemned to nostalgia and possessed of a mythic call that no writer could resist."[24] He later set *Love in the Time of Cholera* in the Caribbean city he has called the most beautiful in the world, Cartagena de Indias, the walled city where Sir Francis Drake plied his "pirate" trade, as García Márquez calls it, and where neither Europe nor the United States are particularly noticed. Its beauty is introverted.

He only returned to Aracataca once, at the age of sixteen, when his grandmother died and he and his mother returned to sell the family home. This trip inspired him to begin his great novel *One*

Hundred Years of Solitude, whose first title was "La Casa" (The House).

After receiving his *bachillerato* (high-school diploma) in 1946, he headed for the Universidad Nacional in Bogotá. There he planned to study law, since law and medicine were the usual occupations for bright young men of his class. Then he read the fiction of Franz Kafka and discovered a type of literature different from that he had been taught in secondary school." In 1946 or 1947 a friend loaned to him a book of Kafka's short stories. He began with *The Metamorphosis* (1915):

> The first line almost knocked me off the bed. I was so surprised. The first line reads, "As Gregor Samsa awoke that morning from uneasy dreams, he found himself transformed in his bed into a gigantic insect." When I read the line I thought to myself that I didn't know anyone was allowed to write things like that. If I had known, I would have started writing a long time ago. So I immediately started writing short stories.[25]

He has said that Kafka made him want to write, that at eight o'clock the next morning, he set out to explore the history of fiction from the Bible to the present.

In his freshman year at the Universidad Nacional he published his first story, "La tercera resignacion" (The Third Resignation), about a boy who lives for eighteen years in a coffin. It won a contest sponsored by the *El Especdador* newspaper and was published in its Sunday supplement. The literary editor, Eduardo Zalamea Borda, proclaimed young "Gabito," as he was called by his friends, "the new genius of Colombian letters!" People told him his work had "Joycean influences."[26]

These comments amused García Márquez, who had never read the works of the Irish author James Joyce. He began to read Joyce's novel *Ulysses* (1922) and discovered the technique of the interior monologue. When he later read the work of British writer Virginia Woolf, he found he liked "the way she uses it better than Joyce."[27] He also discovered that the writer who really invented this technique was the author of the anonymous Spanish picaresque novel, *Lazarillo de Tormes* (1554). In the next six years García Márquez published ten short stories in *El Especdador.* His law studies at the Universidad Nacional were interrupted by the assassination on 9 April 1948 of Liberal politician Jorge Eliécer Gaitán, who had become well known for his inquiry into the banana-zone strike of 1928. The boarding house in which García Márquez was living caught on fire in the upheaval and chaos of "el Bogotázo," the riots that followed the death of the popular leader. The university was shut down, and García Márquez transferred to the Universidad de Cartagena. Once again he was a *costeño,* a man of the coast.

In Cartagena someone told him he needed "a foundation," and so he began to read the works of the ancient Greeks, Sophocles in particular; the influence of his *Antigone* can be discerned in the first novel of García Márquez, *La hojarasca* (1955; translated in *Leaf Storm and Other Stories,* 1972), with its narrative of a community refusing to bury a body. Of Sophocles' *Oedipus Rex,* García Márquez has said, "It's a perfect structure, wherein the investigator discovers that he is himself the assassin . . . an apotheosis of technical perfection."[28] He also read more of William Faulkner, discovering that "his world—the world of the southern United States . . . was very like my world . . . it was created by the same people." He has called Faulkner "a Latin American writer. His world is that of the Gulf of Mexico."[29]

He also began to write a five-hundred-word column for *El Universal,* a newspaper. His topics ranged from parrots to twins to astrology. In 1949 he contracted pneumonia and was bedridden for several months. There was nothing to do but read, and he read, voraciously, the works of Faulkner, Ernest Hemingway, Joyce, and Woolf.

In 1950 he moved to Barranquilla, where he was part of the "Barranquilla group" of young intellectuals led by Ramon Vinyes, an erudite Catalonian book dealer and writer. Every day he would debate with three young reporters at Vinyes's bookshop. "We would argue at the top of our voices," Germán Vargas, one of his fellow reporters, later recalled.[30] García Márquez was now writing a column for the *El Heraldo* newspaper, which was called "La Jirafa" (The Giraffe). He signed it "Septimus," after Septimus Warren Smith, a character in Woolf's novel *Mrs. Dalloway* (1925).

In the afternoons he worked on *Leaf Storm.* Extremely poor, he lived upstairs in a brothel on a street called Calle del Crimen (Street of Crime) and became acquainted with the prostitutes, who were later to figure in his fiction. He remained on *El Heraldo* until 1952. The following year, 1953, he quit journalism briefly, working at several jobs—he even sold encyclopedias, an experience enlivened by the fact that on one of his forays he met the grandson of the man his grandfather had murdered.

In February of 1954, García Márquez moved to Bogotá to work on *El Especdador.* He became the first regular movie critic in Colombia and the first there to praise French motion-picture director François Truffaut's landmark Nouvelle Vague (New Wave) work, *The Four Hundred Blows* (1959). In 1955 García Márquez wrote the serialized nonfiction account of a Colombian Navy sailor named Luis Alejandro Velasco, the only survivor of several crewmen of the destroyer *Caldas* who were swept

García Márquez (right) with Teodoro Petkoff, founder of the Venezuelan political party Movimiento al Socialismo, in 1972

overboard in heavy seas; originally published in *El Espectador,* the tale later appeared in book form as *Relato de un naúfrago* (1970; translated as *The Story of a Shipwrecked Sailor,* 1986). The *El Espectador* serial became controversial when Velasco revealed that his ship had foundered because the vessel had been overloaded with contraband.

Because of the reaction to the Velasco account, it seemed politically expeditious for García Márquez to leave town, and *El Espectador* sent him to Europe to cover a Big Four conference and to Rome in anticipation of the death of the ailing Pope Pius XII, who did not in fact die until 1958. He enrolled for a short time at the Centro Sperimentale di Cinema, where he studied cinema, prefiguring his later interest in screenwriting. In 1956 he moved to Paris. His job as a foreign correspondent came to an end because back in Colombia the dictator Rojas Pinilla shut down *El Espectador.*

In Paris he spent his time writing; sometimes all he had to live on was the money he made returning bottles for their deposits, and he depended on the kindness of a landlady who allowed him to stay in her attic.

He lost weight. He sent his mother a photograph and she replied, "Poor Gabito. He looks like a skeleton."[31] He returned to South America—not to Colombia, but to Venezuela, where he worked on *Momento* and other magazines.

García Márquez proposed to Mercedes Barcha, a pharmacist, before he left for Europe; they were married in March of 1958. He has insisted that he does not even now know exactly how old she is, that there is "a secret part of every personality never revealed to anyone."[32] Their first son, Rodrigo, was born in 1959.

When Rodrigo was born, there was an immediate problem. García Márquez was an atheist. Yet, in order for a child to be officially registered in Colombia, he had to be baptized. Then García Márquez remembered his old classmate at the National University, Camilo Torres Restrepo, who was a priest. García Márquez knew that Torres was "different from other priests."

García Márquez had met Torres in 1947 at the law school, although neither went on to practice law. García Márquez remembers that "everyone was interested in politics at that time, some from the point of view of poetry, some from the point of view of sociology, everyone except Camilo," who would become the most important political figure in Colombia of his day. They were both on the staff of the university magazine, *La Raison*. The whole experience of the university had been a revelation for García Márquez; as he remarked, he "came from the coast," and so "wasn't acquainted with the whole social mechanism of the city."

Torres decided to become a priest and ran away from home to join the seminary at Chinquinquira, only to have his mother pursue him and drag him back from the station. When García Márquez visited Torres at his home a few days later, however, Torres told him that he was still going to be a priest, but he was joining a different order, one more affluent and closer to home. Torres gave him as a going-away present a book from his library, a translation of *A Short History of the World* (1922) by H. G. Wells, in what García Márquez calls "a rustic edition."

When García Márquez went to work on *El Espectador*, in Bogotá, Torres was ordained. His friends were amazed because they were used to another kind of priest. Father Camilo Torres was neither overtly saintly or obsessive. Anything could be discussed with him. "How strange," García Márquez had told Torres when he first joined the seminary, "the last thing I would have thought of was that you would have wanted to become a priest." Once, talking to Torres about another priest, García Márquez had remarked, casually, "Oh, he's the kind of priest who believes in God." Torres bridled. "Wait a minute. I believe in God too." "Yes, you do, but you don't look like you do," García Márquez told him.

A priest who smoked cigars, frequented cafés, and drew the admiration of women attracted the attention of García Márquez. He was happy to know a priest like this, even as, in his fiction, he ponders the kind of man that women like. This pondering is a theme that runs through his work and culminates in *Love in The Time Of Cholera*. Torres lacked sensuality, and even seemed cold, at first appearance, but the attraction he exerted was exceptional.

García Márquez's sister Licia lived with them. When Torres visited, she would lock herself in her room because she felt there was something "wrong with her." She was sinning in being so attracted to a man who was a priest; a similar motif appears in *Chronicle of a Death Foretold* where the sister of the narrator, who is a nun, is also worldly and gets drunk. If García Márquez at times seems anticlerical in his fiction, not least in his depiction of the bishop in *Chronicle of a Death Foretold,* who refuses to set foot on land and baptize anyone, but stops only to collect cockscombs for his soup, it is in part because there was no priest García Márquez could admire except his friend Camilo Torres.

One day Torres turned up at García Márquez's house for lunch, as he did often. He told Mercedes and Gabo about a young man who was a cat burglar. He wanted to rehabilitate himself, but the problem was when people would help by giving him clothes, the police would recognize him in the street and conclude that what he was wearing had been stolen. He would be arrested yet again. It seemed almost a plot from a García Márquez story.

Accepting Torres's recommendation, García Márquez and his wife took the cat burglar under their wing. García Márquez wrote a "testimonial," a certificate for the cat burglar so that when he was given anything, the police would not accuse him of having stolen it. One day the maid arrived and opened the newspaper. "These are your husband's shoes!" she told Mercedes. In the newspaper was a photograph of the cat burglar, who had been killed wearing a pair of shoes García Márquez had given him. He had been carrying his certificate, but he was still killed for wearing the shoes.

Torres agreed to baptize Rodrigo only because Mercedes persuaded him that she at least believed in God and would superintend the child's religious upbringing. It was September of 1959, nine months after the Cuban revolution, and like many Latin American writers and intellectuals, García Márquez was a supporter of Fidel Castro.

The chosen godfather was a Communist. "We are going to make of this child a revolutionary and a guerrilla fighter," he announced. The woman who was to be the godmother admitted that she was not all too sure of the existence of God. Torres was angry. "All you people think about is guns and war," he declared. "We're going to make him a soldier of Christ."

At the chapel, Torres said, "I'm going to baptize him in Spanish so all you atheists and communists will know what this is about." García Márquez believes this may have been the first baptism in Spanish in Colombia, because it was still illegal prior to the reforms of Vatican II that in 1963 allowed the liturgy to be performed in the vernacular rather than Latin.

"He who believes that the body of Christ is now entering this child should kneel," said Torres, according to the baptismal ritual. No one knelt, except for an Indian man who happened to be standing at the door of the chapel. Torres poured the water and concluded the baptism. Then, when they were all out in he street, he expressed his fury. "You are a bunch of sons-of-bitches. You could have knelt at least out of good manners," he told them. "No," García Márquez answered, "because it was a challenge on your part."[33]

Torres, both an activist and a leading figure in "liberation theology," became a national leader in Colombia, arguably the most popular political figure in the country. When his life was threatened by the government and it seemed impossible that his movement, Frente Unido (United Front), could ever take power, he joined the main leftist guerrilla organization, the Ejército de Liberación Nacional (ELN, Army of National Liberation). Camilo Torres died in combat against the Colombian army in February of 1966.

In 1960 García Márquez lived for six months in Havana, working for the Cuban news agency Prensa Latina. He moved to New York City to open a Prensa Latina office there and found himself threatened by Cuban exiles. He kept an iron pipe beside his desk and was not deterred when, while he was driving to his home in Queens, a car drew up alongside, and he spotted a gun pointed at him. He left the news agency only when Jorge Massetti, the friend who had gotten him the job, was fired as Cuba was being taken over by the old Communist Party cadre. García Márquez resigned in solidarity and wound up in Mexico City working for the J. Walter Thompson Agency and other advertising agencies to support his family. In Mexico City he wrote the book that changed his life, *One Hundred Years of Solitude*. His second son, Gonzalo, was born there in 1962.

"There is no way one can relate to contemporary cultural life without going to the United States."

García Márquez

From Alan Riding, "Revolution and the Intellectual in Latin America," *The New York Times*, 13 March 1983, p.28.

To escape the tumult of his extraordinary success, in October of 1967 he moved to Barcelona, where he became friends with Mario Vargas Llosa, who later wrote what remains the only true biography of the novelist, *García Márquez: Historia de un Deicidio* (Garcia Márquez: Story of a Deicide, 1971). He was in Spain to observe the dictatorship of Generalissimo Francisco Franco up close, in preparation for his next book. The atmosphere of Spain under Franco was so cold and repressive, so unlike what he needed, that he returned to the Caribbean for a year, capturing the taste of the indigenous dictatorships. He planned to write this book in one year. It took seven. *The Autumn of the Patriarch* was published in 1975, the year of Franco's death.

Because he had worked for the Cuban news agency, after 1960 the United States government refused to grant García Márquez a visa to enter the country. When he was awarded an honorary doctorate from Columbia University in 1971, because of his politics he was given only a "conditional" or provisional visa, which required an official invitation, with restrictions. In 1984 he was invited to attend a discussion of United States policies in Central America, but because once more he was offered only one of these provisional visas, he refused to participate. His reasons were "principle and personal dignity."

Throughout his career, both in his journalism and in his fiction, García Márquez has been a writer with a pronounced worldview. He believes life would be happier were people to resist the twin temptations of solitude and nostalgia. "[T]he whole disaster of Macondo," he has said, "comes from this lack of solidarity—the solitude which results when everyone is acting for himself alone." Solitude for García Márquez becomes "a political concept" in his effort "to give solitude the political connotation I believe it should have."[34] Both solitude and nostalgia, he reveals, lead to isolation, narcissism, and lack of empathy for others. His work praises compassion over pettiness in the face of a chaotic and absurd universe.

He recognizes as the highest value the capacity for love, which alone allows survival in the face of the absurd. It is a tragic

García Márquez receiving an honorary doctorate from Colombia University in 1971

moment when in *One Hundred Years of Solitude* he indicts Colonel Buendía for his inability to love. García Márquez even told Claudia Dreifus in an interview for *Playboy* magazine that in his work he is "a nymphomaniac of the art" of love.[35] In his work he conveys the joy of sexual connection.

People who love nature and animals, like the Colonel who grows to value his rooster in *El coronel no tiene quien le escriba* (1961; translated in *No One Writes to the Colonel and Other Stories,* 1968), are anointed with the author's approval. Like Florentino Ariza in *Love in The Time Of Cholera,* they can find solace even in the scent of bitter almonds, or in the flavor of the guava. They are capable of solidarity with other human beings. His approach has not been consciously psychoanalytic, however, but intuitive. Referring to a convention of psychoanalysts that met in Buenos Aires to discuss *One Hundred Years of Solitude,* he remarked "What interested me was that the aunt should go to bed with her nephew, not the psychoanalytic origins of this event."[36]

AWARDS AND RECOGNITION

He won prizes from the beginning, from that first scholarship, which took him from home. In 1955 he won a prize from the Bogotá Association of Writers and Artists for "Un día después del sábado" ("One Day After Saturday"), one of the stories that would be published in the collection, *Los funerales de la Mamá Grande* (Big Mama's Funeral, 1961; translated in *No One Writes to the Colonel and Other Stories,* 1968). In 1961 he won the Premio Literario Esso award in Colombia for *La mala hora* (1961; translated as *In Evil Hour,* 1979), when the novel was still only in manuscript form.

One Hundred Years of Solitude was showered with prizes, most notably the Chianciano Award in Italy and the Prix de Meilleur Livre Etranger (Prize for Best Foreign Book) from the Académie Française in 1969. Three years later García Márquez was awarded both the *Books Abroad*/Neustadt International Prize for Literature and the Venezuelan Rómulo Gallegos Prize for *One Hundred Years of Solitude*.

In 1971 he received a doctorate of letters from Columbia University. He has since expressed his amazement that in awarding the doctorate they "should decide to choose me out of twelve men from the whole world," especially since his "path has always been anti-academic." Then he added, "it's as if they gave the Nobel Prize to a bullfighter."[37]

García Márquez accepted the title of *doctor honoris causa,* but refused to wear a tie to the ceremony, his moment of rebellion, all the while believing that, properly, "such things happened to one after death." He also said, "The type of recognition I have always desired and appreciated is that of people who read me and talk to me about my books, not with admiration or enthusiasm but with affection."[38]

There were many Latin Americans at the ceremony. They called out, "Up with Latin America!" At that moment, García Márquez has said, "for the first time, I felt moved and was glad I had accepted."[39]

He has also accepted the French Legion of Honor medal from François Mitterand, whose inauguration he attended in 1981. That same year he received the Serfin Prize.

The most prestigious of his awards was, of course, the Nobel Prize. When he left Colombia for Sweden, he went accompanied by an entourage that included six Colombian dance and music groups. Belisario Betancur, the newly elected president of Colombia, declared that "all of Colombia would be with Gabo." He was a national treasure. Despite all of the acclaim, while in Sweden he remained himself, a *costeño,* wearing not white tie and tails but a white linen "liqui-liqui" suit, the traditional collarless suit of the Carribean coast.

Gabriel García Márquez has often used the prizes he has won to support causes in which he believes. When he received the Rómulo Gallegos prize in 1972, he donated the money to the Venezuelan political reform party Movimiento al Socialismo (MAS, Movement toward Socialism). The $10,000 he received with his *Books Abroad/ Neustadt International Prize for Literature* went to the Committee in Solidarity with Political Prisoners.

In the United States he has been elected an honorary fellow of the American Academy of Arts and Letters.

NOTES

1. Gene H. Bell-Villada, *García Márquez: The Man and His Work* (Chapel Hill & London: University of North Carolina Press, 1990), p. 12.

2. Claudia Dreifus, "*Playboy* Interview: Gabriel García Márquez," *Playboy*, 30 (February 1983): 66.

3. Michael Wood, *Gabriel Garciá Márquez: One Hundred Years of Solitude* (Cambridge & New York: Cambridge University Press, 1990), p. 110.

4. Marlise Simons, "A Talk With Gabriel García Márquez," *New York Times Book Review*, 5 December 1982.

5. Dreifus, "*Playboy* Interview": 67.

6. Alan Riding, "Revolution and the Intellectual in Latin America," *New York Times*, Sunday, 13 March 1983.

7. Rita Guibert, "Gabriel Garciá Márquez," *Seven Voices: Seven Latin American Writers Talk to Rita Guibert* (New York: Knopf, 1973), p. 335.

8. Simons, "A Talk."

9. Guibert, *Seven Voices*, p. 335.

10. Ibid., p. 322.

11. Riding, "Revolution and the Intellectual."

12. Guibert, *Seven Voices*, p. 330.

13. Peter Stone, "Gabriel García Márquez," in *Writers at Work: The Paris Review Interviews: Sixth Series,* edited by George Plimpton (New York: Viking, 1984), p. 339.

14. *Gabriel García Márquez: Magic and Reality,* written, directed, and produced by Ana Cristina Navarro, 60 minutes, Films For the Humanities & Sciences, 1981, video.

15. Dreifus, "*Playboy* Interview": 77.

16. Simons, "A Talk."

17. Ibid.

18. Guibert, *Seven Voices*, p. 323.

19. Quoted in Mario Vargas Llosa, "From Aracataca to Macondo," in *Modern Critical Views: Gabriel Garciá Márquez,* edited by Harold Bloom (New York: Chelsea House, 1989), p. 7.

20. Simons, "A Talk."

21. Dreifus, "*Playboy* Interview": 77.

22. Quoted in Vargas Llosa, *Historia De Un Deicidio* (Barcelona: Barral Editores, 1971), p. 28.

23. *Gabriel García Márquez: Magic and Reality.*

24. "My Thanks," coda to *The General in His Labyrinth,* translated by Edith Grossman (New York: Knopf, 1990), p. 271.

25. Stone, *Paris Review,* p. 320.

26. Stone, *Paris Review,* p. 320.

27. Ibid.

28. Guibert, *Seven Voices*, p. 327.

29. Ibid.

30. Germán Vargas, "Autor de una obra que hará ruido," in *Encuentro liberal* (Bogotá), 29 April 1967, p. 22.

31. Bell-Villada, *The Man and His Work,* p. 52.

32. Dreifus, "*Playboy* Interview": 176.

33. The preceding account of García Márquez and his friend Father Camilo Torres Restrepo is taken from an interview by the author with García Márquez in Mexico City in 1986.

34. Guibert, *Seven Voices*, p. 314.

35. Dreifus, "*Playboy* Interview."

36. Guibert, *Seven Voices*, p. 315.

37. Ibid., p. 336.

38. Ibid.

39. Ibid., p. 337.

GARCÍA MÁRQUEZ AT WORK

GETTING ESTABLISHED

As a beginning writer, García Márquez was prolific. Working as a journalist on *El Espectador* in Bogotá, he recalled, he "used to do at least three stories a week, two or three editorial notes every day, and I did movie reviews. Then at night, after everyone had gone home, I would stay behind writing my novels. I liked the noise of the Linotype machines, which sounded like rain. If they stopped, and I was left in silence, I wouldn't be able to work."[1] So he began.

García Márquez appears to have been in no hurry for his novels to be published. When he went to Europe for *El Espectador,* he left the manuscript of *Leaf Storm* in his desk drawer. Some friends discovered it and took it to a publisher. His habit of showing a manuscript to a small group of friends and requesting suggestions, after which they were to "be silent forever," had borne fruit.[2] It meant that there were always people who knew what he was writing. *Leaf Storm,* his first published novel, appeared in 1955.

Living on credit in a Latin Quarter hotel in Paris in 1957, García Márquez began to write *In Evil Hour.* Then he decided to work instead on *No One Writes to the Colonel.* He wrote eleven drafts. Considering the work a failure, he buried the manuscript "tied with a colored ribbon in the bottom of a suitcase."[3] He returned to Colombia to be married to his fiancée, Mercedes Barcha, then moved to Venezuela and Mexico.

By 1959 he had completed the eight stories of *Los funerales de la Mamá Grande* (Big Mama's Funeral). There they sat until his friend Álvaro Mutis, who was in prison in Mexico City, asked for something to read. In 1962, out of prison, Mutis placed the stories with the University of Veracruz Press, which gave García Márquez a one-thousand-peso advance—about $100. No one noticed the book.

García Márquez's friends also forced him to submit *In Evil Hour* to the competition that it won, but only after they persuaded him to

García Márquez signing books

change the title from "Este pueblo de mierda" (This Town of Excrement). "The truth is," Mario Vargas Llosa has said, "that without the obstinacy of his friends, García Márquez would perhaps still today be an unknown writer."[4] *In Evil Hour* won the Esso Prize in Colombia. Afterward, García Márquez has said that he suffered from writer's block, one that lasted from 1961 to 1964. He told Álvaro Mutis that he would never write again.

His name was becoming known, however. In 1965, at a party held at the Symposium of Intellectuals at Chichén Itzá in the Yucatan, Chilean novelist José Donoso sought out the not-yet-established García Márquez:

> . . . I searched through the rooms and gardens for Gabriel García Márquez because in Chichén Itzá I had read *No One Writes to the Colonel* with astonishment and because someone had said, "Gabo's at this party." At the moment when I was passing this information along to my wife so that she could help me to find him, a man with a black mustache came up to me and asked if I were Pepe Donoso; as we embraced in the Latin American manner, the frenzied *tarántula* passing by absorbed us too.
>
> We were unable to continue talking on that occasion, but we did afterwards. According to what he told me, García Márquez was experiencing a literary dry spell, one that had lasted for nearly ten years. He could not come out of it. His books circulated in very small circles. At least I had the prospect, with *Coronation* about to be published in the United States, that I was going to be able to feel some stimulus to bring about the necessary synthesis in order to finish *The Obscene Bird of Night*. I saw García Márquez as a gloomy, melancholy person tormented by his writer's block, a blockage as legendary as those of Ernesto Sabato and the eternal block of Juan Rulfo. . . .[5]

García Márquez had tried to write his big novel in Barranquilla, feeling the need to return to the life he had led when he was a reporter, with no success. He and his family were driving in their Opel automobile one day along the Mexico City–Acapulco highway, when, suddenly, García Márquez imagined every word of the first chapter of the book he had begun when he was eighteen years old as "La Casa." At that time he had had "neither the vital experience nor the literary means" to complete it, but now "It was so ripe in me that I could have dictated the first chapter, word by word, to a typist," he said later.[6] For the next six months Mercedes took over all the financial details of their lives, while he descended into what he called "The Cave of the Mafia."

"Don't bother me, especially don't bother me about money," he told his wife.[7] Mercedes arranged for loans and pawned household appliances. She borrowed money from his friend Mutis and others. They were more than $10,000 in debt. Eighteen months later there were 1,300 pages of manuscript, along with diagrams and sketches.

The Argentine publisher Editorial Sudamericana had asked to see a novel in progress. The typist, who had the only copies of the chapters of *One Hundred Years Of Solitude,* was hit by a bus; the pages went flying. Unhurt, she picked herself up and reassembled the typescript. Then, on the day they were to mail the typescript, Gabriel and Mercedes arrived at the post-office window only to discover that they did not have the 160 pesos needed for postage. They were able to send only half the typescript. Later that day, García Márquez has said, perhaps with some exaggeration, he mailed the second half of the typescript after pawning the Mixmaster and the hair dryer to get the necessary money. "Well, now all we need is for this novel to be bad," Mercedes said. [8]

He had been, in fact, so ready to write this book that on the galley proofs he changed only one word despite the encouragement of Paco Porrua, the literary editor of Sudamericana, who told him he could make as many changes as he wished.

García Márquez has always been skeptical of the value of literary reputation. *The Story of a Shipwrecked Sailor* had originally been serialized daily for two weeks in a newspaper, published under the name of Luis Alejandro Velasco, who told García Márquez the story, with no mention of the writer; García Márquez wryly remarked "It wasn't until twenty years later that it was published and people found out I had written it. No editor realized that it was good until after I had written *One Hundred Years of Solitude.*"[9]

He was "stunned" with the immediate and extraordinary success of that novel. The publisher announced that he was printing eight thousand copies; García Márquez was astonished since his previous books had never sold more than seven hundred copies. "I asked him why not start slowly," he remembered, "but he said he was convinced that it was a good book and that all eight thousand copies would be sold between May and December. Actually they were all sold within one week in Buenos Aires."[10]

He was established. As Donoso put it, "the Latin American novel did not truly come into the world until the second half of the decade, starting with the scandalously unprecedented triumph of *One Hundred Years of Solitude* by Gabriel García Márquez, a Colombian with a reputation so skimpy that his name barely figured in the Congress of Intellectuals in Concepcion in 1962, despite his having already published *No One Writes to the Colonel.*"[11]

IMAGINATION AND REALITY

"I only write about things I know. People I've seen. I don't analyze."

García Márquez

From Luis Harss and Barbara Dohmann, "Gabriel García Márquez, or the Lost Chord," in *Into the Mainstream: Conversations with Latin-American Writers* (New York: Harper & Row, 1967), p. 320.

"It always amuses me that the biggest praise for my work comes for the imagination, while the truth is that there's not a single line in all my work that does not have a basis in reality. The problem is that Caribbean reality resembles the wildest imagination."

García Márquez

From a 1981 interview with Peter Stone, "Gabriel García Márquez," in *Writers at Work: The Paris Review Interviews: Sixth Series,* edited by George Plimpton (New York: Viking, 1984), p. 322.

Denying he was a "fabulist," he said "I recall our Caribbean reality with such a selective criterion that it seems incredible."

García Márquez

From "Nobel Prize Winner García Márquez Reveals Surprise Memoirs," 21 March 1998 Reuters News Service report of conference in Mexico City.

TECHNIQUES

"A writer can try anything as long as he makes it believable," García Márquez, the master of magic realism, has said. Even as his work blends the realistic and the fantastic, he has called himself a "realist." But reality for García Márquez includes not just actual daily life but "the people's myths, their beliefs, their legends." In life, he has discovered, reality ends up "copying the imagination and dreams."[12] The best example of reality copying the imagination comes from his story "Big Mama's Funeral." The funeral itself is a carnival, a grand affair that is even attended by the Pope, although up to that time no pope had ever visited Latin America, let alone Colombia. Yet, when in 1968 Pope Paul VI became the first pontiff to visit the continent, the country the Pope chose to visit was Colombia.

For García Márquez supernatural elements are part of everyday reality. The Caribbean coast of his origin was an environment combining a mixture of Guajiro Indians, emigrants from the Middle East, and the descendants of black slaves and settlers from Spain. It provided for the novelist a diverse culture tinged by magic, mystery, and the unknowable. "You can't separate reality from fiction," he says. "In my novels I stir them and keep them spinning throughout the book."[13]

The technique he uses most often to render the fantastic entirely credible is specificity. As he himself reveals, if you were to say that 200 elephants passed by, no one would believe you. But if you write that 232 elephants appeared with 7 baby elephants among them, the reader will accept the idea. Thus, in *Love in the Time of Cholera,* he writes that Fernando Ariza loved Fermina Daza for "fifty-one years, nine months, and four days."[14] In *One Hundred Years of Solitude* Colonial Aureliano Buendía organizes not many but "thirty-two armed uprisings," expressing the theme of the meaningless repetitiveness of the wars between the Liberals and the Conservatives that have plagued Colombia.[15]

With specificity comes exaggeration. García Márquez has described the technique another way. "If you say you saw a pink elephant, you won't be believed. If you say you saw seventeen pink elephants flying about that afternoon, your story gains in verisimilitude."[16] He has offered still another example. He remembers his grandmother saying that when the electrician departed, "he would leave the house full of butterflies." He discovered that "when I was writing this, if I didn't say that the butterflies were yellow, people would not believe it."[17] The same problem held true for the ascension of Remedios the Beauty into heaven in *One Hundred Years of Solitude*. Remedios does not just go to heaven, but she travels taking with her the bedsheets that had just been washed and were being put out on the line to dry. "If I used the sheets for Remedios the Beauty," García Márquez has explained, "she would ascend. That's how I did it, to make it credible."[18]

Exaggeration figures in the death of three thousand striking banana workers, which forms the climax of *One Hundred Years of Solitude*. Historically, there was such a massacre, but it is unknown just how many people were killed; the deaths are calculated in the hundreds. To make his point about the horror of this massacre of the army against an unarmed population, García Márquez deliberately raised the death toll to three thousand.

Yet, he has argued, one of his childhood memories was of watching a "long train leave the plantation supposedly full of bananas. There could have been three thousand dead on it, eventually to be dumped in the sea." To the delight of García Márquez, people began to speak of the three thousand dead as fact. He concludes that "sooner or later people believe writers rather than the government."[19]

Exaggeration can also serve the demands of humor. In *Love in the Time of Cholera* the pet parrot of Dr. Juvenal Urbino had "privileges that no one else in the family ever had, not even the children when they were young" (20). In *Chronicle of a Death Foretold* four turkeys, eleven hogs, and four calves have been "sacrificed" for the ill-fated wedding of Angela Vicario and Bayardo San Román.[20]

Another instance of García Márquez's use of magic realism comes in *The Autumn of the Patriarch*, when the old general sells the sea to the United States to repay his country's foreign debt and to prevent the U.S. Marines from being sent to occupy his country. García Márquez has related this image to his own life, pointing out that the dictator who allows the United States to carry away the sea in numbered pieces corresponds to the boy from Aracataca who felt lost when he journeyed to the interior,

Cover for the first edition of *El otoño del patriarca* (1975; translated as *Autumn of the Patriarch,* 1976), García Márquez's novel about a Latin American dictator

because of the absence of the sea. For García Márquez nothing had been worse than to live in the cities of Zipaquirá and Bogotá, greyish cities without a sea.

Yet, an important political point has also been made through the magic of the selling off of the sea. "That actually happened," he has said. "It's happened and will happen many times more."[21] He is referring to the economic exploitation of his country and his continent by the power from the north that historically has seized the wealth of its weaker neighbors through force. His aim as a novelist has been to "close the gap" between literature and politics.[22] "The trouble is that many people believe that I'm a writer of fantastic fiction," García Márquez has said, "when actually I'm a very realistic person and write what I believe is the true socialist realism."[23]

His magic also has a point. In his landmark story "La increíble y triste historia de la cándida Eréndira y de su abuela desalmada" (1972; translated as "The Incredible and Sad Tale of Innocent Eréndira and Her Heartless Grandmother," 1978) glass changes color every time the young man Ulises touches it. This, García Márquez has explained, was his way of expressing the theme that love "upsets life . . . upsets everything."[24]

The novels of García Márquez continually take literary risks. In *One Hundred Years of Solitude* a character shoots himself, and the blood trickles in a thin steam around the town until it finds his mother, the umbilical cord that lasts even beyond death. "The whole book is like that," literary critic Michael Wood writes in his *Gabriel García Márquez: One Hundred Years of Solitude* (1990), "on a knife's edge between the sublime and the vulgar. Like the bolero."[25]

According to García Márquez, each of his novels begins with "a completely visual image."[26] He collects photography books, and he has said that, although the first image he had of *The Autumn of the Patriarch* was of "a very old man in a luxurious palace into which cows come and eat the curtains," "that image didn't concretize" until in Rome he found a photograph that "was just perfect."[27] He told Rita Guibert that the "starting point of *Leaf Storm* is an old man taking his grandson to a funeral."[28] But the actual image with which he began, he later revealed, was "a flash of myself as a little boy, sitting on a chair in the living room."[29] In *No One Writes to the Colonel* he began with his memory of an old man "looking at fish in the market of Barranquilla."

In *One Hundred Years of Solitude* the image through which he began the narrative came from his own life. It was of an old man, the Colonel, his grandfather, taking his grandson, himself, "to the fair to find out what ice is."[30] In *Love in the Time of Cholera* the first image he had was "that of an old couple fleeing by boat. An old couple, happy on a boat, dancing on the deck."[31] Asked about the coincidence that many of these opening images feature an old man, García Márquez replied that "the guardian angel of my infancy was an old man—my grandfather. . . . I'm aware that I always see the image of my grandfather showing me things."[32]

His magic is always placed in the service of a theme and functions as a metaphor rather than being an ornament that exists purely as an example of something fantastic. Remedios the Beauty ascends to heaven because she is so beautiful that she cannot exist in this imperfect world. Considering the political violence that has besieged Colombia for two centuries to have "the same metaphysic as the plague," García Márquez treated that metaphor in two different ways. In his famous story "One Day After Saturday" such a plague kills all the birds. In *One Hundred Years of Solitude* the plague—carrying the same metaphoric meaning—is one of insomnia, "something of a literary trick, since it's the opposite of the sleeping plague."[33]

Voice is one of the strongest elements of his literary style. The narrative voice of his stories, the tone the author adopts toward his subject matter, has its origins in the voice of his grandmother Doña Tranquilina, who told him tales of the supernatural. Yet, her voice was so solemn and her expression so deadpan that he could not help but believe in the reality of whatever she told him.

In the stories and novels of García Márquez, outlandish and fantastic elements are described as if they were entirely natural and commonplace. So in "The Incredible and Sad Tale of Innocent Eréndira and Her Heartless Grandmother" the eponymous protagonist says to her young lover, Ulises, "What I like about you is the serious way you make up nonsense."[34] This, García Márquez has said, is "an absolutely autobiographical statement. It is not only a definition of my work, it is a definition of my character."[35]

In many of his works García Márquez enlists a quasi-omniscient narrative voice. Although the narrator seems to know everything, the deepest secrets in the hearts of his characters, he frequently lapses into the first person, particularly into "we." Never superior to his characters, he is instead a member of the community about which he is writing. He shares their experiences and hence is capable of great empathy with his people. In *Chronicle of a Death Foretold* García Márquez reverts to a first-person narrator who enters the action as a citizen of the town where the events of the story take place. The narrator is a returning journalist who comes home to discover what actually happened: "I returned to this forgotten village, trying to put the broken mirror of memory back together from so many scattered shards" (6).

The voice in a work of García Márquez is often supremely wise, most emphatically in the narrator of *Love in the Time of Cholera,* who talks of "our" history and who often moves away from the story to express generalizations about life. "Life would have been quite another matter for them," he says of Dr. Urbino and his wife, "if they had learned in time that it was easier to avoid great matrimonial catastrophes" than "trivial everyday miseries" (26). "Wisdom comes to us when it can no longer do any good," he remarks. Of Fermina Daza, he notes that "she had never imagined that curiosity was one of the many masks of love"(66).

In his fiction García Márquez seems to hold to the view that temperament is already present at birth. In *One Hundred Years of Solitude* the future Colonel Buendía wept in his mother's womb and was born with his eyes open. Newly arrived in the world, he moves his head "from side to side, taking in the things in the room and examining the faces of the people with a fearless curiosity" (15). Magic, a slight exaggeration, proves to be a more powerful illuminator of truth than strict realism would be.

Eschewing suspense, García Márquez often uses the flash-forward in his descriptions of his characters, so that the reader knows—or thinks he knows—in *One Hundred Years of Solitude* that the eleven-year-old Rebeca will bear the Buendía name until her death because she will never marry and that Colonial Buendía will die by a firing squad. In fact, Rebeca marries a Buendía and so never changes her name, and Colonel Buendía only "faces" that firing squad. Garcíá Márquez also tells us, however, that Remedios was "the last person Arcadio thought about a few years later when he faced the firing squad" (91), and this Arcadio does die.

At times imagery reveals character, as in *Love in the Time of Cholera* when Dr. Urbino's lips turn blue as he reads the eleven-page suicide note of his friend Jeremiah de Saint-Amour. Contradiction and paradox define character as well. In this novel García Márquez describes a woman who will go on living "in the death trap of the poor where she had been happy" (16).

In his treatment of character García Márquez employs psychological realism. In *One Hundred Years of Solitude,* quite logically, Arcadio, who as a child was left to his solitude, becomes a brute in manhood. Despite his use of magic, there is a strong fabric of causality running through the fiction of García Márquez. Indeed, the very fall of Macondo can be causally traced to the obsession with solitude that infected the first José Arcadio Buendía.

However, his characters are also faced with coincidence, nowhere more than in *Chronicle of a Death Foretold* where everyone in the town seems to know of the Vicario brothers' plan to murder Santiago Nasar, and yet no one manages to warn him. There is a warning note, but no one bothers to pick it up. García Márquez continually violates the "rule" that the well-made plot should not turn on accident, the fortuitous, or coincidence; but often his narrative voice furthers the plot in a straightforward way: "Angela Vicario, the beautiful girl who'd gotten married the day before, had been returned to the house of her parents, because her husband had discovered that she wasn't a virgin" (21).

His background as a journalist has contributed to his techniques as a writer. For *The Autumn of the Patriarch* he read about dictators and for ten years talked to people who had lived under dictatorships. Then he made a conscious effort to forget everything he had been told so that he could invent. He wanted this novel to have a Caribbean flavor, and so he moved from Spain back to Barranquilla for the writing; he even traveled from island to island in an effort to create a novel that had a setting that could apply to the Americas in general and not to one country alone. His most successful novels and stories are set in locales in which he has lived.

Setting figures prominently in the works of García Márquez, and more than one critic has noticed a similarity between the imaginary Yoknapatawpha County in which much of William Faulkner's fiction is set and the fictional Macondo of García Márquez. Unlike Faulkner, however, for whom Yoknapatawpha represents the rural Mississippi of his youth, for García Márquez, Macondo does not stand for the Aracataca of his birth, although it resembles it in many ways, not least in its distance from the sea. It stands for any town in the banana zone, for Colombia, and even for Latin America as a whole.

Coming into existence when the world is young, Macondo could stand even for the Garden of Eden, "a truly happy village where no one was over thirty years of age and where no one had died."[36] That it is near an "ashen, foamy, dirty sea"(13) suggests the Fall, the evil that awaits its first happy inhabitants. Not coincidentally, since he will become the conscience haunting all of García Márquez's fiction, Aureliano is the first human being born in Macondo.

Politics alters setting, transforming the lives of individuals, and so Macondo's landscape is altered once the banana company moves in. Macondo becomes now "a field of wooden houses with zinc roofs" (40) coexisting with the almond trees planted by José Arcadio Buendía, and now dusty and broken. The rot of the tropics, the rain that lasts for four years, eleven months, and two days, as García Márquez once again enlists specifics in the service of credibility, represents the moral and historical decline of Macondo. Similarly, the scenes on the Magdalena River in *The General in his Labyrinth* parallel the death of the dream of Simon Bolívar for one unified country, combining the areas he has liberated. Instead a "germ of separation" has infected his world.[37] Venezuela, Colombia, Bolivia, and Peru splinter into separate entities, in a sort of prefiguring of what happened in Yugoslavia during the 1990s.

Politics—the particular perspective of the author—enters the narrative through language. Bolívar is "America's great man," as García Márquez refuses to call this land either "South" or "Latin" America, defining his environment not in relation to the "gringos" in the United States to the north, but with its original name. "Our enemies will have all the advantages until we unify the government of America," Bolívar says.

The labyrinth of the title is both a geographical labyrinth and a labyrinth of deception and intrigue that have prevented the general from realizing his dream. The coldness of Bogotá depresses the fictional Bolívar as it did García Márquez as a young man first traveling to the interior.

Setting in the fiction of García Márquez encompasses not just a geographical place, but equally the history of that place and its culture. His technique is economical: a single phrase may capture an important aspect of the culture, as "the vicious spying of the nuns" (69) in *Love in the Time of Cholera* describes the repressive Catholic culture that helps to separate the lovers Fermina Daza and Florentino Ariza for so long. With exactitude of setting comes a highly specific use of time. Always there are

mustios

pagaron

lo sabíamos porque

de los soldados

había hecho

y sin embargo

civil

era

callejero que por cinco centavos recitaba los versos del
olvidado poeta Rubén Darío y había vuelto feliz con una
morrocota legítima con que le habían premiado un reci-
tal que hizo sólo para él, aunque no lo había visto, por
supuesto, no porque fuera ciego sino porque ningún mor-
tal lo había visto desde los tiempos del vómito negro,
pero sabíamos que él estaba ahí, puesto que el mundo
seguía, la vida seguía, el correo llegaba, la banda muni-
cipal tocaba la retreta de valses bobos bajo las palmeras
polvorientas y los faroles pálidos de la Plaza de Armas,
y otros músicos viejos reemplazaban en la banda a los
músicos muertos. En los últimos años, cuando no se vol-
vieron a oír ruidos humanos ni cantos de pájaros en el
interior y se cerraron para siempre los portones blinda-
dos, sabíamos que había alguien en la casa presidencial
porque de noche se veían luces que parecían de navega-
ción a través de las ventanas del lado del mar, y quienes
se atrevieron a acercarse oyeron desastres de pezuñas y
suspiros de animal grande detrás de las paredes fortifi-
cadas, y una tarde de enero habíamos visto una vaca
contemplando el crepúsculo desde el balcón presidencial,
imagínese, una vaca en el balcón de la patria, qué cosa
más inicua, qué país de mierda, pero se hicieron tantas
conjeturas de cómo era posible que una vaca llegara
hasta un balcón si todo el mundo sabía que las vacas
no se trepaban por las escaleras, y menos si eran de
piedra, y mucho menos si estaban alfombradas, que al
final no supimos si en realidad la vimos o si era que
pasamos una tarde por la Plaza de Armas y habíamos
soñado caminando que habíamos visto una vaca en el
balcón presidencial, y desde entonces nada se volvió a
ver ni nada se volvió a oír en muchos años, sólo la ban-
dada densa de gallinazos que vinieron de donde estaban
siempre adormilados en la cornisa del hospital de po-
bres, vinieron más de tierra adentro, vinieron en oleadas
sucesivas desde el horizonte del mar de polvo donde es-
tuvo el mar, volaron todo un día en círculos lentos sobre
la casa del poder hasta que un rey con plumas de novia
y golilla encarnada impartió una orden silenciosa y em-
pezó aquel estropicio de vidrios, aquel viento de muerto
grande, aquel entrar y salir de gallinazos por las ventanas como sólo era concebible en una casa sin autoridad,
de modo que subimos hasta la colina y encontramos en
el interior desierto los escombros de la grandeza, el
cuerpo picoteado, las manos lisas de doncella con el ani-
llo del poder en el hueso anular, y tenía todo el cuerpo
retoñado de líquenes minúsculos y animales parasitarios
de fondo de mar, sobre todo en las axilas y en las ingles,
y tenía el braguero de lona en el testículo herniado que
era lo único que habían eludido los gallinazos a pesar
de ser tan grande como un riñón de buey, pero ni si-
quiera entonces nos atrevimos a creer en su muerte porque era la segunda vez que lo encontraban en aquella
oficina, solo y vestido, y muerto al parecer de muerte
natural durante el sueño, como estaba anunciado desde
hacía muchos años en las aguas premonitorias de los
lebrillos de las pitonisas. La primera vez que lo encon-
traron, en el principio de su otoño, la nación estaba toda-
vía bastante viva como para que él se sintiera amenazado

también nosotros
nos atrevimos
a entrar

santuario

una vaca en un
balcón presiden-
cial donde nada
se había visto ni
había de verse
otra vez en mu-
chos años hasta
el amanecer del
último viernes
cuando empeza-
ron a llegar
los primeros ga-
llinazos que se
alzaron de don-
de estaban

García Márquez's corrected proof page for *El otoño del patriarca* time cues since time never stands still in the fiction of this author. "On the previous night" he tells the reader, "they had gone to the cinema" (14). The dignitaries arrive "at three o'clock in the afternoon" (21). There is also, of course, the length of Florentino's devotion to Fermina Daza: fifty-one years, nine months, and four days. The narrator of *Love in the Time of Cholera* learns of the events of the murder twenty-seven years later, events that occurred specifically on a Monday.

Despite these various precise references to time that give readers a sense of where they are, however, there is also in some García Márquez narratives such as *One Hundred Years of Solitude* and *The Autumn of the Patriarch* a sense of simultaneity. All events seem to be happening at one time despite the fact that the reader is often reminded that the narrative is moving forward. García Márquez has said that his sense of time in fiction was immediately transformed when he read Virginia Woolf's novel *Mrs. Dalloway* at the age of twenty: "I saw the whole process of decomposition in Macondo and its final destiny."[38] He has pointed to a sentence at the close of his novel that describes his theory of time: "Melquíades had not put events in the order of man's conventional time, but had concentrated a century of daily episodes in such a way that they coexisted in one instant" (421). The chapters of *One Hundred Years of Solitude* are not numbered, the better for the reader to experience the events of the novel as existing in that single moment.

Frequently his use of the flash-forward allows the reader to view a character in terms of the sweep of his entire life. As José Arcadio Buendía plants his almond trees in *One Hundred Years of Solitude,* García Márquez offers a glimpse of Macondo "many years later" after the invasion of the banana planters when those trees, now broken and dusty, still stand on the oldest streets, "although no one knew who had planted them" (40).

Simultaneously, a generous use of the flashback allows García Márquez to provide a biographical treatment of his characters, to show that what they are is a reflection of what they—and their ancestors—have been. So in *One Hundred Years of Solitude* he flashes back to the sixteenth century when "the pirate" Sir Francis Drake so frightened Úrsula Iguran's great-great-grandmother that she sat down on a lighted stove (19). Her descendant is now extremely cautious.

García Márquez is an author who greatly enjoys the process of writing. "Conquering the problem of writing is so delightful," he has said, "and so thrilling, that it makes up for all the work . . . it's like giving birth."[39] He has described the process by which a phrase or an incident that he has collected in his notebook is transformed into a story:

I'll tell you an anecdote which may give you some idea how mysteriously I arrive at a story. One night in Barcelona when we had visitors, the lights suddenly went out. As the trouble was local we sent for an electrician. While he was putting the defect right and I was holding a candle for him to see by, I asked him, "What the devil's happened to the light?" "Light is like water," he said, "you turn a tap and out it comes, and the meter registers it as it comes through." In that fraction of a second, a complete story came to me:

In a city away from the sea—it might be Paris, Madrid, or Bogotá—there live on the fifth floor a young couple and their two children of ten and seven. One day the children ask their parents to give them a rowboat. "How can we give you a rowboat?" says the father. "What can you do with it in this town? When we go to the seaside in the summer we can hire one." The children obstinately persist that they want a rowboat, until their father says: "If you get the top places in school I'll give you one." They get the top places, their father buys the boat, and when they take it up to the fifth floor he asks them: "What are you going to do with it?" "Nothing," they reply, "we just wanted to have it. We'll put it in our room." One night when their parents are at the cinema, the children break an electric light bulb and the light begins to flow out—just like water—filling the whole house three feet deep. They take the boat and begin rowing through the bedrooms and the kitchen. When it's time for their parents to return they put it away in their room and pull up the plugs so that the light can drain away, put back the bulb, and . . . nothing has happened. This becomes such a splendid game that they begin to let the light reach a greater depth, put on dark glasses and flippers, and swim under the beds and tables, practicing underwater fishing. . . . One night, passersby in the street notice light streaming out of the windows and flooding the street, and they send for the fire brigade. When the firemen open the door they find the children had been so absorbed in their game that they had allowed the light to reach the ceiling, and are floating in the light, drowned. Can you tell me how it was that this complete story, just as I've told you, occurred to me within a fraction of a second? Naturally, as I've told it often, I find a new angle every time—change one thing for another or add a detail—but the idea remains the same. There's nothing deliberate or predictable in all this, nor do I know when it's going to happen to me. I'm at the mercy of my imagination, and that's what says *yes* or *no*.[40]

The story was first published as "La luz es como el agua" (1978; translated as "Light Is Like Water," 1993) and collected in *Doce cuentos peregrinos* (1992; translated as *Strange Pilgrims: Twelve Stories,* 1993). The general plot and many of the details in the published version remain the same as in the version García Márquez first imagined.

Despite his declaration that there is "nothing deliberate or predictable" about the origins of his stories, it would be a mistake to say that García Márquez works without a plan, without knowing in advance how a story will conclude. His novels in particular are carefully outlined. Asked by Peter Stone in his 1981 interview for the *Paris Review* whether his "novels ever take unexpected twists," his reply was in the negative:

> That used to happen to me in the beginning. In the first stories I wrote I had a general idea of the mood, but I would let myself be taken by chance. The best advice I was given early on was that it was all right to work that way when I was young because I had a torrent of inspiration. But I was told that if I didn't learn technique, I would be in trouble later on when the inspiration had gone and the technique was needed to compensate. If I hadn't learned that in time, I would not now be able to outline a structure in advance. Structure is a purely technical problem and if you don't learn it early on you'll never learn it.[41]

The humor that suffuses all the fiction of García Márquez emerges most powerfully in his dialogue, speeches which are so witty and so true in their generalizations that they seem capable of being lifted out of the narrative. There is, for example, this exchange between General Bolívar and his British ally, Colonel Wilson, in *The General in His Labyrinth*. In "a voice from another century," Bolívar asks his friend, "What do you suppose London is like now?" Told that it is "the worst time" with "a rain as filthy and dead as road water," Bolívar says in astonishment, "Don't tell me you've conquered nostalgia." Colonel Wilson disabuses him of this utopian view: "On the contrary; nostalgia has conquered me. I no longer put up the slightest resistance to it" (67).

Love in the Time of Cholera includes little dialogue. When dialogue does arise, it becomes all the more powerful. So Dr. Urbino has the following exchange with his parrot, who in his wit and willfulness, his achievements and his stubbornness, is a triumph of magic realism. Just as Dr. Urbino is about to dress for a funeral, the parrot, "whom he loved as if he were a human being" (41), disappears. Before long he is discovered on the lowest branch of the mango tree:

> "You scoundrel!" he shouted.
> The parrot answered in an identical voice:
> "You're even more of a scoundrel, Doctor." (41)

As Fermina Daza and Florentino Ariza are about to consummate a love they have harbored for more than fifty years, on a boat, on the river, bound for nowhere, there is this exchange:

> "If we're going to do it, let's do it," she said, "but let's do it like grownups."

She took him to the bedroom and, with the lights on, began to undress without false modesty. Florentino Ariza was on the bed, lying on his back and trying to regain control, once again not knowing what to do with the skin of the tiger he had slain. She said: "Don't look." He asked why without taking his eyes off the ceiling.

"Because you won't like it," she said. (339)

In the same novel Fermina Daza and Dr. Urbino were able to restore their fragile marriage when he finally became willing to speak one line of dialogue: "'Let me stay here,' he said, 'There was soap'" (29).

Invariably the imagery of García Márquez appeals to the five senses. It is the sense of smell, however, that he uses most frequently. Fermina Daza has so acute a sense of smell that she can sniff the clothes of her husband and know he has been with another woman. His imagery is also metaphoric, a form of his magic realism. Often abstractions or animals are given human qualities. The metaphors are also frequently unexpected: Dr. Urbino's beard is the color of "mother-of-pearl" (4). Another unlikely comparison illuminates the very title of the novel. García Márquez, an inventor of reality as much as he is a describer of it, notes that love and cholera share the same symptom: green vomit.

In *One Hundred Years Of Solitude* the sea becomes a metaphor for the greatest obstacle to human solidarity. García Márquez employs metaphors rather than symbols. He has said that in *One Hundred Years of Solitude* "there isn't a single conscious symbol."[42]

The catalogue or list that is both fantastic and reveals a stream of erudition is another important feature of García Márquez's use of imagery. In *One Hundred Years of Solitude* the gypsies bring "parrots painted all colors reciting Italian arias, and a hen who laid a hundred golden eggs to the sound of a tambourine, and a trained monkey who read minds, and the multiple-use machine that could be used at the same time to sew on buttons and reduce fevers, and the apparatus to make a person forget his bad memories, and a poultice to lose time. . . ." (16).

The technique of the erudite list combining everyday items with archaic or exotic ones is used several times in *Love in the Time of Cholera*. Florentino Ariza lives with the women in a brothel (as the author once did). There the cleaning woman discovers "the number of things that men left after love":

They left vomit and tears, which seemed understandable to her, but they also left many enigmas of intimacy: puddles of blood, patches of excrement, glass eyes, gold watches, false teeth, lockets with golden curls, love letters, business letters, condolence letters—all kinds of letters. (77)

The catalogue of "secret medicines" taken by Dr. Urbino as soon as he arises at the crack of dawn includes: "potassium bromide to raise his spirits, salicylates for the ache in his bones when it rained, ergosterol drops for vertigo, belladonna for sound sleep" (8).

Always utilizing his experience as a journalist, García Márquez did extensive research for *One Hundred Years of Solitude, The Autumn of the Patriarch,* and *The General in His Labyrinth,* which required that he read histories of the life of Bolívar. For *One Hundred Years of Solitude* he has admitted to consulting books on alchemy, navigation, poisons, disease, cookery, home medicines, and Colombia's civil wars, with the twenty-four volumes of the *Encyclopedia Britannica* always by his side.

He asked himself: "How can you tell the sex of a shrimp? How is a man executed by a firing squad? How do you determine quality in bananas?" He insisted, perhaps with tongue in cheek, that he even dropped a character because he was unable to find anybody who could translate seven phrases in Papiamiento: "I had to look up a great deal about Sanskrit; I had to figure out the weight of 7,214 doubloons so as to be certain that they could be carried by four kids. . . ."[43]

Irony continually invades the narratives of García Márquez. For example, in *Chronicle of a Death Foretold* the narrator describes the uselessness of what the women are taught in terms of a list of what they know how to do: "They knew how to do screen embroidery, sew by machine, weave bone lace, wash and iron, make artificial flowers and fancy candy, and write engagement announcements" (31). Dramatic irony comes when the reader learns in *Love in the Time of Cholera* that Dr. Urbino does not like animals, which is ironic both because he loves the parrot and because his wife keeps a large number of pets:

> The first were three Dalmatians named after Roman emperors. . . . Then there were Abyssinian cats with the profiles of eagles and the manners of pharaohs, crossed-eyed Siamese and palace Persians with orange eyes. For several years an Amazonian monkey, chained by his waist to the mango tree in the patio, elicited a certain compassion because he had the sorrowful face of Archbishop Obdulio y Rey. There were all kinds of Guatemalan birds in cages along the passageways, and premonitory curlews and swamp herons with long yellow legs, and a young stag who came in through the windows to eat the anthurium in the flowerpots. (21–22)

To make all this believable, García Márquez adds his customary specificity, most notably in a time cue: "Shortly before the last civil war, when there was talk for the first time of a possible visit by

García Márquez at a press conference in Havana, Cuba, in 1986

the Pope, they brought a bird of paradise from Guatemala . . . " (22). The great irony of *Chronicle of a Death Foretold* comes in the words of one of the murderers in a triumph of economical dialogue: "'We killed him openly,' Pedro Vicario said, 'but we're innocent'" (49).

An examination of two of the short stories of García Márquez—one his best known, "The Incredible and Sad Tale of Innocent Eréndira and Her Heartless Grandmother," and the other the lesser-known "María dos Prazeres" (1979), both collected in *Strange Pilgrims* and equally brilliant although completely different in style—offer glimpses into García Márquez's techniques. The former story is set in an abstract, imaginary landscape, that of a desert, only to end up, with hope implied, by the sea.

The language reveals García Márquez at the height of his power, using metaphors and similes not just as figurative decoration but to further the plot. So the reader learns of the "wind of her misfortune," for Eréndira, an illegitimate child, treated as a slave by her "handsome white whale" of a grandmother (1). When Eréndira accidentally, out of exhaustion, burns down their elaborate house full of useless objects of another era, the grandmother forces her into prostitution so she can earn the money to repay her grandmother for the loss of her possessions.

Appealing to the senses, García Márquez writes of the grandmother's "succulent" (2) back. Her staff, because she is too fat to walk unassisted, is "like a bishop's crosier," the religious reference is ironic because the grandmother is utterly irreligious (2). Magic realism enters as animals are granted human sensibilities, a frequent technique employed by García Márquez, whose works are filled with the love of nature and all its creatures. Here the goat commits "suicide from desolation when the wind of misfortune blew" (3). The pet ostrich drinks from a bowl of water like a dog.

Exaggeration enters in the form of the "fourteen barefoot servant girls" (3) who once tended to the needs of this unholy family. Eréndira needs "six hours just to set and wind the clocks" (3). This statement seems like exaggeration, yet behind the image is a truth more potent than material reality. Eréndira works so hard, at so many tasks, that it must seem to her as if it takes at least six hours to set the clocks.

Despite fantastic elements, the dialogue is crisp and brings with it harsh reality. "My poor child," the grandmother tells Eréndira, "Life won't be long enough for you to pay me back for this mishap" (7). They travel onto the desert in search of smugglers as customers, dragging with them the bones of Eréndira's father and grandfather. A driver with whom they hitch a ride echoes the words of García Márquez's own grandfather, the Colonel: "This thing weighs as much as a dead man" (11).

The structure is episodic, and the plot furthered by numerical specificity as the grandmother counts down from the million pesos she insists she is owed. Soon she is owed "eight hundred seventy-two thousand three hundred fifteen pesos, less the four hundred and twenty which she's already paid me, making it eight hundred seventy-one thousand eight hundred ninety-five" (12). The grandmother figures that only "eight years, seven months, and eleven days" (15) more are needed to pay off the debt. The real meets the fantastic in Eréndira's complaint: "I've got ground glass in my bones"(16).

Because Eréndira is so innocent, she seems beautiful. At fourteen years of age and weighing only ninety pounds, she satisfies every man who sleeps with her. One of the men who experiences her charms is named Ulises, his name suggesting his bravery as a traveler, a boy "with lonely maritime eyes" (16). Anything connected with the sea in the work of García Márquez is at once positive. In a Romeo and Juliet motif, Ulises searches for a way to help Eréndira escape. There is gentle humor in García Márquez's insistence that despite her trade, Eréndira is still as innocent as Ulises, who "smells of flowers" (22):

"I never saw the sea," she said.
"It's like the desert but with water," said Ulises. (20–21)

Eréndira, like the Spanish picaro of the anonymous sixteenth-century novel *Lazarillo de Tormes,* has many adventures. She is kidnapped by missionaries and taken into a convent where she hears a nun play the clavichord, "her heart hanging by a thread" (29), the image offering a physical description of mental anguish. Ulises does not forget her. He is the son of a Guajiro Indian, a group appreciated by García Márquez, and it is his Guajira mother who notices that glass changes color when he touches it. "Those things happen only because of love," she says (32). Eréndira at one point escapes and attempts to shoot her pursuers with a pistol. However, García Márquez, in a splash of humor, makes the weapon "no good" because "[i]t used to belong to Sir Francis Drake" (43). Drake is a villain who, like a ghost, haunts the fiction of García Márquez, appearing at the unlikeliest moments and seemingly never to be put to rest.

Suddenly, close to the end of the story, in violation of the "rules" of writing fiction, a narrator appears. He is selling encyclopedias, as García Márquez once did. He comes upon the tent of Eréndira, whom her grandmother has now tied up with a dog chain. They have arrived at the sea, the place beyond human society, which is the realm of cruelty. Ulises stabs the grandmother, and what emerges from her wounds is "oily blood, shiny and green, just like mint honey" (58). Magic serves to make a point here, too: the grandmother was so brutal that she was scarcely human, and even her blood is an inhuman green. Eréndira escapes once more, but this time from Ulises. Abandoned, Ulises weeps, "from solitude and fear" (59). Eréndira runs, is still running "beyond the arid winds and the never-ending sunsets" (59), as if only in perpetual motion can evil be escaped and freedom enjoyed.

"María dos Prazeres" seems to be a much more realistic and straightforward narrative. It is set in a specific place, the city of Barcelona, in Spain. The story proceeds in what seems a straightforward manner. María has spent her life as a whore. She is now seventy-six years old and has a dream that she is about to die. At once, carefully, she begins to make arrangements for her demise. As the story opens, she is visited by a man from the undertakers. For García Márquez, humor can enliven the darkest moments and the most impoverished existence. Humor erupts at the beginning as María tells the young man: "I've lived in Catalonia for over fifty years, and this is the first time anyone has ever come to an appointment on time."[44]

Distinguishing this story over many others of García Márquez is the sense that history is alive and remains real for everyone, even an obscure former prostitute eking out a meager existence in Barcelona. In the work of García Márquez no one escapes from history, and even the apartment house in which María lives bears "the bullet holes of some inglorious battle" (103). Her apartment is furnished from "the chests of silks and brocades, which the Fascists had stolen from residences abandoned by the Republicans in the stampede of defeat" (103), another reminder of the Spanish Civil War, which changed the face of Spain for more than one generation.

María examines the plan of the cemetery and finds "the three adjacent, identical, anonymous graves where Buenaventura Durruri, killed in the Civil War, and two other anarchist leaders lay buried" (99). Their gravestones are blank, but every night someone writes their names on the stones, only for the guards to wipe them clean the next day so that no one will know who rests there. María allies herself with these Loyalist heroes who had been defeated by the fascist Generalissimo Francisco Franco in 1939.

She wants to rest in a grave near theirs, a wish deeply respected by the author and apparent in the kindliness of the tone of the narrator who describes her feelings. When the guard's back is turned, she writes Durruti's name on the first stone—in lipstick, "with a firm pulse and a heart stirred by nostalgia" (105). That firm pulse foreshadows the ending of the story.

Despite this strong political theme, magic enters the story through the person of María's dog, Noi, who demonstrates more humanity than do most of the people. When, upset that a visitor has arrived early in the morning, he jumps on a table and is reprimanded, two tears roll down his muzzle. María believes, and García Márquez with her, that animals should be taught to do the natural things they enjoy instead of useless acts like doing their business on a schedule.

María teaches Noi to cry over her grave site and to travel by himself to the cemetery on Sundays by memorizing the Ramblas bus route. Testing his progress, on one Sunday María follows him. She spots Noi "distant and serious among the Sunday flocks of children waiting for the traffic light to change at the Paseo de Gracia" (106). By naming the specific street, García Márquez helps the reader believe that a dog can wait for a traffic light to change. Even at this magical moment, however, the historical theme is woven into the imagery of the story. Along the route may be observed "the deep silences of the crippled war veterans tossing bread crumbs to pigeons." The consequences of war are long. María even feels "the same repressed tension that preceded the days when the anarchists had taken over the streets" (107).

Only near the end of the story does García Márquez secure the reader's compassion for María. In a flashback, told in a voice without pity or sentimentality, he describes the life history of his character. His use of magic and his disturbances of verisimilitude exist simultaneously with a biographical appreciation of character:

> She had told the Count that her mother sold her in the port of Manaus when she was fourteen years old, and that the first mate of a Turkish ship used her without mercy during the Atlantic crossing, and then abandoned her, with no money, no language and no name, in the light-filled swamp of the Paralelo. (109)

This passage provides an example of the intertextuality or cross-referencing within the works of García Márquez—María is the same age as Eréndira, fourteen, when she is sold into prostitution, one by her mother, the other by her grandmother.

The Count is the last of María's former clients, and they have been meeting once a month. Now, on the radio, as the fortuitous enters the story, they hear on the radio that "General Francisco Franco, eternal dictator of Spain, had assumed responsibility for deciding the fate of three Basque separatists who had just been condemned to death" (110).

The Count is elated. "'Then they'll be shot without fail,' he said, 'because the Caudillo is a just man.'" The moment serves as an epiphany for María, as she recognizes that she has nothing in common with the Count, who has revealed himself to be a fascist sympathizer. The fury she expresses is strong and deep, another foreshadowing. "'Well, you'd better pray he doesn't,' she said, 'because if they shoot even one of them I'll poison your soup'" (110).

María orders an anarchist's tombstone, one with neither name nor dates, although she cannot rest beside her fallen heroes; those places are taken. The ending of the story is as unexpected as life itself.

In a rainstorm, María and Noi are given a ride by a young chauffeur. "Shall I come up?" he suddenly asks María (113). García Márquez closes his story on an even more powerful epiphany. Suddenly María realizes that she has been mistaken in the meaning of "the premonitory dream that had changed her life for the past three years"—"'My God,' she said to herself in astonishment. 'So it wasn't death!'" (114).

It was not her death that she had dreamed, but an equally dramatic experience: the return of life. Her life had been so hard that she had mistaken the one for the other, a motif that provides this story with a profound catharsis. The unexpected ending of "María dos Prazeres" reveals once more the deeply humane perspective of Gabriel García Márquez, his affection for all of life, and his compassion especially for those whose path has been thorny.

SUBJECT TO REVISION

García Márquez, working from "intuition," has from the time of *One Hundred Years of Solitude,* which marked the triumphant end of his years of apprenticeship, seemed to revise his work less than many other authors. He has said that for him one of the most difficult aspects of writing is the first paragraph:

> I have spent many months on a first paragraph, and once I get it, the rest just comes out very easily. In the first paragraph you solve most of the problems with your book. The theme is defined, the style, the tone. At least in my case, the first paragraph is a kind of sample of what the rest of the book is going to be.[45]

The truth of this observation is manifest in the first paragraph of a novel of his maturity, *Love in the Time of Cholera:*

> It was inevitable: the scent of bitter almonds always reminded him of unrequited love. Dr. Juvenal Urbino noticed it as soon as he entered the still darkened house where he had hurried on an urgent call to attend a case that for him had lost all urgency many years before. The Antillean refugee Jeremiah de Saint-Amour, disabled war veteran, photographer of children, and his most sympathetic opponent in chess, had escaped the torments of memory with the aromatic fumes of gold cyanide. (3)

At once the reader is introduced to the "scent of bitter almonds" that hovers around the courtship of Fermina and her previous suitor, Florentino Ariza. Fermina Daza is not present, but in the word "love" she is already invoked in the last name of the suicide victim (*Amour* is French for "Love") whom Dr. Urbino has arrived to tend. The tone is one of rueful nostalgia, the emotion with which Florentino will endure five decades.

The theme of the seeming transitoriness of all things is present, and along with it the powerful reach of time, appearing here as a paradox: "he had hurried on an urgent call to attend a case that had for him lost all urgency many years before" (3), yet it is in fact an urgent case. The words "unrequited love," which appear in the first sentence, introduce the theme that will carry the story to its happy conclusion.

Early in his career, García Márquez changed his approach. His first influence was William Faulkner, an influence that appears in *Leaf Storm*. Afterward García Márquez wrote works that take place "in a village where there is no magic." He has termed *Los funerales de la Mamá Grande, No One Writes to the Colonel*, and *In Evil Hour* "journalistic literature," in which he had turned away from the example of Faulkner to that of Ernest Hemingway.[46] He stopped writing for five years after completing *In Evil Hour*, only to emerge in *One Hundred Years of Solitude* with a style that embodied characteristics of both Faulkner and Hemingway but was also completely his own. What García Márquez admired about Faulkner is that he "was surprised at certain things that happened in life, but he writes of them not as surprises but as things that happen every day."[47] It was the noncommittal voice of García Márquez's grandmother.

He originally planned to contain "the whole development" of *One Hundred Years of Solitude* within one house, "and anything external would be just in terms of its impact on the house."[48] Later he abandoned the working title, "The House," and brought into the story the external world, though limiting the action to the town of Macondo. He has said, "I had to live for twenty years and write four books of apprenticeship [*Leaf Storm, Los funerales de la Mamá Grande, No One Writes to the Colonel*, and *In Evil Hour*] to discover that . . . the story had to be told simply, the way my grandparents told it."[49]

His process of revision has altered with time. When he first began to write, he would complete a work without a break, creating a complete first draft. Afterward he would make corrections on the manuscript, make copies and correct it yet again.[50] By 1971 he was revising "line by line as I work, so that by the time a page is finished it's practically ready for the publisher. If it has a blot or a slip it won't do for me."[51] When he receives galley proofs, he is nearly finished—on the galley proofs for *One Hundred Years of Solitude* he changed only one word.

The most complex process of revision occurred with *The Autumn of the Patriarch*. He had begun with the idea of writing the entire story using the format of the dictator being tried in a people's court and then revealing his memories through an interior monologue. He later rejected this approach, discarding everything, he said, but the name of the main character. This statement is, of course, ironic since in the final version of the novel the dictator has no name. In the final version the story is told through a variety of voices, including that of the dictator's mother, and it begins not in a people's court but with the death of the patriarch. It was

ON WILLIAM FAULKNER AND ERNEST HEMINGWAY

"I don't know who said that novelists read the novels of others only to figure out how they are written. I believe it's true. We aren't satisfied with the secrets exposed on the surface of the page: we turn the book around to find the seams. In a way that's impossible to explain, we break the book down to its essential parts and then put it back together after we understand the mysteries of its personal clockwork. The effort is disheartening in Faulkner's books, because he doesn't seem to have an organic system of writing, but instead walks blindly through his biblical universe, like a herd of goats loosed in a shop full of crystal. Managing to dismantle a page of his, one has the impression of springs and screws left over, that it's impossible to put back together in its original state. Hemingway, by contrast, with less inspiration, with less passion and less craziness but with a splendid severity, left the screws fully exposed, as they are on freight cars. Maybe for that reason Faulkner is a writer who has had much to do with my soul, but Hemingway is the one who had the most to do with my craft—not simply for his books, but for his astounding knowledge of the aspect of craftsmanship in the science of writing."

García Márquez

From "Gabriel García Márquez Meets Ernest Hemingway," *The New York Times,* 26 July 1981.

his most complex work, and he felt he was doing well if he could finish four lines a day; the novel took seven years to complete.

In an example of intertextuality, García Márquez did allow an echo from *One Hundred Years of Solitude* into *The Autumn of the Patriarch.* He has an "idealistic young foreigner ask the patriarch for help to 'wipe out once and for all every conservative regime from Alaska to Patagonia,'" a phrase from the earlier novel. The visitor is the author's alter ego and surrogate, Colonel Aureliano Buendía.

His routine for writing has been the same for years. He awakens early, listens to the news, may read from six A.M. until eight, and then write from eight until one. Later this became from nine until two-thirty. He found that unlike the days of his youth when he was down and out in Paris, he could no longer write in hotels or borrowed rooms or on borrowed typewriters. In the early 1970s, when his sons were young, he could write "without any sort of interruption until half past two."[52]

His wife, Mercedes, filtered telephone calls. When his sons, Rodrigo and Gonzalo, came home, noise began in the house. Lunch was between half past two and three, in the Spanish style. When he awoke from his siesta at four, he read and listened to music. He always listens to music, he says, "except when I'm writing because I attend to it more than to what I'm writing."[53]

While he was working on *Love in the Time of Cholera,* and they lived by the sea in Cartagena, Mercedes packed a lunch and went to the beach and waited for him there with friends. She did not inform him who would be present on a given day, so he never knew whom to expect, an experience he enjoyed. After lunch he had a siesta and then went out into the streets "to look for places where my characters would go, to talk to people and pick up language and atmosphere. So the next morning I would have fresh material I had brought from the streets."[54]

CRITICAL RECEPTION

García Márquez, ever in the habit of consulting his closest friends on a manuscript, showed the first three chapters of *One Hundred Years of Solitude* to his friend, the Mexican novelist Carlos Fuentes. In a Mexican magazine Fuentes wrote of his ecstatic response:

> I have just finished reading the first seventy-five pages of Cien Años de Soledad. They are absolutely magisterial. . . . all "fictional" history coexists with "real" history, what is dreamed with what is documented, and thanks to the legends, the lies, the exaggerations, the myths . . . Macondo is made into a universal territory, in a story almost biblical in its foundations, its generations and degenerations, in a story of the origin and destiny of human time and of the dreams and desires by which men are saved or destroyed.[55]

When *One Hundred Years of Solitude* was published, the praise was unanimous. As Klaus Müller-Bergh put it in *Books Abroad,* it created "an earthquake, a maelstrom."[56] Chilean poet Pablo Neruda was quoted in *Time* magazine as calling *One Hundred Years of Solitude* "the greatest revelation in the Spanish language since the *Don Quixote* of Cervantes."[57] Novelist William Kennedy wrote in the *National Observer* that *One Hundred Years of Solitude* "is the first piece of literature since the Book of Genesis that should be required reading for the entire human race."[58] Regina Janes, in her book *Gabriel García Márquez: Revolutions in Wonderland,* describes it as a "total novel" that treats Latin America, "socially, historically, politically, mythically, and epically." It was "at once accessible and intricate, lifelike and self-consciously, self-referentially fictive."[59]

Critics have seen García Márquez not just as an individual writer telling his distinctive stories but as the soul of Latin American writing, one who brought the fiction of that continent to a world audience. José Donoso, in his chronicle of "The Boom" in Latin American writing, was the first to note that García Márquez was representing more than himself. Formerly a writer whose reputation was "skimpy," with *One Hundred Years of Solitude* García Márquez inspired a frenzy of interest in Spanish American writing:

> It has to be asserted that the Boom—noisy and vulgar and tarnished with the flattery and envy by which it is known today—gave a reason for publishers to pull hair from their beards in frustration for having rejected such-and-such a manuscript in which they did not know how to recognize quality; and it gave a reason, too, for the novelists but only a few—to be able at last to impose modest conditions by means of literary agents, who soon began to collect Latin Americans. All of this begins with *One Hundred Years of Solitude.*[60]

Mario Vargas Llosa has spoken of the publication in Buenos Aires of *One Hundred Years of Solitude* as "a literary earthquake throughout Latin America. The critics recognized the book as a masterpiece of the art of fiction and the public endorsed this opinion, systematically exhausting new editions, which, at one point, appeared at the astounding rate of one a week."[61] By the late 1990s it had sold more than twenty million copies and had been translated into thirty languages.

In the United States the same view prevailed. García Márquez, wrote John Sturrock in the *New York Times Book Review,* "is one of the small number of contemporary writers from Latin American who have given to its literature a maturity and dignity it never had before."[62] In the *Washington Post* David Streitfield went further, arguing that "Gabriel García Márquez combines both respect (bordering on adulation) and mass popularity (also bordering on adulation)."[63]

Critics have noted as well the historical and sociological values of the novel; writing in the *Saturday Review,* Robert G. Mead Jr. pointed out that "although [*One Hundred Years of Solitude*] is first and always a story, the novel also has value as a social and historical document"; Mead noted that "Macondo may be regarded as a microcosm of the development of much of the Latin American continent."[64]

The critical reception of his other novels has been nearly as enthusiastic. In *TLS: The Times Literary Supplement* Bill Buford called *Chronicle of a Death Foretold* "a mesmerizing work that clearly establishes Marquez as one of the most accomplished, and the most 'magical' of political novelists writing today."[65] In the *New York Review of Books* Robert M. Adams wrote of this novel that "the investigation of an ancient murder takes on the quality of a hallucinatory exploration, a deep groping search into the gathering darkness for a truth that continually slithers away." [66]

Love in the Time of Cholera, which would be the master work of any other novelist, received great acclaim. In the *New York Times Book Review* the novelist Thomas Pynchon argued that it "would be presumptuous to speak of moving 'beyond' *One Hundred Years of Solitude* but clearly García Márquez has moved somewhere else, not least into deeper awareness of the way in which, as Florentino comes to learn, 'nobody teaches life anything.'"

Calling *Love in the Time of Cholera* "a shining and heartbreaking novel," Pynchon asserts that "the Garcíamárquesian voice we have come to recognize from the other fiction has matured, found and developed new resources, been brought to a level where it can at once be classical and familiar, opalescent and pure, able to praise and curse, laugh and cry, fabulate and sing and when called upon, take off and soar."[67]

In the daily *New York Times* Michiko Kakutani called it "a rich commodious novel, a novel whose narrative power is matched only by its generosity of vision."[68] And writing about *Of Love and Other Demons* (1994), R. Z. Sheppard in *Time* magazine wrote that it could stand as a summary of all the author's work. García Márquez, Sheppard wrote, "demonstrates once again the vigor of his own passion: the daring and irresistible couplings of history and imagination."[69]

In the course of the long career of García Márquez there have been some small voices of dissent. Most have centered on *The Autumn of the Patriarch,* the most experimental and least accessible, perhaps, of his novels. Writing in *The Washington Post Book World,* J. D. O'Hara complained about this novel that for all his "magical realism," García Márquez "can only remind us of the many real-life parallels; he cannot exaggerate them." O'Hara wrote that "although he can turn into grisly cartoons the squalor and paranoia of actual dictatorships, he can scarcely parody them; reality has anticipated him again."[70] Perhaps he means that reality is so powerful that García Márquez has no need of his repertoire of techniques, exaggeration, parody, and magic, to make his point. Hence the novel lacks the stylistic necessity of his earlier works. Equally disappointed, Walter Clemons in *Newsweek* found *The Autumn of the Patriarch* "both oversumptuous and underpopulated . . . an extended piece of magnificent writing."[71]

Even the exquisite *Chronicle of a Death Foretold* has been attacked. In the right-wing *National Review* D. Keith Mano wrote that because the narrator "has been sequestered as a juror might be . . . he cannot comment or probe: and this rather kiln-dries the novel." Mano is disappointed that the main characters "are left without development or chiaroscuro. They seem cryptic and surface-hard: film characters really . . . Beyond a Warren Report-meticulous detective reconstruction, it is hard to care much for these people. Emotion, you see, might skew our clarity."[72]

Mano is demanding of García Márquez an approach that was never his, a form of psychological realism that would enlist the reader to identify emotionally with his characters. García Márquez prefers, rather, always to remain at a certain distance, to reveal people by their actions, and to leave the reader with the same degree of mystery about his characters that people experience toward other people in everyday life where no one truly knows another human being.

Other critics, such as Michael Dorris writing of *Love in the Time of Cholera* in the *Chicago Tribune* book section, apply their own definition of "political correctness" to the novels, and so find García Márquez wanting. Dorris wrote that García Márquez portrayed an "anachronistic" world of machismo and misogyny, as if there were some flaw in an author depicting accurately the culture of a given era.[73] More solidly, Ronald Wright has written in the *Globe and Mail* (Toronto) that *Love in the Time of Cholera* was not so much a love story as a meditation "on the equivocal nature of romanticism and romantic love."[74]

An admirer of García Márquez, Gene H. Bell-Villada has attacked this novel for "an overabundance of detail (of 'metonymy,' as theorists might say), a discursiveness that at times becomes long-winded, and, in the middle chapters particularly, a somewhat loose and episodic structure," even as he notes that this is García Márquez's "most joyous book."[75]

In Colombia *The General in His Labyrinth* was greeted by considerable controversy. Some objected to García Márquez's making Bolívar less than a saint and rather a man who uses obscenities and enjoys a bounty of available women, most younger than himself. Others complained that he infused this novel with his own prejudices, a preference for the tropical Caribbean culture and a scorn for the *cachaco* or upland *bogotano* Colombians, those who dwell in the interior of the country. Some, perhaps the loudest and most vociferous, argued that García Márquez had sided with Bolívar to the detriment of his political contemporaries.

In *TLS* John Butt objected that García Márquez had left "much unexplained about the mental processes of the Liberator." Butt fails to take into account that this was a documentary novel based on historical fact and that the information he desires may simply not have been available. "We learn far more about Bolívar's appearance, sex-life, surroundings and public actions than about his thoughts and motives," Butt wrote.[76] However, this may be all that is known about Bolívar.

Other critics have attacked García Márquez for plagiarism, for borrowing plots and themes from other authors and presenting them as his own. As Rita Guibert notes, at a writers' conference in Bonn in 1970 a critic named Günther Lorenz claimed that *One Hundred Years of Solitude* was a plagiarism of Honoré Balzac's *La Recherche d'absolu* (1834; translated as *The Philosopher's Stone,* 1844). Luis Cova García published an article titled "Coincidence or Plagiarism?" in the Honduran review *Ariel* suggesting the same. A French professor named Marcelle Bargas, whose specialization was Balzac, agreed that "the vices of one society and period, as depicted by Balzac, had been transferred to *One Hundred Years of Solitude*."[77]

Confronted by these attacks, García Márquez defended himself. He denied having read Balzac's novel before writing *One Hundred Years of Solitude*, though he did read it after learning of the charges of plagiarism; he told Guibert that "even if I were prepared to accept the fact that I had read it before and decided to plagiarize it, only some five pages of my book could have come from *La Recherche*, and a single character, the alchemist." He went on to ridicule the critics who were charging him with plagiarism: "I ask you, five pages and one character against three hundred pages and some two hundred characters that don't come from Balzac's book. I think the critics ought to have gone on and searched two hundred other books to see where the rest of the characters came from."[78]

Echoing Lillian Hellman, who once taught a course at Harvard University in "Stealing" in which she argued that writers always borrow ideas and techniques from others, García Márquez told Guibert, "I'm not at all afraid of the idea of plagiarism. I can myself say where I find Cervantes or Rabelais in *One Hundred Years of Solitude*—not as to quality but because of things I've taken from them and put there. But I can also take the book line by line—and this is a point the critics will never be able to reach—and say what event or memory from real life each comes from." The practice of writers borrowing from other writers—in both plot and technique—has gone on as long as literature has existed.

"If I had to write Romeo and Juliet tomorrow, I would do it," García Márquez declared, "and would feel it was marvelous to have the chance to write it again." The most important book in his life has been Sophocles' *Oedipus Rex*, and he told Guibert that he once thought of writing a story called "Oedipus the Mayor": "In this case I wouldn't have been charged with plagiarism because I should have begun by calling him Oedipus"—this idea later formed the basis for the motion picture *Edipo alcalde* (Oedipus Mayor, 1996). He has concluded that "the idea of plagiarism is already finished."[79]

García Márquez has also been accused of sexism, of differentiating men and women, so that in his works men are figures of power while women are awarded a completely different set of traits. Some critics, such as Robin Fiddian, have found in his persistent depiction of women as "vulnerable mother-figures" a "conservative sexual ideology which, in its perpetuation of given assumptions about the function of gender in social relations, may actually further that system's interests."[80] Indeed such Earth Mother figures do appear in abundance in *One Hundred Years of Sol-*

itude, from the matriarch Úrsula, to the prostitute Pilar Ternera, to Nigramanta, who comforts Aureliano Babilonia.

So Fiddian notes in *Love in the Time of Cholera* "an early description [which] depicts Juvenal and Fermina's house as a place which displays throughout the good judgment and careful attention of a woman who had her feet firmly on the ground" raises the spectre of a sexist mystique that attributes a priori one set of characteristics (for example, pragmatism and reliability) to women, another quite distinct set to men, who are depicted as helplessly idealistic and impractical."[81]

Luis Harss, writing earlier, expressed a view similar to Fiddian's, noting that there is a decided sexist implication in García Márquez's assigning of one set of characteristics to men, qualities that include access to power and to the outer world, and another to women that involve power only in the home:

> In García Márquez men are flighty creatures, governed by whim, fanciful dreamers given to impressible delusions, capable of moments of haughty grandeur, but basically weak and unstable. Women, on the other hand, are solid, sensible, unvarying and down to earth, paragons of order and stability. They seem to be more at home in the world, more deeply rooted in their nature, closer to the center of gravity, therefore better equipped to face up to circumstances.[82]

Dust jacket for the first U.S. edition of García Márquez's novel *Crónica de una muerte anunciada* (1981), in which an entire town knows that a man will be murdered and yet no one tries to prevent the killing

Indeed, some of his own statements seem to add fuel to the views of these critics. Often García Márquez has contrasted women and men. "Men waver," he has said, "but women survive. Thanks to women, history is able to continue its normal course." It seems, he has added, "as if men are the protagonists of history, but if they are, it is because someone is giving them support from behind and that someone is a woman. My women are more in touch with reality." Men, he concludes, are impatient, untrustworthy, and in fact, are "weaklings."[83]

Elsewhere he has asserted that "it's the power of women in the home—in society as it's organized, particularly in Latin America—that enables men to launch out into every sort of chimerical and strange adventure, which is what makes our America."[84]

García Márquez has acknowledged that the commentaries about gender offered by critics created a problem for him "because I now find it more difficult to work on that material." To the critics who attacked him for machismo, García Márquez has a quick answer. "What I most definitely am is antimachista. *Machismo* is cowardly, a lack of manliness."[85] García Márquez has replied as well that he cannot be accused of sexism since he has assigned to his women traits ordinarily offered to male characters in fiction: "My women are masculine."[86]

Whatever the reception to his work, he does not make adjustments based upon critical feedback. He says he does not "pay much attention to the critics." Nor does he "compare what I think with what they say. So I don't really know whether I agree with them or not. . . ."[87]

At times he has been annoyed by a critic's interpretation of his work. Melvin Maddock of *Life* magazine asked, referring to *One Hundred Years of Solitude*, "Is Macondo meant to be taken as a sort of realistic history of Latin America? Or does García Márquez intend it as a metaphor for all modern men and their ailing communities?"[88] García Márquez denied both of these explanations. Asked about Maddock's questions, he replied playfully that "I merely wanted to tell the story of a family who for a hundred years did everything they could to prevent having a son with a pig's tail, and just because of their very efforts to avoid having one they ended by doing so." He has approved of the comment of another critic who, more modestly, praised *One Hundred Years of Solitude* as being "the first real description of the private life of a Latin American family."[89]

He admits that when he first began to publish his fiction, the words of the critics used to interest him. By the 1970s this was no longer true. He has found that "they seem to have said very little that's new." There was another danger. There came a point when he

THE WRITER AS CRAFTSMAN

"Writing something is almost as hard as making a table. With both you are working with reality, a material just as hard as wood. Both are full of tricks and techniques. Basically very little magic and a lot of hard work are involved. And as Proust, I think, said, it takes ten percent inspiration and ninety percent perspiration. I never have done any carpentry but it's the job I admire most, especially because you can never find anyone to do it for you."

García Márquez

From 1981 interview with Peter Stone, "Gabriel García Márquez," in *Writers at Work: The Paris Review Interviews: Sixth Series,* edited by George Plimpton (New York: Viking, 1984), p. 325.

discovered that "in a way they were telling me what my next book ought to be like." The critics were "rationalizing" his work, and he caught himself finding "things that were not convenient for me to discover," even as they may have been true. "My work stopped being intuitive," he noticed. [90]

Above all talents, he has praised intuition as being the most useful for a novelist. Toward critics, he retains a decided distrust. He threw out, he has confessed, a drawer full "of working notes, diagrams, sketches and memoranda" that he had used in the creation of *One Hundred Years of Solitude* in part "so that the way the book was constructed shouldn't be known—that's something absolutely private."[91] That distrust was also expressed in his evasive statement to the press when he returned to Colombia from Spain to work on *The Autumn of the Patriarch:* "I said that I was coming back because I had forgotten what a guava smelled like."[92]

Throughout his career he has continued to practice the craft of journalism, finding that "it keeps me in contact with the real world, particularly political journalism and politics."[93]

NOTES

1. Peter Stone, "Gabriel García Márquez," in *Writers at Work: The Paris Review Interviews: Sixth Series,* edited by George Plimpton (New York: Viking, 1984), pp. 318–319.

2. *Conversations with Latin American Writers: Gabriel García Márquez,* interviewed by Silvia Lemus, 44 mins., Films for the Humanities & Sciences, 1998, video.

3. Rita Guibert, "Gabriel Garcia Marquez," in her *Seven Voices: Seven Latin American Writers Talk to Rita Guibert* (New York: Knopf, 1973), p. 307.

4. Ibid.

5. José Donoso, *The Boom in Spanish American Literature: A Personal History,* translated by Gregory Kolavakos (New York: Columbia University Press in association with the Center for Inter-American Relations, 1977), pp. 96–97.

6. Quoted in Guibert, *Seven Voices,* p. 306.

7. William Kennedy, "The Yellow Trolley Car in Barcelona and Other Visions: A Profile of Gabriel García Márquez," in his *Riding the Yellow Trolley Car: Selected Nonfiction* (New York: Viking, 1993), p. 258.

8. Claudia Dreifus, "Playboy Interview: Gabriel García Márquez," *Playboy,* 30 (February 1983): 172.

9. Stone, *Paris Review,* p. 317.

10. Ibid., p. 337.

11. Donoso, *The Boom,* p. 89.

12. *Gabriel García Márquez: Magic and Reality,* produced by Harold Mantell, 60 mins., Films for the Humanities & Sciences, 1981, video.

13. Ibid.

14. *Love in the Time of Cholera,* translated by Edith Grossman (New York: Knopf, 1988), p. 53.

15. *One Hundred Years of Solitude,* translated by Gregory Rabassa (New York: Harper & Row, 1970), p. 106.

16. García Márquez quoted in *García Márquez: The Man and His Work* by Gene H. Bell-Villada (Chapel Hill & London: University of North Carolina Press, 1990), p. 109.

17. Stone, *Paris Review,* p. 324.

18. Ibid.

19. Ibid., p. 326.

20. *Chronicle of a Death Foretold,* translated by Gregory Rabassa (New York: Harper & Row, 1982), p. 18.

21. Ibid.

22. Ibid., p. 323.

23. Ibid., p. 326.

24. Dreifus, *Playboy* interview: 74.

25. Michael Wood, *Gabriel García Márquez: One Hundred Years of Solitude* (Cambridge & New York: Cambridge University Press, 1990), p. 76.

26. Guibert, *Seven Voices,* p. 323.

27. Stone, *Paris Review,* p. 328.

28. Guibert, *Seven Voices,* p. 323.

29. Marlise Simons, "A Talk With Gabriel García Márquez," *New York Times,* 5 December 1982.

30. Guibert, *Seven Voices,* p. 323.

31. Marlise Simons, "Love and Age: A Talk with García Márquez," *New York Times Book Review,* 7 April 1985.

32. Guibert, *Seven Voices,* p. 323.

33. Stone, *Paris Review,* p. 325.

34. "The Incredible and Sad Tale of Innocent Eréndira and Her Heartless Grandmother," in *Innocent Eréndira and Other Stories,* translated by Rabassa (New York: Harper & Row, 1978), p 22.

35. Dreifus, *Playboy* interview: 74.

36. *The Autumn of the Patriarch,* translated by Rabassa (New York: Harper & Row, 1976), p. 9.

37. *The General in His Labyrinth,* translated by Grossman (New York: Knopf, 1990).

38. Stone, *Paris Review,* p. 329.

39. Guibert, *Seven Voices,* p. 321.

40. Ibid., pp. 318–319.

41. Stone, *Paris Review,* p. 329.

42. Dreifus, *Playboy* interview: 174.

43. Guiber, *Seven Voices,* p. 326.

44. "María dos Prazeres," in *Strange Pilgrims: Twelve Stories,* translated by Grossman (New York: Knopf, 1993), p. 98.

45. Stone, *Paris Review,* p. 331.

46. Ibid., p. 323.

47. Kennedy, *Riding the Yellow Trolley Car,* p. 253.

48. Stone, *Paris Review,* p. 337.

49. Wood, "Chronology, 1961–1967," in his *Gabriel García Márquez.*

50. A revised proof page for *El otoño del patriarca* is reproduced in his interview with Stone, *Paris Review,* p. 314.

51. Guibert, *Seven Voices,* p. 324.

52. Guibert, *Seven Voices,* p. 311.

53. Ibid.

54. Simons, "Love and Age."

55. Quoted in Kennedy, *Riding the Yellow Trolley Car,* p. 261.

56. Klaus Müller-Bergh, "Relato de un náufrago: García Márquez's Tale of Shipwreck and Survival at Sea," *Books Abroad,* 47 (Summer 1973): 460.

57. Quoted in "Magic, Matter, and Money: Pioneers Who Have Explored Four Aspects of Reality," *Time,* 120 (1 November 1982): 88.

58. William Kennedy, "All of Life, Sense and Nonsense, Fills an Argentine's Daring Fable," *National Observer,* 9 (20 April 1970): 23.

59. Regina Janes, *Gabriel García Márquez: Revolutions in Wonderland* (Columbia: University of Missouri Press, 1981), p. 7.

60. Donoso, *The Boom,* p. 89.

61. Mario Vargas Llosa, "From Aracataca to Macondo," in *Modern Critical Views: Gabriel García Márquez,* edited by Harold Bloom (New York: Chelsea House, 1989), p. 5.

62. John Sturrock, "Shorter Márquez," *New York Times Book Review,* 16 July 1978, p. 3.

63. David Streitfield, "The Intricate Solitude of Gabriel Garcia Marquez," *Washington Post,* 10 April 1994, p. F1.

64. Robert G. Mead Jr., *"One Hundred Years of Solitude,"* *Saturday Review* (7 March 1970): 34–35.

65. Bill Buford, "Haughty Falconry and Collective Guilt," *TLS: The Times Literary Supplement* (London), 10 September 1982, p. 965.

66. Robert M. Adams, "Big Little Book," *New York Review of Books,* 30 (14 April 1983): 3.

67. Thomas Pynchon, "The Heart's Eternal Vow," *New York Times Book Review,* 10 April 1988, pp. 48–49.

68. Michiko Kakutani, "García Márquez Novel Covers Love and Time," *New York Times,* 6 April 1988, p. C21.

69. R. Z. Sheppard, "Love Among the Ruins," *Time,* 145 (22 May 1995): 73.

70. J. D. O'Hara, "Sick, Simpering Tyrant," *The Washington Post Book World,* 14 November 1976, p. 14.

71. Walter Clemons, "A Dictator's Debris," *Newsweek,* 88 (8 November 1976): 105.

72. D. Keith Mano, "A Death Foretold," *National Review* (10 June 1983): 700.

73. Michael Dorris, *Chicago Tribune,* 31 October 1993.

74. Ronald Wright, *Globe and Mail* (Toronto), 21 May 1988.

75. Bell-Villada, *The Man and His Work,* pp. 201–202.

76. John Butt, "The Liberator in Defeat," *TLS: The Times Literary Supplement,* (London)14–20 July 1989, p. 781.

77. Guibert, *Seven Voices,* p. 316.

78. Ibid.

79. Ibid., p. 317.

80. Robin Fiddian, "A Prospective Post-script: Apropos of Love In *The Times Of Cholera,"* in *Gabriel García Márquez: New Readings,* edited by Bernard McGuirk and Richard Cardwell (Cambridge: Cambridge University Press, 1987), p. 201.

81. Ibid., p. 202.

82. Quoted in Bell-Villada, *The Man and His Work,* p. 100.

83. *Gabriel García Márquez: Magic and Reality.*

84. Guibert, *Seven Voices,* p. 316.

85. Ibid.

86. Quoted by Luis Harss and Barbara Dohmann, "Gabriel García Márquez, or the Lost Chord," *Into the Mainstream: Conversations with Latin-American Writers* (New York: Harper & Row, 1966), p. 327.

87. Ibid., p. 313.

88. Quoted in Guibert, *Seven Voices,* p. 314.

89. Ibid.

90. Ibid., p. 313.

91. Ibid., p. 326.

92. Stone, *Paris Review,* p. 327.

93. Stone, *Paris Review,* p. 328.

GARCÍA MÁRQUEZ'S ERA

GARCÍA MÁRQUEZ'S COUNTRY

Gabriel García Márquez was born in Colombia, the fourth largest country in South America. It is situated in the northern part of the continent, just southeast of Panama, and is bordered on the east by Venezuela and Brazil and on the southwest by Ecuador and Peru. Colombia commands coastlines on both the Pacific Ocean and the Caribbean Sea. Politically, Colombia is divided into thirty-two administrative departments and the special capital district.

The national language is Spanish. Founded by Spanish conquistadores in 1538, the capital of the country is Bogotá, formerly known as Santa Fe de Bogotá; García Márquez uses the original name in *The General In His Labyrinth*. Bogotá is located in the interior in the Andean highlands and has a culture, as well as a climate and philosophy, diametrically opposed to that of the coast. The people of Bogotá and the interior are called *cachacos*, and those of the coast, *costeños*. Four hundred miles of jungle and mountains separate the two regions.

An understanding of the history of Colombia is necessary to an understanding of the fiction of García Márquez. As Regina Janes notes, he himself "once remarked that the reader of *Cien años de soledad* who was not familiar with the history of his country, Colombia, might appreciate the novel as a good novel, but much of what happens in it would make no sense to him."[1]

As early as colonial times, when it was part of the Viceroyalty of New Granada (encompassing most of present-day Colombia, Venezuela, and Ecuador), Colombia was already a society with strictly stratified classes. Those at the apex of society were people of Spanish blood who had been born in Spain, the *peninsulares*. This elite formed the basis of an oligarchy that would continue in power in Colombia until the end of the twentieth century. All other Colombians occupied a lower position in the social hierarchy.

Criollos, people of Spanish descent born in Colombia, were regarded as inferior to the *peninsulares,* but they were socially superior to the largest class, which would become the largest group throughout Latin America, the mestizos. The mestizos were of mixed Spanish and Indian blood. By the end of the twentieth century most Indians had either been assimilated or had intermarried with Colombians of Spanish or African descent, and only 1 percent of the Colombian population was considered to be of pure Indian stock. The mother of Ulises in "The Incredible and Sad Tale of Innocent Eréndira and Her Heartless Grandmother" is a Guajira Indian and is treated with respect and admiration by the author. García Márquez also treats with special sympathy those at the bottom of the social ladder, the *zambos,* people of mixed African and Indian blood, descended from black slaves and indigenous Americans. The disenchanted groom of *Chronicle of a Death Foretold,* Bayardo San Román, is a *zambo.*

Simón Bolívar, Liberator of Colombia and the protagonist of García Márquez's historical novel, *The General in His Labyrinth* (1990)

Sixty percent of the population is mestizo; blacks and mulattos compose about 20 percent of the population, many residing in the Caribbean Coastal Lowlands, the birthplace of García Márquez. The Bantu noun for *banana* is in fact *macondo,* the name García Márquez chose for his fictionalized version of the *Zona Bananero* (Banana Zone); in his youth there was even an actual banana plantation called "Macondo." The Spanish had imported African slaves to the colony of New Granada, an event that appears in the fiction of García Márquez in *Chronicle of a Death Foretold.*

The author's point of view toward the slave trade is apparent in this novel. Santiago Nasar, the perhaps innocent victim, "pointed to an intermittent light at sea and told us that it was the soul in torment of a slave ship that had sunk with a cargo of blacks from Senegal across from the main harbor mouth at Cartagena de Indias."[2] The image is interpolated into the narrative purely to express the author's indignation at the history of degradation that is the legacy of his countrymen.

This legacy is one that García Márquez himself claims. When he traveled to Angola on a journalistic assignment in the 1970s, he pronounced himself a "mestizo."[3] Later he added to that description of his racial heritage. "Not long ago," García Márquez says in the documentary movie *Magic and Reality,* "I realized that I was a mulatto."[4] However, as the grandson of Colonel Nicolás Márquez, the leading figure in the town of Aracataca, his position was high.

It was in Colombia that the revolutionary movement to throw off Spanish colonial rule in South America began on 20 July 1810, when *criollo* leaders in Bogotá declared their independence from both the puppet government that had been installed in Spain by Napoleon Bonaparte and the *peninsulare*-dominated resistance council. The colonial elites argued among themselves about whether they should form a national government that was federalist, resembling the United States, or centralist and more authoritarian. The great federalist leader was named Camilo Torres—namesake of García Márquez's college friend Father Camilo Torres Restrepo; the centralists were led by Antonio Nariño. Civil war loomed before the independent country was even established. The question of the separation of church and state was a deciding issue. These disagreements led to the so-called Patria Boba (Foolish Fatherland) period, with the factions splitting the former colony into several small republics that squabbled among themselves, thus allowing the Spanish to reconquer much of the territory by 1816.

Simón Bolívar, who became known as El Libertador (The Liberator), took charge of the independence forces. He managed to enlist the masses in the war against Spain, and after the last major royalist force was defeated at the Battle of Boyaca in August of 1819, independence was secured.

Bolívar became the first president of the new country, Gran Colombia, which encompassed present-day Colombia, Ecuador, Panama, and Venezuela. Later appointed dictator, he was forced to resign in 1830, and both Ecuador and Venezuela soon seceded from Gran Colombia.

The followers of Bolívar, and those of Francisco de Paula Santander, the first vice president, formed the core of the Conservative and Liberal parties, which formally came into existence around the elections of 1849. Before long these two parties, heirs to the earlier centralist and federalist factions, would enter into the series of civil wars that are reflected in many of the novels of García Márquez. These civil wars ran from the nineteenth into the twentieth century.

The Liberals were intent on creating a new society and on dismantling the colonial legacy. They favored the separation of church and state, free trade, restrictions on presidential power, freedom of the press, freedom of religion, and the abolition of slavery. The Liberals are the party of Colonel Aureliano Buendía.

The Conservatives were committed to maintaining the traditions and institutions established during the colonial period, which they saw as essential to preserving their cultural and national identity. They strongly supported the church retaining all of the power with which the Spanish had invested it. They saw no reason to reduce government control of the economy or to abolish slavery. The Conservatives proposed a society rooted in the traditions of authoritarian Spain and sought to eliminate any new freedoms that might challenge the status quo.

Liberals were represented by the color red and Conservatives by the color blue; when the new mayor arrives in Macondo in *One Hundred Years of Solitude* and demands that all the houses be painted blue, the reader immediately knows his political orientation. Hundreds of thousands of people have died in Colombia over the difference in color, red or blue.[5]

Colonel Nícolas Márquez, the grandfather of the author, fought in the wars between the Liberals and the Conservatives as a Liberal. His grandson, however, rejects

A TRADITION OF CONFLICT

The following list of the major civil wars in Colombia in the nineteenth century does not include minor uprisings, bloodless coups, abortive plots, or riots.

Rebellion of 1830-1831. 10 August to 28 April. Attempt by General Rafael Urdaneta to establish a dictatorship.

Rebellion of 1839; or, Rebellion of the Minor Convents. July to August. Uprising in opposition to the closing of religious houses.

Rebellion of 1840-1842; or, War of the Supreme Commanders. Several uncoordinated federalist revolts.

Rebellion of 1851-1852. May 1851 to January 1852. Conservative revolt.

Rebellion of 1854. 17 April to 4 December. Brief dictatorship of General José María Melo.

Rebellion of 1859-1862; or, Federal War. Established Liberal-dominated United States of Colombia (1863-1885).

Rebellion of 1876-1877. July 1876 to April 1877. Conservative revolt.

Rebellion of 1884-1885. 17 August 1884 to 26 August 1885. Liberal revolt.

Rebellion of 1895. 22 January to 15 March. Series of unsuccessful Liberal revolts.

Rebellion of 1899-1903; or, War of the Thousand Days. 17 October 1899 to 1 June 1903. Liberal revolt.

Source: Robert H. Davis, *Historical Dictionary of Colombia*, second edition (Metuchen, N.J. & London: Scarecrow Press, 1993).

Dust jacket for the first U.S. edition of García Márquez's
novel about Simón Bolívar

the Liberals and Conservatives both as equally contemptible representatives of the ruling oligarchy. As García Márquez puts it in *One
Hundred Years of Solitude,* the only real difference between the Liberals and the Conservatives is that the Liberals go to Mass at five
o'clock and the Conservatives go at eight.

Since colonial days, the upper class has been closely identified with the religious hierarchy. The priesthood has been largely
made up of men of upper-class or upper-middle-class origins who
have shared the values of the ruling oligarchy. They continued social
relationships with the friends of their youth, sharing authority and
an understanding that excluded participation by anyone not of the
traditional elite. The bishop in *Chronicle of a Death Foretold,* who
refuses to set his feet on land to say mass for the people anxiously
awaiting his arrival, reflects the view of García Márquez toward this
religious hierarchy. There are, however, a few positive images of
priests in the work of García Márquez, such as the priest nicknamed
"Pup" in *Leaf Storm* and the Camilo Torres–like priest in *The Autumn
of the Patriarch.*

The Liberals and Conservatives have succeeded in maintaining a traditional pyramidal structure for Colombian society. Members of the ruling oligarchy constitute themselves in informal and small decision-making groups. Called *roscas*, the name of a twisted pastry, these groups trade favors among themselves and maintain intricate social and political ties—twisted and contorted like the pastry after which they are named. The *roscas* are a form of "old boy network" by which the ruling oligarchy dispenses patronage, thus perpetuating its power—if one does not belong to a *rosca*, one is not really part of the upper or upper middle classes.

This oligarchy of two parties has thwarted the emergence of other parties organized around socioeconomic interests instead of traditional loyalties. Colombia, Michael Wood writes, has had "a democracy of the upper classes . . . a contest between rival oligarchies."[6] Despite the unraveling of the social order, the traditional parties continued in the second half of the twentieth century to believe that government leadership was the prerogative of a paternalistic upper class whose members made the decisions for the nation and its people, a perspective abhorrent to a socialist such as García Márquez.

Historically, when moderate factions within each party have been in power, the Liberals and the Conservatives have worked out their differences, since, as García Márquez notes, there is not much difference ideologically between them. Although the parties were once clearly ideologically opposed, since the early twentieth century both have supported the status quo and have generally opposed altering the existing social structure.

During periods when radical factions were in control, one party has sought through violent means to eliminate the rival party's participation in the political process, as during the so-called War of the Thousand Days (1899–1902), of which Colonel Márquez was a veteran and in which more than one hundred thousand were killed, and the period known as La Violencia (The Violence, 1948–1966), which claimed nearly three hundred thousand lives. Ostensibly a democracy since 1886 under a constitution that established executive, legislative, and judicial branches with a separation of powers, from the moment of independence Colombia has been beset by anarchy and civil war.

GARCÍA MÁRQUEZ'S ERA AND TIME IN HISTORY

If he were born in 1928, and not 1927 as his father claimed, then the year of the birth of García Márquez would coincide with the famous strike of banana workers near Santa Marta, a pivotal event in the history of Colombia. Based in Boston, the United Fruit Company—known as *La Compañía* to Colombians—had brought a kind of prosperity to the area in the early part of the twentieth century, culminating in 1915–1918, but by 1928 the boom time had long passed.

Although the United Fruit Company helped the local economy somewhat, this U.S. company was never really integrated into the local community. United Fruit operations in the area around Santa Marta and Aracataca included residential compounds that were fenced in, so that the North Americans could maintain their own schools and social life apart from the local inhabitants. United Fruit even ran its own railroad and its own private irrigation system. Workers were paid in scrip that could be redeemed only in company stores that sold goods brought on the company-owned transport ships, which otherwise would have had to return from New Orleans empty. The company hired most of its workers through subcontractors to avoid Colombian labor laws that regulated working conditions and benefits.

When the trouble began, United Fruit insisted that it had no employees on its payroll. Workers' employment cards were burned so they could not prove how long they had worked and could not prove their eligibility for pensions, a theme that is developed in *No One Writes to the Colonel*. In *One Hundred Years of Solitude* the spokesmen of the banana company argue sophistically that since all workers were hired temporarily, they were never really employees; the court to which the workers have turned agrees, issuing a decree that the workers do not, in fact, exist. As Janes points out, this incredible assertion, that the workers do not exist, is not García Márquez's invention but is the actual judicial ruling in favor of United Fruit.[7]

When García Márquez was a child, he heard conflicting accounts of the massacre that followed the strike; some of his neighbors said that no one had actually been killed while others claimed a relative—an uncle or a brother—had been among those who died.[8] In the official version of the event, General Cortés Vargas, the military commander sent by the Conservative government in Bogotá to quell the strike, reported that the crowd was all men, and that only nine had died in the massacre itself, with others being killed later. In *One Hundred Years of Solitude* the crowd is comprised of men, women, and children, and three thousand die. García Márquez has admitted to exaggeration; three thousand was probably the entire population of the town.

In the 1940s, before one more uneasy alliance between the Liberals and Conservatives could be cobbled together, Colombia was overtaken by La Violencia, nearly twenty years of murder and mayhem between Conservatives and Liberals. La Violencia was set off on 9 April 1948 by the assassination during the lunch hour on the streets of Bogotá of the popular Liberal leader Jorge Eliécer Gaitán.

Gaitán had been in favor of radical reform and had investigated the notorious banana strike of 1928; his progressive views split the Liberal Party and allowed the Conservatives to win in the election of 1946. Gaitán restrained his followers from a violent uprising, but strikes and police repression grew.

The *Bogotázo,* the outpouring of rage and the rioting following the murder of Gaitán, was a profound experience for the young García Márquez, who was then a student at the National University; he later recalled:

> . . . the people of Bogotá went mad in the streets. I was in my pension ready to have lunch when I heard the news. I ran toward the place, but Gaitán had just been put into a taxi and was being taken to the hospital. On my way back to the pension, the people had already taken to the streets and they were demonstrating, looting stores and burning buildings. I joined them. That afternoon and evening, I became aware of the kind of country I was living in, and how little my short stories had to do with any of that.[9]

More than two thousand people were killed in the *Bogotázo.* The National Police, largely Liberal in their sympathies, sided with the rioters, giving weapons to the crowd and sometimes joining them in fighting with the Conservative-dominated army troops who had been summoned to Bogatá to suppress the riots. Stories that García Márquez had written while he was a student went up in flames along with the pension in which he had been living.

The violence had actually begun in the early 1940s, with violent attacks on rural Liberals by Conservatives opposing the Liberal agenda. After Gaitán's assassination La Violencia raged even more profoundly. It extended deep into the countryside but erupted again in the capital as well. In 1949 there was even a gun battle between Liberal and Conservative congressmen on the floor of the legislature—one Liberal legislator was killed and four others wounded. In the provincial capital of Barranquilla, a crowd of Liberals almost succeeded in taking over the city. They seized the provincial government building and raised a red flag.

The objective of La Violencia became to eliminate any of one's countrymen belonging to the opposite party. The entire country was in a state of anarchy. Conservative and Liberal villages wiped each other out with extreme brutality. The army, having been purged of Liberals, could not quell the violence. The wars fought by Colonel Buendía in *One Hundred Years of Solitude* are, in fact, a composite of the civil wars of the nineteenth century and La Violencia of the twentieth.

The Liberals boycotted the presidential election of 1949. The Conservative candidate, Laureano Gómez Castro, running unopposed, succeeded to the presidency in 1950 and immediately ordered that even greater force be used against the resistance in the countryside. Military expenditures grew to nearly one-quarter of the national budget.

By the middle of 1952 as much as a third of the national territory was controlled by forces opposed to the government. At the height of La Violencia, some twenty thousand armed rebels operated in Colombia, some organizing themselves into guerrilla groups and establishing their own "independent republics" in the jungles.

Gómez Castro went on to draft a proposed new constitution in 1953. Fascist in outline, the constitution would have increased the powers of the presidency and expanded the role of the church within the political system. Although unsuccessful in amending the Constitution of 1886, he canceled pro-Labor laws, curtailed civil liberties, and censored the press.

Gómez Castro was overthrown by a military coup on 13 June 1953. It was the military leadership's first intervention in the political sphere in nearly a century. The coup leader, General Gustavo Rojas Pinilla, promised to bring an end to La Violencia. Emulating the Argentine dictator General Juan Domingo Perón's populist program, Rojas Pinilla tried to create a broad-based movement that would bring rural peasants and urban workers together, thus circumventing the control that the Liberal/Conservative oligarchy had traditionally had in the political realm. He failed to create this new power base but succeeded in angering the oligarchy.

Rojas Pinilla had declared an amnesty to those who would lay down their arms, and at first many of the fighters accepted his offer. Within a year, however, violence broke out again. Enlisting Cold War ideology, the Rojas Pinilla government now labeled the rebels in the countryside "communists." The Constitution of 1886 was abolished in 1954, and Rojas Pinilla created a new, rubber-stamp government. The armed forces of Colombia had more than doubled, from fourteen

Fabio Vásquez Castaño (at left) and Víctor Medina Morón, the leaders of the
ELN, with García Márquez's college friend Father Camilo Torres Restrepo (on far
right) in 1966, shortly before Father Torres was killed in combat against the
Colombian army

thousand men in 1948 to thirty-two thousand troops in 1956, and the
National Police had been brought under the command of the armed
forces.

Out of control, Rojas Pinilla had a law enacted that made
showing disrespect to the president punishable by imprisonment or
fines. At the notorious Bullring Massacre in February of 1956, many
were killed or injured at a bullfight after refusing to join in a demon-
stration of loyalty to the regime. Near the end of his regime Rojas
Pinilla shut down the Liberal newspaper *El Espectador* leaving foreign
correspondent García Márquez stranded in Europe with no income.

By early 1957 the oligarchy had had enough of Rojas Pinilla's
rule. Meeting in secret, the leaders of the Liberals and Conservatives
agreed to stop fighting one another and united in opposition to Roja
Pinilla. Faced by widespread demonstrations and having lost the support of both the church and key military leaders, Rojas Pinilla was

pressured by the military to resign his office in May of 1957. He was allowed to select his successors, who promised a return to civilian rule. They handed power over to the Liberal and the Conservative elites, who instituted a National Front coalition government, which, through a plebiscite in December of 1957, restored the Constitution of 1886, divided legislative power equally along party lines, and introduced some reforms, such as female suffrage.

Most importantly, the National Front agreement stipulated that the two parties would alternate the presidency every four years for a period of twelve years (later extended to sixteen years). The first National Front president, the Liberal Lleras Camargo, was elected in August 1958; partially because of reforms he enacted, fighting in the countryside diminished. Nonetheless, La Violencia persisted, and in 1965 the Conservative president Guillermo León Valencia declared the country under a state of siege, which decree was not formally lifted until 1982.

The novels that grew out of La Violencia, García Márquez insisted in a 1960 essay, were bad: writers concentrated on the details of the violence with no larger perspective, so that their books consisted of descriptions "de los decapitados, de los castrados, las mujeres violados, los sexos eparicidos y las tripas sacadas"[10]; that is, they offered details of the atrocities of decapitated people, castrated men, women who were raped, with no sense of the cause of these events. In his own work the influence of La Violencia may be observed both in *No One Writes to the Colonel* in the sinister murder of the Colonel's son and in *In Evil Hour* in the animosity between the dentist and the mayor.

Although the National Front government managed to diminish the violence between Liberals and Conservatives, disaffection with the traditional oligarchy continued. In 1964 Fabio Vásquez Castaño and Victor Medina Morón founded the Ejército de Liberación Nacional (ELN; Army of National Liberation) in the department of Santander. This group was inspired by the Cuban Revolution and by the methods employed by Fidel Castro and his band of guerrilla fighters to defeat Cuban dictator Fulgencio Batista y Zaldívar. The ELN, comprised mainly of student radicals, focused its activities in the countryside, attempting to win over the local peasantry and conducting raids on small towns where the guerrillas would rob banks and liberate prisoners from local jails. There were occasional skirmishes with the army. Another major revolutionary movement inspired by the Cuban example, Fuerzas Armadas Revolucionarias de Colombia (FARC; Revolutionary Armed Forces of Colombia), began guerrilla operations in 1966.

García Márquez's college classmate Father Camilo Torres Restrepo joined the ELN in October of 1965, after he had been laicized by the church and stripped of his powers and privileges as a priest. Although he had become the most popular political leader in the country, addressing thousands in his speeches, he had been unable to see a path to actual power.

Father Torres explained his extraordinary decision in this way: "I don't want to let them kill me as they did Gaitán on the Carrera Séptima. They will have to kill me in the mountains. They killed Gaitán in the city, and his death did not point to any solution. If they kill me in the mountains, my death will show the way."[11] Torres was killed in the mountains in a battle with the Colombian armed forces in February of 1966.

García Márquez himself was profoundly influenced by the Cuban Revolution. Like other Latin American writers, he looked toward Cuba as the nation opposed to cultural colonialism. Cuba became an emblem for ending the economic dependence of the region upon the United States and for putting an end to economic exploitation.

This resistence to U.S. economic and cultural domination was a dominant theme for many writers of the Boom, the sudden flourishing of the Latin American novel in the late 1960s. In *The Boom in Spanish American Literature* José Donoso notes that prior to the 1960s the works of Latin American writers were distributed only in their own countries. The publishers explained that this was to "keep foreign currency within the country." Donoso and others noticed that "there was more than enough currency to import Walt Disney comic books."[12]

The relations of Colombia with the United States have been strained since 1903 when Theodore Roosevelt's administration was involved in the revolt of Panama, which until then had been a part of Colombia. García Márquez sees the neighbor to the north, a country with no exclusive right to call itself "America," as having exploited Colombia in particular and the continent in general.

In his fiction García Márquez has been vehemently critical of the role of the United States in Colombian history. The depiction in

THE SWORD OF THE LIBERATOR

The following is translated and excerpted from the M-19 proclamation left in the National Museum in Bogotá, Colombia, in 1974, after guerrillas stole Simón Bolívar's sword:

"Our freedom is not secured. It doesn't exist.... We Latin Americans live in hunger. We're impoverished by injustice. We feel our culture being castrated, deformed, sold-out. . . . The Spanish chains broken by Bolívar today are replaced by the gringo dollar. And from Bolívar's heritage, every four years representatives of the oligarchy alternate positions, those assassins of the Colombian people. For these reasons Bolívar's fighting continues, Bolívar has not died. His sword breaks through the cobwebs of the museum. . . . into our hands."

From Dario Villamizar, *Aquél 19 Será* (Bogotá: Planeta, 1995), p. 56.

One Hundred Years of Solitude of a U.S.-owned company in Macondo, modeled on the actions of the United Fruit Company in the Caribbean Coastal Lowlands in the first decades of the twentieth century, reveals a heartless exploiter with no concern for the welfare of the workers on its plantations. In the novel, as in history, the pillaging of the country by the U.S. company culminates in a massacre. In *The Autumn of the Patriarch* the country is so ravaged economically by its foreign debt to the United States that the dictator, rather than accept the alternative of the landing of U.S. Marines, chooses to sell off the sea. García Márquez's love of the sea runs through all of his fiction; loss of the sea amounts to the loss of national identity.

The United States has also been involved, if more indirectly, in other Colombian problems. Beginning in the 1970s Colombian narcotics traffickers emerged as a dominant economic force, with most of the drugs going to meet the voracious demand of U.S. consumers. By 1999 Colombia had begun to include income earned from growing illegal drugs in calculations of the size of the national economy. Traditional export earnings on coffee, bananas, flowers, sugarcane, and cotton are still important, as are those from the sale of oil, gold, silver, and emeralds; however, income from drugs is as much as four billion dollars a year.[13] Colombia produces half of the world's supply of cocaine, most of it destined for the U.S. market.

With the rise in the drug trade came a wave of violence in Colombia; by the middle of the 1980s, much of Colombia had slid into chaos, with the powerful drug kingpins openly defying the national government and out to torture, intimidate, or murder anyone who openly opposed their operations, striking at journalists, politicians, law enforcement, and judicial authorities with seeming impunity. Kidnappings in Colombia had become especially endemic; García Márquez even wrote a full-length nonfiction book, *Noticia de un secuestro* (1996; translated as *News of a Kidnapping*, 1997), describing the kidnapping of ten people, mostly journalists, by gunmen from Pablo Escobar's Medellín drug cartel. The victims included a friend of García Márquez, Maruja Pachón, who was kidnapped because she was the sister of the widow of Luis Carlos Galán Sarmiento.

A presidential candidate, Galán had been gunned down in August 1989 in the presence of his eighteen bodyguards. He was the founder of the Movimiento Nuevo Liberalismo (MNL; New Liberalism Movement) faction of the Liberal Party, which supported the extradition of Colombian nationals to stand trial in the United States. Extradition was a policy the drug lords feared and violently opposed. In Colombia they could escape imprisonment or be jailed in relative luxury, but they knew the U.S. authorities would treat them far more harshly.

This set of kidnappings, illustrating the control of civilian life in Colombia by the drug cartels, was, García Márquez wrote, "only one episode in the biblical holocaust that has been consuming Colombia for more than twenty years."[14] Colombia had become a society where people, as García Márquez wrote, "tended to believe the lies of the Extraditables more than the truths told by the government" (132). "Extraditables" were those leaders of the drug trade whose crimes extended to the United States and whom the U.S. Department of Justice was eager to try in its courts; their campaign of terror was aimed at forcing the Colombian government to grant them protection from extradition, and their slogan was "We prefer a grave in Colombia to a cell in the United States" (22).

By the 1990s no one in Colombia was safe. "Are you dealers or guerrillas?" Maruja had demanded of her kidnappers (9). They might have been either. Bombs explode daily, some set by the drug traffickers, others the work of urban guerrillas.

Although the direct impact of the narcotics traffickers has lessened since the early 1990s when the dominant Cali and Medellín cartels were largely suppressed, the drug kingpins have not been the only ones contributing to the violence and anarchy in Colombia. Since their inception in the 1960s, guerrilla groups in Colombia have continued to fight the central government. In addition to the ELN and the somewhat larger guerrilla movement FARC, other, smaller guerrilla groups appeared on the scene, such as the Maoist group Ejército Popular de Liberación (EPL; Popular Liberation Army) and the Movimiento 19 de Abril (M-19; 19th of April Movement).

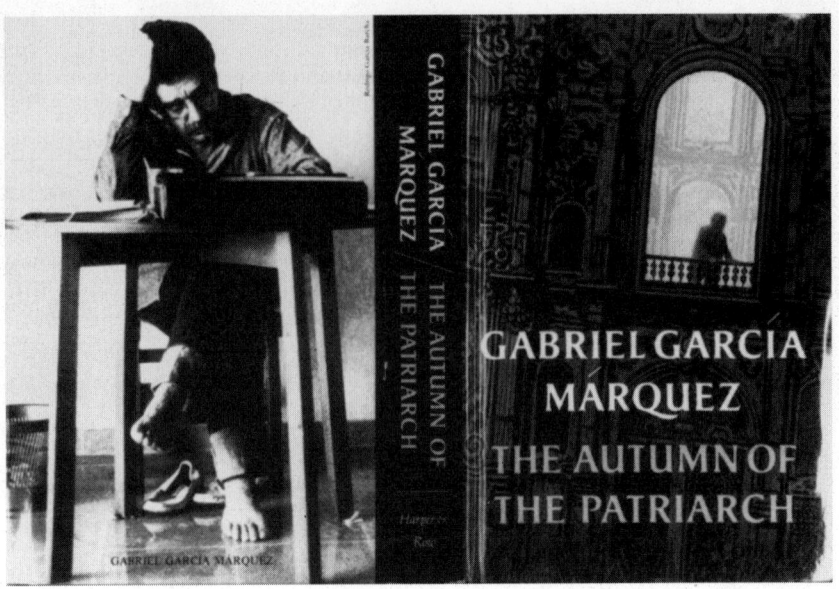

Dust jacket for the first U.S. edition of *El otoño del patriarca*

The M-19 group became notorious for two actions. In January 1974 guerrillas broke into a museum in the capital and stole Bolívar's sword, in a symbolic gesture meant to identify their actions with those of the Liberator. Although a ceasefire was signed in 1984 between most of the guerrilla movements and the government, the ELN refused to sign, and the agreement broke down.

M-19 guerrillas stormed the Palace of Justice in 1985, taking several hostages. Ostensibly, they were motivated by the government's alleged failure to live up to the provisions of the 1984 agreement, although it is also widely believed that they were acting on behalf of the drug cartels, which wanted them to destroy court records relating to U.S. extradition requests. When the government troops recaptured the building, more than one hundred people, including twelve supreme court justices, were killed. In 1990, however, M-19 signed an agreement with the government in which the organization renounced violence, voluntarily disarmed, and became a legitimate political party. The sword of the Liberator was also returned to the government.

Meanwhile, in the 1990s the ELN stepped up its assaults on the system. The group has attacked petroleum pipelines and drilling sites to draw attention to the exploitation of Colombia's natural resources by foreign companies. In 1999 the ELN decided that by kidnapping ordinary citizens they could make their point more dramatically. Their war would be against everyone.

In April of 1999 the ELN hijacked an Avianca domestic flight bound from Bucaramanga, for thirty years an ELN stronghold, to Bogotá, with forty-one people on board. This action was followed by the abduction of more than one hundred people from a church in Cali during Sunday mass on 30 May. Several hostages were released because they made deals with the ELN, agreeing to sell their property and possessions and turn the proceeds over to the guerrillas. The government argued that the ELN had now reverted to the same tactics as the late drug lord Pablo Escobar, who had been killed by police in 1993.

The peace efforts instituted by President Andrés Pastrana have focused, however, on the FARC, which was granted control over four departments or counties. Unlike the ELN, the FARC has chosen to negotiate with the existing government. The FARC has included among its demands the curbing of right-wing military groups, over which the government insists it has no control. The *Colombia Country Report on Human Rights Practices for 1998,* issued by the U.S. State Department, estimated that up to seventeen thousand guerrillas had significant control of approximately 65 percent of the country's municipalities and, where the perpetrator could be positively identified, were responsible for approximately 21 percent of all "politically motivated extrajudicial killings," while right-wing paramilitary groups, with between five thousand and seven thousand members, accounted for more than 75 percent of such murders. The State Department report went on to note that the Colombian national average for successful prosecutions was less than 3 percent.[15] In 1998 President Pastrana agreed to withdraw all army and police forces from an area of roughly fifteen thousand square miles (about the size of Switzerland) that includes the town of San Vicente Del Caguán, ceding sovereignty to the FARC.

In September of 1999 President Pastrana was in New York City speaking before the United Nations General Assembly, asking for international monetary aid to help resolve his country's continuing slide into anarchy. The Colombian government was seeking more than one billion dollars worth of U.S. military aid; although Pastrana and other government officials emphasized that this materiel would be directed against the drug trade, as both the ELN and FARC are now engaged in this trade, many observers were worried that the United States might be pulled into the civil war. With the insurgents apparently more powerful than ever, it seemed unlikely that the Colombian government could resolve the situation militarily. While Pastrana was in the United States, it was reported that García Márquez was prepared to act as an intermediary between Colombia, the United States, Cuba, and the Colombian insurgents.

The sympathies of García Márquez toward the guerrilla movement may be observed in the fate of the murderer Pedro Vicario in *Chronicle of a Death Foretold*. "Without love or a job," both of which are necessary for a good life, Pedro Vicario reenlists in the armed forces. "One fine morning," however, as the weather cooperates with justice, his patrol "went into guerrilla territory singing whorehouse songs and was never heard of again" (83). The guerrillas have brought about justice where the civic authorities have failed.

LIFESTYLE AND CULTURE

García Márquez was born into a rigid and highly stratified class society. Status differences were pronounced. Social mobility was limited. There was almost no middle class. Class consciousness, particularly in the interior, was high and permeated social life.

As first cousins, García Márquez's maternal grandparents, Colonel Nicolás Márquez Iguarán and Tranquilina Iguarán Cotes, belonged to the most eminent family in the local aristocracy of Aracataca. Colonel Márquez had fought under the great Liberal general Rafael Uribe Uribe, and Aracataca, as a result of his efforts, had become a Liberal city. Until the age of eight García Márquez lived in their large, commodious house and enjoyed certain privileges.

As for Colombia as a whole, the elite lived primarily in Bogotá. They modeled their lifestyles on European and North American norms and dictated them to the rest of society. They emphasized racial and cultural purity and wealth derived from property. The only approved forms of employment for this class were landowning, law, medicine, or architecture. Journalism was also considered respectable by the time García Márquez entered manhood. Aid from relatives often enabled families to maintain the facade of prosperity, and the children of the elite were often sent to school in Europe or the United States.

People defined themselves by their ancestry, and regional and local connections were emphasized. Only after the 1940s did mestizos, predominantly peasants, move from the highlands, where the Spanish conquerors had mixed with Indian women, into the cities.

The new rich, people who had worked their way up through entrepreneurial skills and entered banking, commerce, and industry, were not accepted as socially equal to the old elite. Upper-class children received the best educations, attending one of the country's exclusive private schools and then one of the national universities. García Márquez, whose family was impoverished, was fortunate to receive one of the few available scholarships and was thus able to study at better schools.

During the coming-of-age of García Márquez, Colombia was a society so centered on class privilege that people were judged by the degree to which they spoke Spanish in a pure manner most similar to *castellano,* the official language of Spain, a language free of Latin American inflections or references. They prided themselves as well on the eloquence of their spoken Spanish. The elite of Bogotá considered their capital "the Athens of South America"; however, they have virtually no literary tradition.

In an early article, "La literatura Colombiana: un fraude a la nación" (Colombian Literature: A Fraud on the Nation), García Márquez pointed to the absence among Colombian writers of a sense of national identity, of what distinguished the culture and people of Colombia. He set out to accomplish that task. In creating that missing national literature, he took as his model *The Plague* (1947), a work in which Albert Camus, as García Márquez notes, recounts "a brief episode of the human race in which not even the germs of the plague are definitely bad, nor its victims necessarily good."[16]

For writers like García Márquez their lifestyle involves an acute disenchantment with the politics of the United States. Latin American intellectuals of the Left have long distrusted the motives of their neighbor to the north. "What the United States Government wants in Central America are governments it can control," he has said.[17] An important part of his life involves his political commitment, in particular a struggle for an independent politics for the region.

Because of his well-publicized friendship with the Cuban leader, when Cuban-trained guerrillas from M-19 made a minor incursion by boat from Panama, the Colombian government tried to get them to admit that it was García Márquez who "had coordinated the landing with Fidel Castro."[18] García Márquez sued the Colombian military for abuse of authority for making these accusations. The charges were preposterous; yet, part of his lifestyle has included periodic visits to Cuba, where, he has said, his discussions with the Cuban leader have focused on matters of literature. In 1982 he stopped off in Cuba after he accepted the Nobel Prize in literature in Sweden, and he was a guest of Castro at the historic visit of Pope John Paul II to Cuba in January of 1998.

Personally, García Márquez has considered himself in his culture and frame of reference, like his hero Simón Bolívar—who was born in Caracas, Venezuela—a man of the coast, a *costeño*, a Caribbean man. The northern coast, with its diverse population, has been a place of the supernatural, of fantastic stories told by old women. Supernatural elements are a part of everyday reality. It is from this style of life that he has drawn inspiration for his technique of magic realism.[19]

The northern coast of Colombia, which embraces the cities of Barranquilla, Santa Marta, and Cartagena de Indias and the smaller towns of Riohacha and Aracataca as well, is a place where a man does not bundle up in a suit and tie. It is an area where behavior is free and easy and often spontaneous, distinct from the manners of Bogotá, where the women are dressed in the fashions of Paris.

Historically, the interior of Colombia has produced nearly all of the country's military men and its clergy. Few generals have been *costeños*, and no bishop or archbishop has hailed from the northern coast, where the very idea of seclusion, of the asceticism that characterizes both of these professions, is alien.[20] The coast is a place gifted in the celebration of being alive; there in *One Hundred Years of Solitude* José Arcadio Buendía has to struggle to find a single image of God.

Far from the emphasis on purity of blood and one's antecedents that has created a repressive atmosphere in Bogotá and the interior, the coast welcomes people of diverse backgrounds and mixed blood. It offers a melange of cultures coming together in its carnivals and celebrations, which are depicted in García Márquez's story "Big Mama's Funeral." Spain and Africa mix.

"People here," he has said, describing the coast, "sense the presence of phenomena or other beings, even if they are not here. These must be influences of ancient religions, of Indians and blacks.

This world's full of spirits you find all over, in Puerto Rico, in Cuba, in Brazil. In Santo Domingo and in Vera Cruz."[21]

As a consequence of the slave trade, García Márquez has written, "it became possible to distinguish as may as eighteen different degrees of mestizos," who were not permitted to hold high positions in the national government or even to enroll in secondary schools. He attributes to Bolívar himself the missed opportunity of creating a democratic society. Bolívar, he has written, "lost the first opportunity to eradicate this deplorable legacy." Instead, yielding to repression as a means of gaining power, behaving abominably, and setting an early example of the ruthlessness and violence that have beset Colombia throughout its history, he "ordered the execution of eight hundred Spanish prisoners, even those lying wounded in a hospital."[22]

García Márquez and his friend Fidel Castro in Cuba, summer 1978

The coast, García Márquez has said proudly, is comprised of "bandits . . . dancers, adventurers, people of gaiety." The people are descendants of pirates and smugglers who had intermarried with black slaves; "they are people capable of believing in anything."[23] In his childhood he heard stories of people able to move chairs simply by looking at them and of a man who could deworm cows by simply standing in front of them. In particular, he has said that he admires the first inhabitants of his native land, the Indians, for two qualities: "a talent for creativity, the supreme expression of human intelligence," and "a fierce commitment to self-improvement."[24]

In his essay "For the Sake of a Country Within Reach of the Children" García Márquez describes the people of the coast as having "discovered the political miracle of living as equals despite their differences." Such a political culture is a far cry from that of Bogotá and Colombia as a whole, which is "a centralized, bureaucratic nation, creating out of colonial lethargy the illusion of national unity."[25]

In the heat of the Caribbean even passing time loses its relevance. "The feeling of cold," he has said, "is something the people born in Bogotá cannot imagine."[26] So it was traumatic for this man of the coast to come into contact with Bogotá, which, he says, has marked him, has impressed him, but which only reminded him that he was not a *cachaco,* but a *costeño.*

Before he travelled to the interior, it had been difficult for García Márquez to conceive of living in a city without the sea. He received his secondary education in an old colonial convent in Zipaquirá one thousand meters above sea level. He remembers it as a school "in a town with a narrow mentality, distant and gloomy." Having been born near the Caribbean, he found this place "a punishment, and a frozen town, an injustice."[27] It reeked of the Spanish colonial culture, which was not his. He spent most of his time reading.

The coast is a place of sexual freedom, where the brothel, as depicted in *Chronicle of a Death Foretold,* is a positive place, one concealing "the incapacity for love" and even "the hesitations of old age." Simultaneously, women have suffered in Colombia from a "cult of virginity,"[28] whose consequences he describes in *Chronicle of a Death Foretold.*

Catholicism has imposed a double standard upon Colombia, even on the free and easy coast. Men have been offered a degree of sexual freedom, symbolized by the brothel, where, in *Chronicle of a Death Foretold,* all of the young men of the town experience their sexual initiation, including the narrator, who found his experience with María Alejandra Cervantes sublime. The authority of the church is represented by the ringing of bells that draw the free young man back to the world of repression and denial.

García Márquez has offered one clarification. The concept that every young man in the village had been initiated by María Alejandra Cervantes was another of his exaggerations. "In fact, brothels cost too much for the young," he has said. Sexual initiation "actually starts with servants at home. And with cousins. And with aunts."[29] He adds that it was not easy in his youth to have a relationship with a woman who was not a prostitute. Prostitutes provided both company and companionship. He has remarked, playfully, that he married "not to eat lunch alone."[30]

Life in Colombia does not differ markedly from that of the characters in *One Hundred Years of Solitude.* Colombians of the present, whom García Márquez has called "the unfortunate seed of Colonel Aureliano Buendía," are members of "a sentimental society where action takes precedence over reflection, impulsiveness over reason, human warmth over prudence. We have an almost irrational love of life but kill one another in our passion to live." Most Colombians today are descended from both the invading Spanish conquistadores and the indigenous people who were the first inhabitants: "five centuries later the descendants of both," García Márquez laments, "still do not know who we are."[31]

NOTES

1. Regina Janes, "Liberals, Conservatives, and Bananas: Colombian Politics in the Fictions of Gabriel García Márquez," in *Gabriel García Márquez,* edited by Harold Bloom (New York: Chelsea House, 1989), p. 125.

2. *Chronicle of a Death Foretold,* translated by Gregory Rabassa (New York: Harper & Row, 1982), pp. 66–67.

3. Gene H. Bell-Villada, *García Márquez: The Man And His Work* (Chapel Hill & London: University of North Carolina Press, 1990), p. 22.

4. *Gabriel García Márquez: Magic and Reality,* written, directed, and produced by Ana Cristina Navarro, 60 minutes, Films for the Humanities & Sciences, 1981, video.

5. Ibid.

6. Michael Wood, *Gabriel García Márquez: One Hundred Years of Solitude* (Cambridge & New York: Cambridge University Press, 1990), p. 8.

7. Janes, "Liberals, Conservatives, and Bananas," p. 142.

8. Ibid., p. 140.

9. Peter Stone, "Gabriel García Márquez," *Writers at Work: The Paris Review Interviews—Sixth Series,* edited by George Plimpton (New York: Viking, 1984), pp. 320–321.

10. Quoted in Janes, "Liberals, Conservatives, and Bananas," p. 126.

11. Gérman Guzman, *Camilo Torres* (New York: Sheed & Ward, 1969), p. 237.

12. José Donoso, *The Boom in Spanish American Literature,* translated by Gregory Kolvakos (New York: Columbia University Press/Center for Inter-American Relations, 1977), p. 25.

13. Larry Rohter, "Colombia Adjusts Economic Figures to Include Its Drug Crops," *New York Times,* Sunday, 27 June 1999.

14. "Acknowledgements" to *News of a Kidnapping,* translated by Edith Grossman (New York: Knopf, 1997).

15. *U.S. Department of State Colombia Country Report on Human Rights Practices for 1998,* released by the Bureau of Democracy, Human Rights, and Labor, 26 February 1999. http://www.state.gov/www/global/human_rights/1998_hrp_report/colombia.html

16. Bell-Villada, *The Man and His Work,* p. 87.

17. Claudia Dreifus, "*Playboy* Interview: Gabriel García Márquez," *Playboy,* 30 (February 1983): 72.

18. Ibid.: 73.

19. *Garcia Marquez: Magic and Reality.*

20. Ibid.

21. Marlise Simons, "A Talk with Gabriel García Márquez," *New York Times Book Review,* 5 December 1982.

22. "For the Sake of a Country Within Reach of the Children," *A Country for Children,* edited by Benjamin Villegas (Bogotá: Villegas Editores, n.d.), pp. 7–8.

23. Dreifus, "*Playboy* Interview": 74.

24. "For the Sake of a Country," p. 8.

25. Ibid., pp. 6–7.

26. *García Márquez: Magic and Reality.*

27. Ibid.

28. Ibid.

29. Dreifus, "*Playboy* Interview": 177.

30. Ibid.: 178.

31. "For the Sake of a Country," p. 5.

GARCÍA MÁRQUEZ'S WORKS

BOOKS

La hojarasca. Bogotá: Sipa, 1955. Translated by Gregory Rabassa as "Leaf Storm" in *Leaf Storm and Other Stories*. New York: Harper & Row, 1972; London: Cape, 1972. Gabriel García Márquez's first novel, this book is the one he professes to like best: "It's the most spontaneous, the one I wrote with most difficulty and with fewer technical resources. I knew fewer writers' tricks, fewer nasty tricks at the time."[1] The story begins with the death of the doctor who refused to care for the casualties of a minor battle nearby; "I've forgotten everything I knew about all that" (14), he insisted when the wounded were brought to his door. He was then condemned to a "labyrinthine solitude" (65). The whole town hated him and now rejoices to see him dead.

The story is told by a woman, her father, the colonel, and her son, but the real hero is the colonel, who comes to see to a decent burial for the doctor. The colonel had befriended him because the doctor had arrived carrying a "letter of recommendation" from "The Intendant General of the Atlantic Coast" (17), Colonel Aureliano Buendía.

In a flashback the reader learns that the settling of the town was accomplished in a gentle and good way, with the people so kind that they had their horses sleep under mosquito netting. There is a priest who at seventeen had been a colonel in the civil war of 1885 and goes by his childhood name of "Pup." Unlike most of the clerics in the fiction of García Márquez, he is a priest who is "a whole man who fulfills his duties as a man" (69), perhaps suggestive of García Márquez's friend Camilo Torres. "I think the Pup will be made a saint," the colonel remarks, "we've never seen anything like him in Macondo" (69).

Macondo banana plantation near Aracataca, from which García Márquez took the name of the fictional town that is the setting for *One Hundred Years of Solitude* and many of his other works

All that changed with the arrival of a banana company "pursued by a leaf storm" (intro.). When the United Fruit Company departs, Macondo is a ruined town: "Ivy invades the houses, weeds grow in the alleys, walls crumble" (93). The author describes the effects on the community of imperialism without ever using that word, or the word "exploitation," or even the name, United Fruit.

El coronel no tiene quien le escriba. Originally published in the Bogotá magazine *Mito*, 4 (May–June 1958): 1–38. Published in book form: Medellín: Aguirre, 1961. Translated by J. S. Bernstein in *No One Writes to the Colonel and Other Stories*. New York: Harper & Row, 1968; London: Cape, 1971. The colonel of the title was on the losing side in the last civil war and so is condemned to wait fruitlessly for his pension from a government for which he has no sympathy. Like many of the works of García Márquez, it opens on a funeral, "the first death from natural causes which we've had in many years" (6), a reflection not only of the civil wars but also of La Violencia.

Now seventy-five years old and starving, the colonel sleeps fitfully in his "revolutionist's cot" (14). He has waited fifteen years for his veteran's pension. Each Friday when the mail arrives, he is disappointed. "No one writes to the colonel," the postmaster tells him scornfully (21).

The colonel's son, a rebel, was shot down for "distributing clandestine literature" (11). The colonel's asthmatic wife urges him to sell his son's fighting cock for food, but he will not. His pride forbids it. Better to suffer, García Márquez implies, than be like the colonel's friend Sabas, the only leader of his party who has escaped persecution, who has grown rich by buying up the property of his defeated partisan comrades. Even as the life of the colonel is scarcely bearable, he insists, speaking for the author, that "it's never too late for anything" (37).

La mala hora. Madrid: Pérez, 1962. Revised edition: Mexico City: Ediciones Era, 1966. Translated by Rabassa as *In Evil Hour*. New York: Harper & Row, 1979; London: Cape, 1980. García Márquez submitted the typescript to a literary competition, which it won. When it was published in Spain, the publisher revised the book, cutting out objectionable passages and removing all Latin American idioms. García Márquez repudiated the work as unauthorized, restored the cuts and original language, and had it republished in Mexico in 1966. The setting is once again Macondo. The story opens with the shooting of a singer named Pastoro, one more in a series of acts of meaningless violence. At first the evil seems mere gossip, the writing of derogatory lampoons about certain citizens. *In Evil Hour* culminates in the disintegration of the entire community.

The civil wars between the Liberals and the Conservatives have bred lifelong animosity and bitterness, so that the dentist refuses to treat the mayor with anesthesia. "You people kill without anaesthesia" (58), the dentist tells his political enemy, in a scene that also appears in the short story "Un día de estos" (translated as "One of Those Days"), part of the collection *Los funerales de la Mamá Grande* (1962). "The only newspapers left in the country are the official ones," the barber says, "and they won't enter this establishment as long as I am alive" (43).

He has put up the sign "*Talking Politics Prohibited*" (45), which also appeared in the tailor shop in *No One Writes to the Colonel*. Among the other townspeople is the priest Father Angel, the same priest who appears in *Leaf Storm.*

Politics is a life-and-death matter here, and after the last elections the police confiscated and destroyed the electoral documents of the opposition party. The majority of the town's inhabitants lack means of identification.

By the end of the book, it emerges that the mayor is ruling only by a state of siege. Working in an armored office with a steel door, he declares a curfew. Yet, he cannot prevent disorder as it emerges that the lampoons are not a form of harmless mischief but a means of undermining the authoritarian Conservative government. "Clandestine propaganda" (146) makes its appearance, as it did in *No One Writes to the Colonel.* The mayor and his three hired assassins roam the streets, but La Violencia is upon the residents of Macondo. "Sooner or later it had to happen," García Márquez writes, "the whole country is patched up with cobwebs" (149).

The reader is told that "they're organizing guerrilla groups against the government in the interior again" (149). The jails of Macondo are full, while "men are going into the jungle to join up with guerrilla bands" (183). Sleepy Macondo has joined the second tumultuous half of the twentieth century.

Los funerales de la Mamá Grande. Jalapa, Mexico: Editorial de la Universidad Veracruzana, 1962. Comprises the short stories "La siesta del martes," "Un día de estos," "En este pueblo no hay ladrones," "La prodigiosa tarde de Baltazar," "La viuda de Montiel," "Un día después del sábado," "Rosas artificiales," and "Los funerales de la Mamá Grande," translated by Bernstein as "Big Mama's Funeral: Tuesday Siesta," "One of These Days," "There Are No Thieves in this Town," "Balthazar's Marvelous Afternoon," "Montiel's Widow," "One Day after Saturday," "Artificial Roses," and "Big Mama's Funeral" in *No One Writes to the Colonel and Other Stories.* The death that opens this collection of short stories set in Macondo is that of Carlos Centeno, a thief who has chosen the profession of robber because he was so frequently injured when he was a boxer. He is finally killed by a revolver that had not been fired "since the days of Colonel Aureliano Buendía" (70).

Big Mama is a mythic figure who stands for the power structure strangling Colombia. Her dying in "Big Mama's Funeral," a story without a plot, represents the dying of the old order, a death that had always seemed impossible. Yet, "Her hour had come"(58), and she dies sterile and a virgin. As a tiny oligarchy owns most of the wealth of Colombia, so it takes "twenty-four folios" (159) to catalogue all of Big Mama's possessions. She dies before she can "finish her list of her invisible estate" (161), although the narrator obliges:

> The wealth of the subsoil, the territorial waters, the colors of the flag, national sovereignty, the traditional parties, the rights of man, civil rights, the nation's leadership, the right of appeal, Congressional hearings, letters of recommendation, historical records, free elections, beauty queens, transcendental speeches, huge demonstrations, distinguished young ladies, proper gentlemen, punctilious military men, His Illustrious Eminence, the Supreme Court, goods whose importation was forbidden, liberal ladies, the meat problem, the purity of the language, setting a good example, the free but responsible press, the Athens of South America, public opinion, the lessons of democracy, Christian morality, the shortage of foreign exchange, the right of asylum, the Communist menace, the ship of state, the high cost of living, republican traditions, the underprivileged classes, statements of political support (161).

This list is a catalogue of all that is of value, as well as all the evils that have plagued Colombia. Like the finest satirists, García Márquez offers clues to his own perspective. He denounces "the priority of traditional power over transitory authority, the predominance of class over the common people, the transcendence of divine wisdom over human improvisation" (163). That divine is epitomized by Father Anthony Isabel of the Holy Sacrament of the Altar in the story "One Day After Saturday"; only when he is nearing one hundred years of age is the heart of Father Anthony Isabel penetrated by "all the goodness, the misconduct and the sufferings of the town" (139). Meanwhile the veterans of Colonel Aureliano Buendía's camp are still without their pensions and arrive at the funeral to state their case to the President of the Republic.

His country, García Márquez laments, is "Drowning in the pandemonium of abstract formulas" (161). He suggests at the close of "Big Mama's Funeral" that someone should "tell this story, lesson and example for future generations" (170). He hopes to live to the day after Big Mama's funeral when "the garbage men will come and will sweep up the garbage from her funeral, forever and ever" (170), and replace it with a new, more humane social order.

Isabel viendo llover en Macondo (Isabel Watching It Rain in Macondo). Buenos Aires: Estuario, 1967.

Cien años de soledad. Buenos Aires: Editorial Sudamericana, 1967. Translated by Rabassa as *One Hundred Years of Solitude.* New York: Harper & Row, 1970; London: Cape, 1970. García Márquez has called his masterpiece the "least mysterious" of his books: "I tried to take the reader by the hand so as not to get him lost at any moment."[2] He has also distinguished it from earlier of his books that belonged to "a kind of premeditated literature that offers too static and exclusive a vision of reality."[3]

One Hundred Years of Solitude is the saga of the Buendía family. It begins in a Garden of Eden, Macondo at its founding. This paradise will be lost to them by their own errors no less than by the invasion of the United Fruit Company, which seizes its banana plantations.

José Arcadio Buendía and Úrsula Iguarán begin their family when the world is young in "a truly happy village where no one was over thirty years old" (9). Yet, a Buendía ancestor had been born with a pig's tail, and the line of the Buendías comes to an end in the middle of the twentieth century when, out of an incestuous union, a last child is born with a pig's tail. It is, García Márquez has said, "the story of a family obsessed by incest."[4]

The men of the family consist of two basic types: the emotional and the sensual, represented by those sons named José Arcadio, and the cool, rationalist men named Aureliano. In time, they mix and intertwine. Neither does better than the other.

The first Aureliano enters politics on the side of the Liberals. He discovers that the Liberals are no more principled than the Conservatives, and he becomes ruthless. During the civil wars he also fathers seventeen sons, all named Aureliano, by women who enter his tent in the dead of night to partake of his genetic bounty. The Conservatives will murder them all.

Disgusted by himself, Aureliano, now Colonel Aureliano Buendía, retreats into his solitude. Love deserted him with the death in childbirth of his barely pubescent bride, Remedios. Politics deserted him when he perceived that power was the aim of both sides, with principle not a factor at all. Although he faces the firing squad in the first line of the novel, he does not die. Later he says to Úrsula, "'Tell him,' the colonel said, smiling, 'that a person doesn't die when he should but when he can'" (248).

The disillusionment of Colonel Aureliano Buendía is matched by the discovery of his great-nephew José Arcadio Segundo that the Americans have massacred three thousand rebellious striking banana workers and their families and shipped their bodies, like bananas, in freight trains to be dumped into the sea.

There are ghosts in this novel, such as that of Prudencio Aguilar, murdered by José Arcadio Buendía, who walks the earth with "immense desolation," longing for "living people" (23). Solitude is a problem in the next world no less than in this one. And there are miracles that are real, such as ice. Nature expresses its disdain for human intransigence, so that after the departure of the banana company, it rains for "four years, eleven months and two days" (320), a purging and a ruining phenomenon. Time is unreliable. It "stumbled and had accidents and could therefore splinter and leave an eternalized fragment in a room" (355).

Throughout this extraordinary novel solitude is a "pox," the enemy of humanity and community. The solitariness of Colonel Aureliano Buendía from childhood was a sign that he would prove finally to be "incapable of love" (254). He flounders, "Lost in the solitude of his immense power" (171). No less solitary has been his father, José Arcadio Buendía, whose inventions include a daguerreotype laboratory that he hopes to use to "obtain scientific proof of the existence of God" (54). He is confident that sooner or later he "would get a daguerreotype of God" (54), something García Márquez views as a pointless enterprise. José Arcadio Buendía winds up mad, living under a chestnut tree.

"The letters I find most interesting are from people who ask me where I got this theme or that passage or such and such a character. Because they feel it is about something or someone they know. They will say: So and so is just like my aunt. Or: I have an uncle just like him. And: that episode happened exactly like that in my village. How did you know about it? People from all over Latin America wrote such things, especially after 'One Hundred Years of Solitude.' They felt it was part of their lives."

García Márquez

From Marlise Simons "The Best Years Of His Life: An Interview with Gabriel García Márquez," *The New York Times*, 10 April 1988.

If Úrsula, the earth mother of the story, survives beyond any normal life expectancy, the other Buendía women fare less well. Rebeca, who loves Úrsula most but who is not her biological daughter, grows old alone, her face "wrinkled by the aridity of solitude" (224). At the end, Amaranta Úrsula and her nephew Aureliano Babilonia become "more and more integrated in the solitude of a house that needed only one last breath to be knocked down" (415). The Buendía line has been exhausted, along with the community of Macondo. Ruined, they die together, neither to be offered "a second opportunity on earth" (422). The last Buendía child is devoured by red ants.

The final conceit is that of the gypsy Melquíades's manuscript, which generations of Buendías have attempted to decipher. The manuscript turns out to be this novel, the chronicle of their destiny, which has now been fulfilled. Reading it with intense concentration, Aureliano Babilonia, with the self-absorption that has meant the ruin of the Buendías, does not notice what is happening to his baby. Seduced by solitude, infected with nostalgia, the Buendías, like Colombia, lack a future.

Dust jacket for the first U.S. edition (1979) of García Márquez's novel *La mala hora* (1962), about political violence in a small Colombian town

This novel, García Márquez has said, is "not a history of Latin America" but a "metaphor for Latin America."[5] The Buendías have failed in solidarity with their fellows. With an apocalyptic stroke by the author, they are wiped from the earth as if they had never existed.

La novela en América Latina: Diálogo (The Novel in Latin America: Dialogue). By García Márquez and Mario Vargas Llosa. Lima, Peru: Milla Batres, 1969. This work is a discussion between García Márquez and Vargas Llosa on contemporary Latin American fiction.

Relato de un náufrago. Barcelona: Tusquets, 1970. Translated by Randolph Hogan as *The Story of a Shipwrecked Sailor*. New York: Knopf, 1986. This work was originally published in 1955 as a series of installments running for fourteen consecutive days in the newspaper *El Espectador* (Bogotá) under the name of Luis Alejandro Velasco, the twenty-year-old sailor of the title. There is "not a single invented detail in the whole account," García Márquez has said.[6] The series created a stir because it was published during the dictatorship of Rojas Pinilla and revealed that Velasco, hailed as a hero by the government for surviving after being swept overboard from a Colombian navy destroyer in a storm, had actually been the victim of corruption and incompetence: his ship was overloaded with contraband, including refrigerators, television sets, and washing machines, which had caused the ship to wallow in relatively calm seas and brought about the deaths of seven sailors.

García Márquez wrote in his 1970 preface that two years after the story was originally published, "Colombia fell to the mercy of other regimes that were better dressed but not much more just, while in Paris I began my nomadic and somewhat nostalgic exile that in certain ways also resembles a drifting raft" (ix). He has also revealed that he would have preferred that *The Story of a Shipwrecked Sailor* not be published in book form: "I agreed without thinking about it very much, and I am not a man to go back on his word" (ix).

La increíble y triste historia de la cándida Eréndira y de su abuela desalmada (The Incredible and Sad Story of Innocent Eréndira and Her Heartless Grandmother). Barcelona: Barral, 1972. Comprises "Un señor muy viejo con unas alas enormes," "El mar del tiempo perdido," "El ahogado más hermoso del mundo," "Muerte constante más allá del amor," "El último viaje del buque fantasma," "Blacamán el bueno vendedor de milagros," "La increíble y triste historia de la cándida Eréndira y de su abuela desalmada."

Ojos de perro azul (Eyes of a Blue Dog). Rosario, Argentina: Equiseditorial, 1972. This collection of García Márquez's first ten stories was unauthorized.

Cuando era feliz e indocumentado (When I Was Happy and Uninformed). Caracas: Ojo del Camello, 1973. This collection consists of articles written for the Venezuelan magazine *Momento* in 1958.

El Negro que hizo esperar a los ángeles. Buenos Aires: Ediciones Alfil, 1973. Originally published as "Nabo, el negro que hizo esperar a los ángeles," *El Espectador* (Bogotá), Suplemento Dominical, 157, 18 March 1951, pp. 17–23.

Chile, el golpe y los gringos (Chile, the Coup and the Gringos). Bogotá: Editorial Latina, 1974. This book is a collection of journalistic essays on Chilean politics.

Cuatro cuentos (Four Stories). Mexico City: Comunidad Latinoamericana de Escritores, 1974. Comprises "Monólogo de Isabel viendo llover en Macando," "En este pueblo no hay ladrones," "Los funerales de la Mamá Grande," "Un hombre muy viejo con unas alas enormes."

El otoño del patriarca. Barcelona: Plaza & Janes, 1975. Translated by Rabassa as *The Autumn of the Patriarch*. New York: Harper & Row, 1976; London: Cape, 1977. García Márquez has termed this book, his most experimental novel, "an extremely long poem about the loneliness of a dictator."[7] He considers it a more important literary achievement than *One Hundred Years of Solitude*

The novel opens with the death of the "great man" (61), an irony, and the flapping of the wings of vultures "stirr[ing] up the stagnant time inside" the palace (1). Lacking a linear plot, lacking even paragraphing, *The Autumn of the Patriarch* is a meditation on dictatorship. It closes with the stopping of "the uncountable time of eternity" (269), reflecting that the dictator, like Generalissimo Francisco Franco of Spain, seemed as if he would live forever.

During the course of his reign, among his atrocities was selling the country to foreign powers, the English, the Dutch, and the gringos of North America, who take away the sea. When he dies, "his whole body was sprouting tiny lichens and parasitic animals from the depths of the sea" (6) that he has betrayed. The only wealth remaining to the country is his personal fortune.

García Márquez freely enlists the magic of exaggeration. When he dies, the dictator is between 107 and 232 years of age. The damage he inflicts is so incalculable it can only be depicted through the means of magic. The face of the despot is pictured not only on coins but even "on condom labels" (4). By the end he has not been seen by anyone "since the days of the black vomit" (5). A plague descends on the country, an emblem of his cruel regime. A cow is observed on the palace balcony.

To avoid assassination he has brought a double named Patricio Aragones into the palace, who succumbs to a poison dart. When he dies, a "fishwife" (27) laments, "what's going to become of us without him" (28), since people have grown accustomed to his paternalism, as in the Soviet Union people had wept at the death of Joseph Stalin. "We had ended up not understanding what would become of us without him" (219), García Márquez writes, again using the "we" that prevents his narrator from placing himself above and superior to the people about whom he is writing.

A cacophony of narrators tells this story. At times it is the mother of the despot, Benedición Alvarado. At others, it is the general. Sometimes one of his victims steps forward to tell the story. García Márquez sympathizes neither with "the liberals who had sold the federalist war" nor "the conservatives who had bought it" (31). The despot has them all machine-gunned. When he opens schools, it is to teach sweeping. When he massacres the generals, the only survivor is an Indian named General

Saturno Santos, "who knew Indian secrets of how to change his form at will" (58). Only the supernatural can save anyone from this dictator.

He has packed two thousand kidnapped children in boxcars to be dispersed throughout the country, an image similar to the one in *One Hundred Years of Solitude,* evoking Hitler's shipping of the Jews to concentration camps during the Holocaust. When his only friend, Major General Rodrigo de Aguilar, allies himself with one of the many American ambassadors, the despot has his old friend roasted, stuffed with pine nuts and aromatic herbs, and served up at a banquet on a silver tray with "a garnish of cauliflower and laurel leaves" (124) to be served to the assembled military.

In a novel about power, García Márquez does not neglect the psychological element. The despot "squandered the earnings of power in order to have as an old man what he had lacked as a child" (61). He grew up without his father, about whom he knows only that he was a "back-trail" fugitive (131). In the most darkly humorous segment of the story, he attempts to have his mother, Benedición Alvarado, canonized by the church. For the nuncio's skepticism about this idea, the palace of the Apostolic Nunciature is sacked; the nuncio is then dragged through the streets, tortured, and cast adrift on the shipping lane that the cruise ships follow to Europe as a lesson to foreigners.

As a man, the despot is isolated, lonely, and paranoid. He is sexually voracious, a rapist who cannot sustain love for his wife and the son whom he makes a major general before the umbilical cord is cut. His wife, Leticia, and this boy are torn to pieces in the market and devoured by sixty stray hunting dogs "with frightened yellow eyes" (197) who, magically, had studied newspaper clippings containing their photographs. The cruelty of his regime devastates him as much as it does his victims.

He has survived for so long that no one can even remember a time when he was not there. His countrymen are a people without a history, bearing responsibility for their servitude. When the old dictator finally dies, Liberals, Conservatives, and priests divide the plunder. The author has a final word for his readers: "one learns too late that even the broadest and most useful of lives only reach the point of learning how to live" (267).

Todos los cuentos de Gabriel García Márquez, 1947–1972 (All of the Stories of Gabriel García Márquez, 1947–1972). Barcelona: Plaza & Janes, 1975. This collection of short stories includes those previously published in *Los funerales de la Mamá Grande, La increíble y triste historia de la cándida Eréndira y de su abuela desalmada,* and *Ojos de perro azul.*

Crónicas y reportajes (Chronicles and Reports). Bogotá: Instituto Colombiano de Cultura, 1976.

Operacion Carlota (Operation Carlota). Lima, Peru: Mosca Azul, 1977. A nonfiction account of Cuban military aid to Angolan rebels.

Periodismo militante (Militant Journalism). Bogotá: Son de Máquina, 1978.

Innocent Eréndira and Other Stories. New York: Harper & Row, 1978; London: Cape, 1979. Translated by Rabassa. Comprises "The Incredible and Sad Tale of Innocent Eréndira and Her Heartless Grandmother," "The Sea of Lost Time," "Death Constant Beyond Love," "The Third Resignation," "The Other Side of Death," "Eva Is Inside Her Cat," "Dialogue with the Mirror," "Bitterness for Three Sleepwalkers," "Eyes of a Blue Dog," "The Woman Who Came at Six O'clock," "Someone Has Been Disarranging These Roses," "The Night of the Curlews."

De viaje por los paises socialists: 90 dias en la "Cortina de Hierro" (Journey to the Socialist Countries: 90 Days behind the "Iron Curtain") Cali, Colombia: Ediciones Macondo, 1978. This work recounts García Márquez's 1957 trip through Eastern Europe.

Obra periodistica (Periodical Works). Barcelona: Bruguera, 1981–1982. Three volumes in four: volume 1: *Textos consteños;* volume 2: *Entre Cachacos I* and *Entre Cachacos II;* and volume 3: *De Europe y America (1955–1960).* This book is a collection of García Márquez's early journalism.

Crónica de una muerte anunciada. Bogotá: Oveja Negra, 1981. Translated by Rabassa as *Chronicle of a Death Foretold.* New York: Harper & Row, 1982; London: Cape, 1982. Once more, a García Márquez work of fiction begins with a death. Santiago Nasar is knifed to death by the brothers of Angela Vicario after her new husband, Bayardo San Román, returns her to her parents' house. San Román has discovered that she is not a virgin, and Angela claims that Nasar was her seducer. García Márquez never reveals whether in fact Santiago Nasar was guilty of deflowering Angela. Suspense comes in the unraveling of how Santiago came to be murdered.

The narrator is a journalist who resembles García Márquez. He falls in love with a thirteen-year-old girl, about the same age as was Mercedes, García Márquez's wife, when he first met her. One of his names is even Márquez, and it is to one of the narrator's relatives, his aunt Wenefrida Márquez, that the victim cries out at the end: "They've killed me, Wene child" (120). The town itself is a microcosm of Colombia. Having been born in this town, the narrator knows those who were involved in the murder and so hopes to get to the bottom of the crime, though it had happened twenty-seven years earlier.

Irony suffuses this novella. Although everyone, including a policeman, knows that the murder will happen, and the two murderers even tell people they plan to kill Santiago Nasar, hoping that they will be stopped, the murder occurs, bloody and inevitable. Chaos lies beneath the surface of everyday life in this town, where the autopsy is performed by Father Carmen Amador, his ineptness creating another "massacre" (74). He calls the stab wound in the victim's hand "a stigma of the crucified Christ" (75). Witnessing this autopsy, Colonel Lazaro Aponte, "who had seen and caused so many repressive massacres," is so appalled that he becomes "a vegetarian as well as a spiritualist" (76).

There are also, as always in the fiction of García Márquez, links between this novel and his other works. The father of Bayardo San Román, General Petronio San Román, is a Conservative who defeated Colonel Aureliano Buendía in the "disaster of Tucurinca" (33). The mother of the narrator hates General San Román for having given "the orders for Gerineldo Márquez to be shot in the back" (34). In *Chronicle of a Death Foretold* García Márquez creates an epic in novella form. The fate of the community is as much in balance as that of Santiago Nasar.

El olor de la guayaba: Conversaciones con Plinio Apuleyo Mendoza. Buenos Aires: Editorial Sudamericana, 1982. Translated by Ann Wright as *The Fragrance of Guava*. London: Verso / New York: Schocken Books, 1983. This book consists of interviews of García Márquez by his friend Plinio Apuleyo Mendoza.

Viva Sandino. Managua: Editorial Nueva Nicaragua, 1982. Republished as *El secuestro: Relato cinematográfico*. Salamanca, Spain: Lóguez / Managua : Editorial Nueva Nicaragua, 1983. Republished again as *El asalto: El operativo con que el FSLN se lanzó al mundo: Un relato*. Montevideo, Uruguay: Forum Editora, 1985. This unproduced screenplay is about the final assault on the National Palace during the Nicaraguan revolution.

El rastro de tu sangre en la nieve; El verano feliz de la Señora Forbes. Bogotá: Dampier, 1982. These two stories were translated by Grossman as "The Trail of Your Blood in the Snow" and "Mrs. Forbes' Summer of Happiness" in *Strange Pilgrims: Twelve Stories* (1993).

Dust jacket for the 1978 collection that includes the novella "The Incredible and Sad Tale of Innocent Eréndira and Her Heartless Grandmother," about a young girl driven into prostitution by her grandmother

Persecución y muerte de minorías: dos perspectivas polémicas (Persecution and Death of Minorities: Two Polemical Perspectives). Buenos Aires: Juárez Editor, 1983. This work on Vietnam was written in collaboration with Guillermo Nolasco-Juarez.

La aventura de Miguel Littín, clandestino en Chile. Bogotá: Oveja Negra; Madrid: El País, 1986; México: Editorial Diana, 1986. Translated by Asa Zatz as *Clandestine in Chile: The Adventures of Miguel Littín.* New York: Holt, 1987; Cambridge: Granta/Penguin, 1989. A nonfiction work that recounts the exiled Chilean moviemaker Miguel Littín's experiences secretly filming life under the dictatorship after returning to his homeland in disguise in early 1985.

El amor en los tiempos del cólera. Published simultaneously: Bogotá: Oveja Negra, 1985; Barcelona: Bruguera, 1985; Buenos Aires: Editorial Sudamericana, 1985. Translated by Edith Grossman as *Love in the Time of Cholera.* New York: Knopf, 1988; London: Cape, 1988. Dedicated to his wife, Mercedes, this novel is a meditation on love and a love story. After fifty years of loving her in silence, Florentino Ariza declares himself to Fermina Daza, freshly widowed. In the background of the story is a repressive Catholic culture, complete with meddling nuns. Fermina Daza, who had been married to Dr. Juvenal Urbino, has lived a lifetime without Florentino Ariza, to whom she is restored at this last moment.

The country is suffering from a plague, an analogue for the civil wars that had long divided the country. Once again the author expresses his antagonism toward Bogotá, where "it had been drizzling since the year one" (324). No wonder Fermina Daza had allowed herself to fall into "mists of disenchantment" (283) and the reunion had to wait for fifty-one years, nine months, and four days (53).

Setting his story in the Caribbean north, in particular in the venerable city of Cartagena de Indias, García Márquez suffuses the story with the superstitions that form part of that culture. "There is another important character," he has said, "one that has no name and that is the society of the Caribbean coast, its prejudice and superstitions, its old-fashioned ways. This is what really drives the story."[8]

Even a scientist like Dr. Juvenal Urbino participates in fantasies, magic, and myths. In his respiratory exercises, he breathes toward the side where the roosters are crowing because the air is better there. He is so excellent a physician that "he could tell what was wrong with a patient just by looking at him" (9–10), a skill García Márquez learned of in his youth in Aracataca. At times his views seem outlandish only to be true: Dr. Urbino views all medication as poison and believes that 70 percent of common foods hasten death.

In this novel the things of this world can seem so wonderful that they are magical: these include the "Catalonian condoms with iguana crests that fluttered when circumstances required" (101) and a Bengalese magnifying glass sold in the local market. A curlew sings "every hour on the hour" (107) when Dr. Urbino arrives home from Paris, as if the bird were trying to reconcile him to his shabby, "rubble-strewn" homeland (107).

The real magic is in the love between the widowed Fermina Daza and her old admirer Florentino Ariza, whose "driving need for love" (167) will admit no obstacle, not least the ravages of age. Over the years of his love nine civil wars have erupted, "always the same war" (191) between the Liberals and the Conservatives. A child shoots his brother for saying God was a member of the Conservative Party, an example of how absurd García Márquez finds the history of Colombia's perpetual "violencia." Visiting the river, Florentino does not know whether the bloating corpses he encounters there died of cholera or of the civil war; there is no difference between them.

If the culture is itself an important character, so is the narrator, who constantly instructs and comments. He understands that only by the irrational do we endure the inevitable hardships of life: "that the heart's memory eliminates the bad and magnifies the good, and that thanks to this artifice we manage to endure the burden of the past" (106). He is also wise in matters of love, the subject of this book: "one can be in love with several people at the same time, feel the same sorrow with each, and not betray any of them" (270).

Despite a lifetime of many loves, Florentino never forgets Fermina Daza. His mother had said that the only disease he ever had was cholera, confusing cholera with love, which is the central metaphoric conceit of this book, for "the symptoms of love were the same as those of cholera" (62). The author demonstrates as well that "the physical act . . . is only a part of the feat of love" (246). Love also exists in the mundane, the ordinariness of life, and Florentino discovers the letter for which he had been waiting for half a century floating in a puddle.

At the end, only on a riverboat cruise, never on the wartorn, decimated land, can they love each other. When at last they go to bed, he is impotent, and she withered. When they finally accomplish the act, it is "hurried and sad" (340). Yet, they try again, "much later, when the inspiration came to them without their looking for it" (341). Love triumphs even at the moment when it is accompanied by death, symbolized by the cholera epidemic.

In this most buoyant and joyous of his novels, García Márquez declares that love grows "more solid the closer it comes to death" (345). Cholera stands for impending death, and so the false cholera epidemic, which they use to keep the ship afloat and the world at bay, is figuratively real. The ultimate magic of García Márquez is the magnificence of real life, not just the magic of love.

García Márquez conveys his own point of view through the perceptions of the captain of the boat:

> The Captain looked at Fermina Daza and saw on her eyelashes the first glimmer of wintry frost. Then he looked at Florentino Ariza, his invincible power, his intrepid love, and he was overwhelmed by the belated suspicion that it is life, more than death, that has no limits. (348)

Fittingly, the intrepid lover Florentino Ariza is awarded the last word. Asked by the Captain how long they will be able to "keep up this goddamn coming and going," Florentino, who "had kept his answer ready for fifty-three years, seven months, and eleven days and nights," replies, "Forever" (348).

El cataclismo de Damocles. Bogotá: Oveja Negra, 1986. Translated in *El cataclismo de Damocles/The Doom of Damocles*. San José, Costa Rica: Universidad para la Paz, Editorial Universitaria Centroamericana, 1986. This book comprises the text of a speech given by García Márquez at the inaugural ceremony of the Ixtapa Summit of the Group of Six in Mexico in 1986.

El general en su laberinto. Published simultaneously: Bogota: Editorial Oveja Negra, 1989; Buenos Aires: Editorial Sudamericana, 1989; Mexico City: Editorial Diana, 1989; Madrid: Mondadori, 1989. Translated by Edith Grossman as *The General in His Labyrinth*. New York: Knopf, 1990; London: Cape, 1991. In this historical novel, based upon considerable research, García Márquez tells the story of the last of the Great Liberator, Simón Bolívar. Feverish and dying, Bolívar makes a final voyage down the Magdalena River. In a coda titled "My Thanks," the author offers his personal homage to the man he believes is the greatest figure in the history of the Americas. "I would recount," he decided, "a tyrannically documented life without renouncing the extravagant prerogatives of the novel" (272).

The year is 1830. Bolívar is only forty-six years old, but prematurely aged. He has already liberated the Americas from tyrannical Spanish rule. He dreams, however, of one united America, free of separatism and civil wars. He had wished to create "the largest country in the world: one nation, free and unified, from Mexico to Cape Horn" (48). In the course of this novel, he realizes that this dream was but an illusion. Nor is the public grateful for his sacrifice; it even despises the insurgents who demanded of them that they make sacrifices for their liberation. "He won't leave and he won't die" (13), they whine. Bolívar falls into a neurotic state of despair.

García Márquez reveals, however, that the people are not wholly in the wrong. They have achieved their freedom only to be "at the mercy of local tyrants." The "idea of integrity" will fail because it is "unfavorable to the local privileges of the great families" (203). Liberal, humane, and compassionate, Bolívar had intended to create a true republic. Instead, "everything we created with our hands is being trampled by others" (18).

This Bolívar is a great man. Using paradox, a seeming contradiction that is in fact true, García Márquez writes that Bolívar "knew how to put himself on equal footing with his subordinates" (63). He reveals "the untold sorrow that other people's suffering caused him" (106). Bolívar is a hero because he feels more for others than for himself. He loves dogs and horses and flowers. Like the author, this fictional Bolívar feels great affection "for the very noble and heroic city of Cartagena de Indias" that "has been celebrated a thousand times as one of the most beautiful cities in the world" (169–170).

He is a learned man who speaks English, and Spanish "in the educated forms of Madrid" (77). He is so proficient a lover that a young girl, whom he does not touch, leaves his room chastely in the morning with the parting words, "No one is a virgin after a night with Your Excellency" (183).

Magic arrives in the author's introduction of animals in the form of the menagerie of Bolívar's mistress, Manuela Sáenz: "three monkeys educated in the art of palace obscenities, a bear trained to thread needles, and nine cages of parrots and macaws that railed against Santander [an unreliable general] in three languages" (153).

Through Bolívar, García Márquez chastises his fellow Colombians for believing that "every Colombian is an enemy country" (240). Speaking from the vantage of the present, referring to Colombia's history of civil wars and violence, he notes that "The only ideas that occur to Colombians are for ways to divide the nation" (252). "The only wars here will be civil wars" (185), Bolívar predicts. While he is still alive, the first coup d'état occurs, "and the first of the forty-nine civil wars we would suffer in what remained of the country" (199).

Bolívar knew that the first step "was to distance the military from power" (19), a task that has since proven impossible in Latin America. Writing of the time of Bolívar, García Márquez also expresses his anger at the suffering visited upon the Americas by the neighbor to the north, the United States: "It's omnipotent and terrible, and its tale of liberty will end in a plague of miseries for us all" (223), the general says.

Bolívar departs, carrying two special books from Napoleon Bonaparte's personal library, Rousseau's *Social Contract* and Montecuccoli's *The Art of War*. Once more, García Márquez pokes fun at the weather of Bogotá, a frequent conceit in his work: "someone attempted to detain him until the weather cleared, although both of them knew it would not clear for the rest of the century" (36). Bolívar remains stoical and controlled, elegant, refined and humane, and so worldly that "he had learned from the French the custom of talking about food while he ate" (45).

A typical García Márquez dialogue occurs when one officer jokes that "The fact that no one's seen [Bolívar's copper mines] doesn't mean the mines don't exist" (62). Someone else volunteers that they're "in the Department of Venezuela" (62). A third retorts, "At this stage I even wonder if Venezuela exists" (62). At the height of misery, García Márquez insists, humor is never far away.

Toward the end, Bolívar is infected by nostalgia: "He stood with his eyes closed, inhaling the heartbreaking aroma of days gone by" (107). He "will continue to be the greatest Colombian anywhere on earth" (72) for his fragile dream of the "most invincible league of nations the world had ever seen" (74). Having given away all of his personal wealth, he becomes a repository of the ideals of the author.

García Márquez combines his magic with a strong sense of psychological causality. In the last pages of this highly personal novel, he reveals that Bolívar lost his father at the age of three, his mother when he was nine, and his wife when he was only twenty. It was then that he decided for the rest of his life "to escape the servitude of formalized love" (149). He would never again marry. That moment chronicled "his birth into history" (253). The last sentence of the novel reiterates the homage of García Márquez, who declares that with the death of Simón Bolívar also died "the final brilliance of life that would never, through all eternity, be repeated again" (268).

Primeros Reportajes. Caracas: Consorcio de Ediciones Capriles, 1990. This collection of articles originally appeared in 1956–1957 in the Venezuelan weekly *Elite.*

Notas de prensa, 1980–1984. Madrid: Mondadori, 1991. These collected articles originally appeared in the Spanish press.

Doce cuentos peregrinos. Published simultaneously: Buenos Aires: Editorial Sudamericana; Bogotá: Editorial Oveja Negra; Mexico City: Editorial Diana; Madrid: Mondadori, 1992. Translated by Grossman as *Strange Pilgrims: Twelve Stories.* New York: Knopf, 1993; London: Cape, 1993. Translation abridged as *Bon Voyage, Mr. President and Other Stories.* London: Penguin, 1995. This short story collection comprises "Buen viaje, señor presidente," "La santa," "El avión de la bella durmiente," "Me alquilo para soñar," "'Sólo vine a hablar por teléfono,'" "Espantos de agosto," "María dos Prazeres," "Diecisiete ingleses envenenados," "Tramontana," "El verano feliz de la señora Forbes," "La luz es como el agua," "El rastro de tu sangre en la nieve"; translated as "Bon voyage, Mr. President," "The Saint," "Sleeping Beauty and the Airplane," "I Sell My Dreams," "'I only came to use the phone,'" "The Ghosts of August,"

Irene Papas as the grandmother in *Eréndira* (1983), the motion-picture adaptation of García Márquez's novella "The Incredible and Sad Tale of Innocent Eréndira and Her Heartless Grandmother," for which he wrote the screenplay

---

"María dos Prazeres," "Seventeen Poisoned Englishmen," "Tramontana," "Miss Forbes's Summer of Happiness," "Light Is like Water," "The Trail of Your Blood in the Snow."

Diatriba de amor contra un hombre sentado: monologo en un acto (Diatribe of Love against a Seated Man: Monologue in One Act). Santa fe de Bogotá: Arango Editores, 1994. García Márquez's first published play, it was first performed in 1988 at the Cervantes Theater, Buenos Aires.

Del amor y otros demonios. Published simultaneously: Barcelona: Mondadori; Bogotá: Norma; Buenos Aires: Editorial Sudamericana; Mexico City: Editorial Diana, 1994. Translated by Grossman as *Of Love and Other Demons.* New York: Knopf, 1995.

This novel begins with the account of the narrator, a journalist, who witnesses the opening of a crypt in a convent; the crypt is full of beautiful hair, flowing from the skull of a twelve-year-old marquise who had died two hundred years before. From this point, the novel recounts the story of Sierva Maria Todos los Angeles, the neglected daughter of a

Spanish aristocrat, who grows up with her family's African slaves, immersed in their culture. After she is bitten by a dog, the local authorities of the Inquisition decide that she may be possessed by the demon of hydrophobia, and she is sent to a convent, where she undergoes a series of tortuous exorcisms. In this novel García Márquez examines the idea of love as a form of possession—one of the inquisitors falls in love with Sierva—but the novel is also a study of clashing cultures: Spanish and American, European and African.

Noticia de un secuestro. Barcelona: Mondadori, 1996. Translated by Grossman as *News of a Kidnapping*. New York: Knopf, 1997; London: Cape, 1997. In the acknowledgments García Márquez describes writing this story of his friend Maruja Pachón, who was kidnapped by the Pablo Escobar drug ring, as an "autumnal task, the saddest and most difficult of my life." Although this book is a work of nonfiction, García Márquez enlists the same techniques he uses in his novels. The characters reside among contradictions; the president's security adviser, Rafael Pardo, is a lyric poet whose socks do not match. A Beatles fan, he also fashioned peace accords with the M-19 guerrilla group. There is even a moment of magic realism. As the kidnapped journalist "Pacho" contemplates escape, "a wave of nausea rose from his stomach, froze his tongue, and emptied out his heart" (218).

Once more a García Márquez narrator speaks in the first person, here the plural "we." He allies himself with his fellow Colombians who must live in a landscape of terror. García Márquez makes it clear he admires his compatriots for surviving under such conditions.

SCRIPTS AND SCREENPLAYS

García Márquez studied briefly at the Centro Sperimentale di Cinema in Rome in the late 1950s, indicating his fascination with the motion-picture medium. His first foray into motion pictures occurred even before he went to Europe; in 1954 he collaborated with several members of "the Barranquilla group" on *La langosta azul* (The Blue Lobster), a twenty-nine minute black-and-white silent experimental piece. Hernando Martinez Pardo has called it the first serious effort to renew the Colombian cinema. The story involves the radioactive poisoning of lobsters discovered by a "gringo," whose presence disturbs a peaceful coastal fishing village. Martinez Pardo describes the work as "a surrealist experiment whose best moments are not only symbolic but also function as film journalism."[9] García Márquez has continued to write for both motion pictures and television.

Juego peligroso. 1966. 94 minutes. Made in Mexico in Spanish, directed by Luis Alcoriza and Arturo Ripstein. García Márquez wrote the "HO" segment, about a man who picks up newlyweds on the highway to Rio de Janeiro only for the car to be wrecked and the man's wife to find him alone with the bride.

Tiempo de morir (A Time to Die). 1985. Made in Mexico 1985 and directed by Jorge Ali Triana, the writing credit going to Gabriel García Márquez, with dialogue by García Márquez and Carlos Fuentes. García Márquez actually wrote this screenplay in 1965, and it was his first screenplay not to be adapted from one of his stories. The screenplay was published in *Revista de Bellas Artes* (Mexico), 9 (May–June 1966): 21–58.

In the outline, the story is similar to *Chronicle of a Death Foretold* in which the outcome is known from the beginning and destiny is enacted. A man returns to his hometown after eighteen years in prison for having killed another man in a duel. He meets his former love and his victim's two sons, who vow revenge. The eldest son taunts the killer; the younger attempts to get to know him and understand why he killed his father. Yet, it is the younger who eventually kills the man, in spite of the fact that he has discovered that his father was killed in a fair fight. Tarot cards predict tragedy for the younger son; the rumor that the man who killed his father is invulnerable is, of course, ironic. *Tiempo de morir* ends on a Colombian *vallenato* based on the death of the father and suggesting that the entire story has passed into legend.

Un Domingo feliz (A Happy Sunday). Televisión Española / International Network Group, S.A. 1988. 90 minutes. Filmed in Spain and directed by Olegario Barrera, with script by García Márquez, Eiseo Alberto, and Olegario Barrera. A young boy from a wealthy family runs away from home and falls in with a young musician, who shows him the seamy nightlife of Caracas.

Fabula de la Bella Palomera. Released in the U.S. as *Fable of the Beautiful Pigeon Fancier*. Televisión Española / International Network Group, S.A. 1988. 78 minutes. Made in Brazil in Spanish, directed by Ruy Guerra. The movie is set in a small Caribbean town in 1892. A rich brewery owner, Don Orestes, falls in love with the married Fulvia, who raises pigeons, which the two use to send messages to each other.

Milagro en Roma (Miracle in Rome). 1988. 90 minutes. Filmed in Colombia in Spanish, and directed by Lisandro Duque Naranjo with writing credits to Duque Naranjo and García Márquez. The seven-year-old daughter of a minor bureaucrat dies; when a corrupt priest sells the cemetery to a developer twelve years later, her body is exhumed and is discovered to be perfectly preserved. The father takes the body to Rome for the Pope to decide whether or not this is a miracle and if she is the first Colombian saint.

Yo soy el que tu buscas (I'm The One You're Looking For). Televisión Española / Österreichischer Rundfunk / Taurus Film. 1988. 90 minutes. Made in Spain and directed by Chavarri, with writing credits to Chavarri, Juan Tebar, and García Márquez. Natalia, a fashion model, is coming home from work late at night and is raped. Obsessed with thoughts of revenge, she searches for her attacker.

The Two Way Mirror. Gabriel García Márquez' Scriptwriters' Workshop / The Fundacion del Nuevo Cine Latinoamericano / Producciones Amaranta / RM Associates. 1990. 27 minutes. Made in Mexico in Spanish. Directed by Carlos Garcia Agraz, with writing credits to Gabriel García Márquez and Susana Cato. In 1990, Susana, about to be married, looks into an antique mirror and sees the image of a handsome soldier looking back at her. He is Nicolas, who lived in 1863.

Contigo en la distancia. Released in the U.S. as *Far Apart.* 1991. 27 minutes. Gabriel García Márquez's Scriptwriters' Workshop / The Fundacion del Nuevo Cine Latinoamericano / Producciones Amaranta / RM Associates. Made in Mexico. Directed by Cuban director Tomas Gutierrez Alea, with a screenplay by García Márquez and Eiseo Alberto.

Maria. 1991. A nine-part television series, the story was adapted by García Márquez from the classic Colombian novel by Jorge Isaacs. It was directed by Lisandro Duque Naranjo.

Saturday Night Thief. 1991. 25 minutes. Made in Mexico in Spanish, directed by Jose Luis Garcia Agraz, with writing credits to García Márquez and Consuelo Garrido.

Edipo alcalde (Oedipus Mayor). Sociedad General de Televisión, S.A. 1996. 100 minutes. Made in Colombia in Spanish, directed by Jorge Ali Triana, with a script by García Márquez, Stella Malagon, and Orlando Senna, this movie is an adaptation of Sophocles' play *Oedipus Rex*, with the setting in modern-day Colombia.

THE ROLE OF THE LATIN AMERICAN WRITER

"Why is it like this?" Mario Vargas Llosa, the Peruvian novelist, asked in a recent essay. "Why is it that instead of being basically creators and artists, writers in Peru and other Latin American countries must above all be politicians, agitators, reformers, social publicists and moralists?"

From Alan Riding, "Revolution and the Intellectual in Latin America," *The New York Times,* 13 March 1983, p. 28.

CRITICAL SUMMARY

"Critics in the United States are those who best understand my works," García Márquez has said.[10]

The most elegant study of García Márquez, and the one that best places his work within twentieth-century literary traditions is *Gabriel García Márquez: One Hundred Years of Solitude* by Michael Wood. Wood begins by locating García Márquez in the context of the "Boom" of Latin American writers that began in the 1960s; he discovers antecedents for García Márquez in the works of Jorge Luis Borges, the Argentinian parabolist, and in the works of Spanish motion-picture director, Luis Buñuel. Wood goes on to invoke James Joyce, Virginia Woolf, Thomas Mann, and William Faulkner as he places García Márquez among the highest practitioners of the art of fiction.

Wood discusses the geographical, political, and social context of *One Hundred Years of Solitude* more shrewdly than other critics. He finds García Márquez among "the most accessible of writers"[11] in a book which is sensible, yet personal, and always admiring of its subject.

The best introduction to Gabriel García Márquez is *Gabriel García Márquez: The Man And His Work* (1990) by Gene H. Bell-Villada. More than any other critic, Bell-Villada is good at placing García Márquez in his Colombian, in particular in his *costeño* context. Bell-Villada offers the most extensive use of biography in an effort to discuss this author. His book is full of quotations from García Márquez himself, drawn from the available interviews, both in English and in Spanish. He is also excellent on the historical and cultural background. "The social division, ideological struggles and geographic differences within Colombia are a constant underlying presence in his work," Bell-Villada writes.[12]

There are two outstanding collections of essays that should be consulted on the subject of this author. *Gabriel García Márquez: New Readings* (1987), edited by Bernard McGuirk and Richard Cardwell, focuses on *One Hundred Years of Solitude* with four of the essays concerning that work. There are also two essays on *Chronicle of a Death Foretold* and one each on *The Autumn of the Patriarch* and *Love in the Time of Cholera*. Clive Griffin's contribution, "The Humor of *One Hundred Years of Solitude*," makes interesting comparisons with Miguel de Cervantes's *Don Quixote* (1605–1615), and draws attention to the similarities between "Cid Hamete Benengeli," the "true author" of *Don Quixote,* and Melquiades of *One Hundred Years of Solitude.*

Modern Critical Views: Gabriel García Márquez (1989), edited by Harold Bloom, surveys the range of themes to be found in the work of

García Márquez, from Colombian politics to his use of magic realism. It opens with Peruvian novelist Mario Vargas Llosa's seminal introductory essay, "García Márquez: From Aracataca to Macondo," which offers important biographical information. The civil wars between Liberals and Conservatives, La Violencia, and the banana strike of 1928 that figures so prominently in *One Hundred Years of Solitude* are discussed in "Liberals, Conservatives and Bananas: Colombian Politics in the Fictions of Gabriel García Márquez," by Regina Janes. This essay introduces the reader to some of the central events of Colombian history that appear in the stories and novels of García Márquez.

The most comprehensive appreciation and discussion of the work of García Márquez remains *García Márquez: Historia de un Deicidio* (1971), by Vargas Llosa. Although this work is available only in Spanish, in it Vargas Llosa simultaneously enlists biography and the study of his novelistic techniques to describe the work of García Márquez.

Vargas Llosa begins with the life of the father of García Márquez, Gabriel Eligio García, who went to Cartagena to enter the university only to find himself without money. He then became "telegrafista de Aracataca."[13] He found, Vargas Llosa writes, not fortune, but "el amor," love. The author's mother, Luisa Santiago Márquez Iguaran, belonged to one of the groups of old families that had looked with disgust at the invasion of the area by those caught up in "la fiebra bananera" (banana fever).

Her parents, the couple who raised Gabriel García Márquez, were not only first cousins, but "constituian la familia mas eminente de esa aristocracia lugarena"[14] (Constituted the most eminent family of the local aristocracy). They opposed the marriage, and as legend has it, when the young couple were separated, local telegraph operators who knew Eligio García helped them to communicate. The story reads, not surprisingly, like a novel, not least in Vargas Llosa's description of the grandmother with her "ojos azules, todavia hermosa"[15] (blue eyes, still beautiful).

Vargas Llosa also discusses the social history of the moment of García Márquez's birth. He analyzes "La Huelga del año 28," the banana strike of 1928, in its wider context, in particular how it is a manifestation of North American capitalism. Like García Márquez, Vargas Llosa is well aware of how the United States established economic hegemony in the area, which included his own country, Peru, and in so doing often destroyed the fledgling local economies, making them dependent and stunting their growth. It was, Vargas Llosa writes, an "invasion economica que no tiene oposicion"[16] (an economic invasion that has no opposition). In the absence of a full-length biography of García Márquez, Vargas Llosa's study remains the most important book written about this author.

For a fuller measure of the author's time in history and the era in which he lived, the following book, also available only in Spanish, *La Violencia en Colombia: Estudio de un Proceso Social* (1963), volume 1, is indispensable. The three authors are German Guzman Campos, the biographer of Camilo Torres Restrepo, and two sociologists, Orlando Fals Borda and Eduardo Umana Luna. They date the outbreak of La Violencia to 1930.

For the South American literary context, read José Donoso's *The Boom in Spanish American Literature* (1977), which provides a full and humorous introduction to the "sudden" interest in Latin American writers. The hero of this volume is, however, not García Márquez, but Carlos Fuentes, the Mexican novelist and author of *The Death of Artemio Cruz* (1962), who reached a position of authority and literary recognition before his friend.

Donoso explains how in Latin America, politics and literature have been inseparable. He also reveals that there has been a solidarity among these writers from diverse countries, and he quotes an Italian critic: "In Italy it would be impossible for a writer like Vargas Llosa to write a book about the work of another writer like García Márquez. And for both of them to be at the same party without one throwing poison into the other's coffee, well, that really would seem like science fiction."[17]

ART IMITATING LIFE

García Márquez drew his inspiration from the Caribbean landscapes of his youth. "When he was born, Aracataca lived off memories," Vargas Llosa has written; his fictions, in turn, "take life from his memories of Aracataca."[18] When García Márquez was twenty-two years old, he returned with his mother to Aracataca where he had not been since he was eight years old. "Nothing had really changed," he has said. "It was as if everything I saw had already been written, and all I had to do was to sit down and copy what was already there . . . for all practical purposes everything had evolved into literature: the houses, the people, and the memories."[19]

Even the details of his courtship of Mercedes Barcha appear in his work. In *Chronicle of a Death Foretold,* he writes that the narrator proposed marriage to Mercedes at the wedding of Bayardo San Román and Angela Vicario: "Many knew that in the confusion of the bash I had proposed marriage to Mercedes Barcha as soon as she finished primary school, just as she herself would remind me fourteen years later when we got married" (43). García Márquez proposed to Mercedes Barcha when she was thirteen years old.

Mercedes reappears in *One Hundred Years of Solitude* as a pharmacist, Gabriel's "stealthy girlfriend" (409) with a "thin neck and sleepy eyes" (418) who is left behind when he goes to Europe. (In the novel he goes because he wins a trip to Paris, however, not as a journalist for *El Espectador*). And in *Love in the Time of Cholera,* there is a reference to the town of Magangue, "where Mercedes was born" (344), as if his life cannot escape spilling into even novels set in earlier times, as if, in this love story, he could not help but include the name of the woman he loves.

García Márquez has called *One Hundred Years of Solitude* "a book based on the experiences of my parents," to which he added "people I met during childhood, popular legends, stories people have told me, newspaper reports and the research I've done. . . ."[20] His work, but this novel in particular, critic Gerald Martin has noted, is driven by a "nostalgic quest—many years later—for that lost time."[21] The small room which Jose Arcadio Buendía has "built in the rear of the house so that no one would disturb his experiments" (4) seems itself a reflection of García Márquez's own garden studio in his Mexico City home.

The trail of yellow butterflies was suggested by a remark of his grandmother about a butterfly following a man. One day she saw a butterfly fly into the winter and said, "a letter is coming today." García Márquez has remarked that "the realistic base of this story is that there was an electrician who came to our house in Aracataca . . . one day, after his visit, my grandmother found a butterfly, which she quickly hit with a dish towel. 'Every time that man comes into this house, we get butterflies,'" she declared. These small incidents are transformed into the group of yellow butterflies that always precedes the appearance of Mauricio Babilonia, the lover of Meme Buendía.[22]

García Márquez had once heard that as a euphemism for a girl who had run away from home with a traveling salesman her parents said she had "ascended into heaven," adding, "if the Virgin Mary could do it, so can our daughter." The incident became the moment where Remedios The Beauty ascends into heaven. García Márquez had feared that this would be unbelievable. He has said that after spying on the maid next door to their house in Mexico City when she was hanging out the wash, he added the detail of Remedios rising with the sheets

AUTUMN OF THE PATRIARCH

"The first political leader to whom García Márquez became both friend and confidante was General Omar Torrijos, who seized power in Panama in 1969. . . . García Márquez says that he and Torrijos became friends after their first meeting turned into a three-day drinking binge. They remained close until Torrijos's death, in a plane crash, in 1981. García Márquez lovingly describes how the moody, lonely Torrijos would stay up drinking whiskey all night, and then, when he wanted sex in the morning, would summon one of six different women he had 'on permanent call.' He also recalls with pride how Torrijos—who rarely read a book—had read and liked 'Autumn of the Patriarch.' 'He told me he thought it was my best book, and I asked him why he thought so. He leaned over to me and said, 'Because it's true; we're all like that.'"

Jon Lee Anderson

From "The Power of García Márquez," *The New Yorker* (27 September 1999): 69.

that she was folding still in her hands. Remedios herself was inspired by a Guajira girl he had met.

There are other autobiographical details as well. In 1925 El Niño caused the death of millions of birds that were washed up on the shores of Ecuador and Colombia, a detail he added to emphasize the spiritual importance of the death of Úrsula; when she dies, thousands of birds fall dead, a plague he also incorporates in his story "One Day After Saturday."

His own personal experience appears in the discovery of ice by Colonel Aureliano Buendía. As a child, "Gabito" was taken to the United Fruit Company store with his grandfather who opened the frozen fish boxes for the child to observe the miracle of ice, and it was he who found them so cold that he said, "But this is boiling." "No, on the contrary," his grandfather said, "it is very cold."[23]

His characters are drawn from people he has known. Like his grandmother, Úrsula is a baker. Eufemia, one of the prostitutes from the brothel where he lived in Barranquilla in the early 1950s, became the character Nigormanta.

His aunt Francisca, like Amaranta, wove her own shroud and, when the job was done, lay down and died, exactly like the character in the novel. There is a priest who levitates when he drinks hot chocolate, reflecting a real priest in Aracataca "who was thought to be so saintly that people said he rose off the ground whenever he raised the chalice during mass." García Márquez had thought of having the priest drink Coca-Cola, but he did not want to give Coca-Cola free advertising, he has said, perhaps with tongue in cheek, so he chose hot chocolate.[24]

Toward the end of the novel, knowing that he had accomplished his goal, García Márquez allows autobiographical details to

García Márquez in Paris with his friend, and fellow Colombian author, Plinio Apuleyo Mendoza, 1981

proliferate. The characters who gather at the bookstore are given their real-life first names Álvaro (Cepeda), Gérman (Vargas), and Alfonso (Fuenmayor).

They are joined by one Gabriel, the only one of the group who "did not doubt the reality of Colonel Aureliano Buendía," not least "because he had been a companion in arms and inseparable friend of his great-great-grandfather Colonel Gerineldo Márquez" (396). The Catalonian bookshop frequented by the final Aureliano is like the Cafe Colombia in Barranquilla, where in 1950 García Márquez met Ramon Vinyes, a Catalonian bookseller, and his three friends. García Márquez pays them homage by calling this group, for Aureliano "the first and last friends that he ever had in his life" (394). In real life, however, García Márquez took with him not a copy of a book by Rabelais, as in the novel, but Daniel Defoe's *Journal of the Plague Year* (1722).

There is more. Amaranta Úrsula, whose sexual relations with her nephew Aureliano bring the Buendía line to its end, hopes to name her sons, "Rodrigo and Gonzolo, never Aureliano and José Arcadio" (387), as García Márquez in fact named his sons. Had he a daughter, she would have been named "Virginia and never Remedios" (387). García Márquez has called Amaranta his second favorite character, because she "most resembles the original Úrsula [his grandmother]— but without the older woman's complexes and prejudices. Amaranta Úrsula is Úrsula again—but emancipated now, with the experiences of the world, with modern ideas."[25]

His grandfather, the colonel, appears first in *Leaf Storm,* and then in *No One Writes To The Colonel;* he too had sought a pension that never came to him, a cause assumed by his widow after his death. His grandfather had shot a man, remarking to his grandson years later, "you don't know how much a dead body weighs"[26] and his experience is echoed in that of José Arcadio Buendía, who is haunted by the ghost of the man he killed, Prudencio Aguilar. Colonel Aureliano Buendía attains the same rank as García Márquez's grandfather did in the War of the Thousand Days, and both have seventeen illegitimate children, a figure given to García Márquez by his mother. The character also includes aspects of the life of General Rafael Uribe Uribe, leader of the Liberal forces and the superior of the grandfather of García Márquez. It was he who signed the Peace of Neerlandia, only to be assassinated in 1914.

So personal was García Márquez's identification with the character of Colonel Aureliano Buendía that after he wrote the scene of the colonel's death, he went upstairs trembling. Mercedes knew at once what had happened.

In 1969 a journalist traveled to Aracataca and found that the house of García Márquez's grandparents was being eaten away by ants, the same way that the last Buendía baby meets its end. With García Márquez, life imitates art as much as art imitates life.

The Autumn of the Patriarch is "based completely on my personal experiences," he has said. The magic element of the United States carrying away the sea in numbered pieces "corresponds to the boy from Aracataca, from Barranquilla, feeling lost because of the lack of the sea when he arrived in Zipaquirá, and then in Bogotá. . . ."[27]

García Márquez was present in Venezuela during the fall of the dictator Peréz Jimenéz, an event that inspired this novel. As Bell-Villada recounts, García Márquez and other journalists were sitting in the foyer at Miraflores, the Venezuelan presidential palace, awaiting word about the governmental transition. Suddenly a general in combat fatigues burst into the room brandishing a machine gun. Then the man "backed out, slowly and silently, streaking the floor with his muddy boots and fled by car to La Guaira airport and safe haven abroad."[28]

This novel was inspired as well by the fall of Fulgencio Zaldívar Batista y Zaldivar in Cuba in 1959. Covering the trial of Batista henchman Jesus Sosa Blanco in a Havana baseball stadium, García Márquez had listened to a recounting of the officer's crimes and heard the death sentence passed on him by the tribunal. When he sat down to write *The Autumn of the Patriarch,* he considered using "the form of a monologue by the dictator as he sat in the middle of the stadium."[29]

His inspiration even went back to his childhood in Aracataca where many Venezuelan exiles lived, including Juan Vicente Gómez. The fact that he had never himself lived under any of the old dictatorships was what inspired him to move to Spain, in order to live under the regime of the fascist dictator Francisco Franco.

The plot of *Chronicle of a Death Foretold* is based on an actual murder that occurred in Sucre, involving Cayetano Gentile, a childhood friend of García Márquez. The murder was committed on 22 January 1951. A man named Miguel Reyes Palencia had married a schoolteacher, only to discover that she was not a virgin. She named as her seducer Gentile, who was a medical student, and who had been one of those who gathered to see the honeymoon couple off.

The couple, however, did not appear at the farewell party. Gentile wrote a letter about the event to García Márquez's father and told him about the incident. He was later killed by the schoolteacher's brothers on his way home. His entrails dangled exactly like Santiago Nasar's. "I'm innocent," he had proclaimed, like Nasar.

Love in the Time of Cholera, which describes the courtship of his parents, is also deeply autobiographical. He has called this novel "a true and literal copy of the love of my parents."[30] During its composition, García Márquez would go to his parents' house every afternoon; he questioned his mother and his father separately. Their versions differed only slightly.

In the process, he discovered to his surprise that in their seventies they "were still—at that time—making love!"[31] So he had a precedent for the sexual relationship between Florentino Ariza and Fermina Daza in their old age.

Even *Of Love and Other Demons* derives from an event the author witnessed as a journalist. As a reporter in Cartagena in 1949 he was assigned to watch while a tomb was opened to transfer burial remains since the convent was being torn down to clear space for a hotel. From the coffin emerged twenty-two meters of human hair, attached to the skull of a young girl who had been buried for two centuries. He added a story told to him by his grandparents about a twelve-year-old aristocrat who had died of rabies, and he began to construct the story of Sierva Maria.

THE WORKS' PLACE IN HISTORY

One Hundred Years of Solitude was widely acknowledged as a literary masterpiece immediately upon publication. Its reputation was only enhanced when Gabriel García Márquez won the Nobel Prize in literature fifteen years later. Certainly, its stature in literary history is assured, not only because it has sold more copies than any book in Spanish since *Don Quixote,* but also because admiration for this work has remained constant.

Chronicle of a Death Foretold must be counted among the finest novellas to be written in the twentieth century; it takes its place alongside Joseph Conrad's *Heart of Darkness* (1902), Thomas Mann's *Death in Venice* (1912), and Franz Kafka's *Metamorphosis* (1915). Although critics were ambivalent about *Love in the Time of Cholera,* and some accused García Márquez of sentimentality, the novel would have been considered an unquestionable masterpiece had it been written by any other author.

Lesser works include *The Autumn of the Patriarch,* which, however, has been compared to the experimental works of James Joyce and William Faulkner, and the historical novel *The General in His Labyrinth.* The verdict of history, of course, is yet to come. A strong case could be made that García Márquez is the finest novelist of the second half of the twentieth century from any country.

ADAPTATIONS

The attitude of García Márquez toward his stories and novels being adapted for the stage or motion pictures has always been ambivalent. Adamantly, he has prevented *One Hundred Years of Solitude* from being adapted for the screen, "since the film viewer sees a face that he may not have imagined."[32] To discourage offers, his agent set a price for the movie rights at one million dollars. When offers were made for it at that price, she raised it to three million. García Márquez has said: "I prefer that it remain a private relationship between the reader and the book."[33]

Asked whether *Love in the Time of Cholera* would be filmed, he replied, "I don't mind as long as it's a Latin American movie. By that I mean one that is directed by a Latin American, that exudes the atmosphere of Latin America, that shows our character, our way of being, our society, because those are the things that define this drama." Acknowledging that he would never be satisfied with any adaptation, he added, "the answer is for me not to get involved."[34]

MOTION PICTURES: Several of the works of fiction of Gabriel García Márquez have been made into motion pictures, most frequently his short stories.

El mar del tiempo perdido was directed in 1977 by experimental moviemaker Solveig Hoogesteijn, who immigrated to Venezuela at the age of one. This movie, adapted from a short story in the 1972 collection *La increíble y triste historia de la cándida Eréndira y de su abuela desalmada,* won Second Prize at the Havana Film Festival in 1981.

Maria de mi corazon (Maria My Dear). Universidad Veracruzano. 137 minutes. Made in Mexico in 1979 in Spanish. Directed by Jaime Humberto Hermosillo, who also wrote the screenplay. A robber and a magician are lovers. In an ending with a twist, after an accident she is picked up by a bus and taken to a mental hospital. Her magic appears to be mental illness, and she is incarcerated as if she were a patient.

La viuda de Montiel. Filmed in Colombia-Venezuela-Cuba-Mexico. 1980. In Spanish, directed by Miguel Littin. Based on the short story of that title by García Márquez.

Eréndira. Cinequanon / Les Films de Triangles / Atlas Saskia Film / Films A2 / Ministère de la Culture de la Republique Française / Austra. 103 minutes. Made in Mexico in 1983 in Spanish, with English subtitles. Directed by Ruy Guerra with Claudia Ohana as Eréndira and Irene Papas as Eréndira's grandmother. This movie is an adaptation by García Márquez of his 1978 novella "The Incredible and Sad Tale of Innocent Eréndira and her Heartless Grandmother." The grandmother is depicted as a witch with a long staff capable of feats of magic.

Cronaca di una morte annunciata (Chronicle of a Death Foretold). France 3 Cinéma / Italmedia Film / Les Films Ariane / Soprofilms. 1987. 109 minutes. A Franco-Italian production, in Italian. Screenplay adapted by Tonino Guerra and Francesco Rosi; the movie was directed by Rosi and shot in the Colombian town of Mompox, which figures in the novel *The General in His Labyrinth.* Rosi was about to show García Márquez the screenplay, but he replied, "Don't show it to me because if I read it the film will probably never be made. I am thinking of my book and you are thinking of your film. I wrote the book alone; you make the film alone." Later, Rosi thanked him.[35]

Un señor muy viejo con unas alas enormes (A Very Old Man with Enormous Wings). Televison Española. 1988. A Cuban-Italian-Spanish production. Filmed in Spanish, it was directed by Fernando Birri and was only the second feature film by the Argentine filmmaker, who is also a director at the new International Film and Television School in Cuba, founded by García Márquez himself. García Márquez wrote the screenplay of "A Very Old Man with Enormous Wings" with Birri, adapted from his much-anthologized short story. In a scene added to the filmed version of the story, the old man is revealed as a trickster or confidence man who takes off his wings when he is alone. The film begins with a quotation from Hebrews 13:2: "Be not forgetful to entertain strangers: for thereby some have entertained angels unaware."

El verano de la señora Forbes (The Summer of Miss Forbes). Televisión Española / International Network Group, S.A. 1988. 90 minutes. Made in Cuba and directed by Jaime Humberto Hermosillo with writing credits to Hermosillo and García Márquez. Two children plan to murder their German governess, Mrs. Forbes, who is cruel and autocratic and has been left in charge of them while their parents are away; while spying on her, they learn of her secret passion.

Mujer que llegaba a las seis. 1991. Made in Mexico, in Spanish, directed by Arturo Flores and Rogelio Jaramillo. Screenplay adapted by Flores, Jaramillo, and María Andrea de León from a story by García Márquez. Reina, a prostitute, enters a cafeteria later than she usually does; the cafeteria owner, her friend, begins to suspect that she may have murdered her last client.

Eyes of a Blue Dog. 49 minutes. Made in the United States in 1994 in English.

STAGE: *Crónica de una muerte anunciada.* New York, Public Theater, 1 August 1990. Written and directed by Salvador Tavora; based on the novel of the same name.

No One Writes to the Colonel. London, Lyric Studio, February 1991. English-language adaptation of García Márquez's novella, produced by Walter Acosta.

Innocent Eréndira and her Heartless Grandmother. New York, Spanish Theater Repertory Company / Repetario Español, 1992. Ofelia

González was awarded the *Village Voice* Obie Award for her role as the grandmother in this adaptation of García Márquez's novella.

Florencia en el Amazonas. Composed by Daniel Catán, Los Angeles Grand Opera, 1995. An opera loosely based on García Márquez's *Love in the Time of Cholera*, with the setting on a riverboat traveling through the jungle and a plot of love. The libretto was developed in 1994 through discussions with García Márquez, the librettist Marcela Fuentes-Berain, who is a García Márquez protege, and the composer, Catán.

PUBLIC RESPONSE

Although García Márquez is not a "realist" in the strict sense of that term, and although his novels are demanding, he is read in Latin America by ordinary people as well as by those interested in literary fiction. Carlos Fuentes has remarked that his cook in Mexico reads García Márquez. An Argentine maid refused to return to work until she had finished what she called "the last page of the history of Macondo," García Márquez has remarked. He has told of an incident in rural Cuba in the early 1970s when a group of peasants asked him what he did for a living.

"I write," he said modestly.
"What do you write?"
"I wrote a book called *Cien años de soledad*."
One of the peasants at once cried out: "Macondo!"[36]

The Panamanian salsa singer Ruben Blades even released an entire album of songs with lyrics based on eight García Márquez stories.

García Márquez has said that his best reviews for *One Hundred Years of Solitude* came from the United States: "They are professional readers . . . some are progressive, others so reactionary, as they are supposed to be; but as readers, they're wonderful."[37]

From the start, his writing attracted a wide following. There was so much enthusiasm among readers for the installments of *The Story of a Shipwrecked Sailor*, and the circulation of *El Espectador* had increased so enormously, that the editor told García Márquez, "I don't know how you're going to manage, but you must get at least twenty installments out of this." He then set about "enriching every detail." His popularity became so great among readers that even the least accessible of his books, *The Autumn of the Patriarch*, sold five hundred thousand copies instantly upon publication.

With its extraordinary public response, *One Hundred Years of Solitude* changed the life of García Márquez. "Before the book I had my friends," he has said, "but now there are enormous numbers of people who want to see me and talk to me—journalists, academics, readers. It's strange . . . most of my readers aren't interested in asking questions, they only want to talk about the book."[38] So wide is the response that he has changed hotels at times, claiming he was leaving town, in order to evade people.

His popularity become "like that of a singer or film star." He has also compared his popularity to that of "a great soccer player or an eminent singer of boleros.[39] Yet, when he writes, he thinks not of his wide readership in the abstract, but of the "four or five particular people who make up my public when I'm writing. As I consider what would please or displease them, I add or subtract things, and so the book is put together."[40]

NOTES

1. Rita Guibert, "Gabriel García Márquez," *Seven Voices: Seven Latin American Writers Talk to Rita Guibert* (New York: Knopf, 1973), p. 326.

2. Ibid., p. 306.

3. Michael Wood, *Gabriel García Márquez: One Hundred Years of Solitude* (Cambridge & New York: Cambridge University Press, 1990), p. 90.

4. Ibid., p. 85.

5. Claudia Dreifus, "*Playboy* Interview: Gabriel García Márquez," *Playboy,* 30 (February 1983): 74.

6. Guibert, *Seven Voices,* p. 309.

7. Ibid., p. 328.

8. Marlise Simóns, "The Best Years Of His Life: An Interview With Gabriel García Márquez," *New York Times Book Review,* 10 April 1988.

9. *South American Cinema: A Critical Filmography, 1915–1994,* edited by Timothy Barnard and Peter Rist. (Austin: University of Texas Press, 1996), pp. 245–246.

10. Dreifus, "*Playboy* Interview": 67.

11. Wood, *Gabriel García Márquez,* p. 15.

12. Gene H. Bell-Villada, *Gabriel García Márquez: The Man And His Work* (Chapel Hill & London: University of North Carolina Press, 1990), p. 41.

13. Mario Vargas Llosa, *Gabriel García: Historia de un Deicidio* (Barcelona: Barral Editores, 1971), p. 13.

14. Ibid., p. 14.

15. Ibid., pp. 16–17.

16. Ibid., p. 22.

17. José Donoso, *The Boom in Spanish American Literature: A Personal History,* translated by Gregory Kolavakos (New York: Columbia University Press / Center for Inter-American Relations, 1977), p. 68.

18. Vargas Llosa, "García Márquez: From Aracataca to Macondo," in *Gabriel García Márquez,* edited by Harold Bloom (New York: Chelsea House, 1989), pp. 5–19.

19. Peter Stone, "Gabriel García Márquez," in *Writers at Work: The Paris Review Interviews: Sixth Series,* edited by George Plimpton (New York: Viking, 1984), p. 321.

20. *Gabriel García Márquez: Magic and Reality,* written and directed by Ana Cristina Navarro, produced by Harold Mantell, 60 min., Films For the Humanities & Sciences, 1981, video.

21. Gerald Martin, "On Magical and Social Realism in García Márquez," in *Gabriel García Márquez: New Readings,* edited by Bernard McGuirk and Richard Cardwell (Cambridge: Cambridge University Press, 1987), p. 96.

22. Dreifus, "*Playboy* Interview": 74.

23. Dreifus, "*Playboy* Interview": 76.

24. Dreifus, "*Playboy* Interview": 176.

25. Ibid. : 76.

26. Vargas Llosa, "From Aracataca to Macondo," p. 7.

27. *Gabriel García Márquez: Magic and Reality.*

28. Bell-Villada, *The Man And His Work,* p. 150.

29. Dreifus, "*Playboy* Interview": 177.

30. *Gabriel García Márquez: Magic and Reality.*

31. *Conversations with Latin American Writers: Gabriel García Márquez,* interviewed by Silvia Lemus., 44 min., Films For The Humanities & Sciences, 1998, video.

32. Stone, *Paris Review,* p. 338.

33. Ibid.

34. Simons, "The Best Years Of His Life."

35. Ibid.

36. Bell-Villada, *The Man And His Work,* p. 5.

37. Guibert, *Seven Voices,* p. 307.

38. Ibid., pp. 310–311.

39. Ibid., p. 306.

40. Ibid., p. 326.

GARCÍA MÁRQUEZ ON
GARCÍA MÁRQUEZ

GABRIEL GARCÍA MÁRQUEZ'S NOBEL PRIZE LECTURE

"The Solitude of Latin America," delivered to the Swedish Academy 8 December 1982. (©The Nobel Foundation, 1982)

Antonio Pigafetta, a Florentine navigator who went with Magellan on the first voyage around the world, wrote, upon his passage through our southern lands of America, a strictly accurate account that nonetheless resembles a venture into fantasy. In it he recorded that he had seen hogs with navels on their haunches, clawless birds whose hens laid eggs on the backs of their mates, and others still, resembling tongueless pelicans, with beaks like spoons. He wrote of having seen a misbegotten creature with the head and ears of a mule, a camel's body, the legs of a deer and the whinny of a horse. He described how the first native encountered in Patagonia was confronted with a mirror, whereupon that impassioned giant lost his senses to the terror of his own image.

This short and fascinating book, which even then contained the seeds of our present-day novels, is by no means the most staggering account of our reality in that age. The Chronicles of the Indies left us countless others. Eldorado, our so avidly sought and illusory land, appeared on numerous maps for many a long year, shifting its place and form to suit the fantasy of cartographers. In his search for the fountain of eternal youth, the mythical Alvar Núñez Cabeza de Vaca explored the north of Mexico for eight years, in a deluded expedition whose members devoured each other and only five of whom returned, of the six hundred who had undertaken it. One of the many unfathomed mysteries of that age is that of the eleven thousand mules, each loaded with one hundred pounds of gold, that left Cuzco one day to pay the ransom of Atahualpa and never reached their destination. Subsequently, in colonial times, hens were sold in Cartagena de Indias, that had been raised on alluvial land and whose gizzards contained tiny lumps of gold. Our founders' lust for gold beset us until recently. As late as the last century, a German mission appointed to study the construction of an interoceanic railroad across the

García Márquez at the Nobel Prize ceremony

Isthmus of Panama concluded that the project was feasible on one condition: that the rails not be made of iron, which was scarce in the region, but of gold.

Our independence from Spanish domination did not put us beyond the reach of madness. General Antonio López de Santana, three times dictator of Mexico, held a magnificent funeral for the right leg he had lost in the so-called Pastry War. General Gabriel García Moreno ruled Ecuador for sixteen years as an absolute monarch; at his wake, the corpse was seated on the presidential chair, decked out in full-dress uniform and a protective layer of medals. General Maximiliano Hernández Martínez, the theosophical despot of El Salvador who had thirty thousand peasants slaughtered in a savage massacre, invented a pendulum to detect poison in his food, and had streetlamps draped in red paper to defeat an epidemic of scarlet fever. The statue to General Francisco Morazán erected in the main square of Tegucigalpa is actually one of Marshal Ney, purchased at a Paris warehouse of second-hand sculptures.

THE CHALLENGE OF THE NOBEL LECTURE

"I have this great opportunity.... I must try and break through the cliches about Latin America. Superpowers and other outsiders have fought over us for centuries in ways that have nothing to do with our problems. In reality we are all alone."

García Márquez

From Marlise Simons, "A Talk with Gabriel García Márquez," *The New York Times,* 5 December 1982.

Eleven years ago, the Chilean Pablo Neruda, one of the outstanding poets of our time, enlightened this audience with his word. Since then, the Europeans of good will—and sometimes those of bad, as well—have been struck, with ever greater force, by the unearthly tidings of Latin America, that boundless realm of haunted men and historic women, whose unending obstinacy blurs into legend. We have not had a moment's rest. A promethean president, entrenched in his burning palace, died fighting an entire army, alone; and two suspicious airplane accidents, yet to be explained, cut short the life of another great-hearted president and that of a democratic soldier who had revived the dignity of his people. There have been five wars and seventeen military coups; there emerged a diabolic dictator who is carrying out, in God's name, the first Latin American ethnocide of our time. In the meantime, twenty million Latin American children died before the age of one—more than have been born in Europe since 1970. Those missing because of repression number nearly one hundred and twenty thousand, which is as if no one could account for all the inhabitants of Uppsala. Numerous women arrested while pregnant have given birth in Argentine prisons, yet nobody knows the whereabouts and identity of their children, who were furtively adopted or sent to an orphanage by order of the military authorities. Because they tried to change this state of things, nearly two hundred thousand men and women have died throughout the continent, and over one hundred thousand have lost their lives in three small and ill-fated countries of Central America: Nicaragua, El Salvador and Guatemala. If this had happened in the United States, the corresponding figure would be that of one million six hundred thousand violent deaths in four years.

One million people have fled Chile, a country with a tradition of hospitality—that is, ten per cent of its population. Uruguay, a tiny nation of two and a half million inhabitants which considered itself the continent's most civilized country, has lost to exile one out of every five citizens. Since 1979, the civil war in El Salvador has produced almost one refugee every twenty minutes. The country that could be formed of all the exiles and forced emigrants of Latin America would have a population larger than that of Norway.

I dare to think that it is this outsized reality, and not just its literary expression, that has deserved the attention of the Swedish Academy of Letters. A reality not of paper, but one that lives within us and determines each instant of our countless daily deaths, and that nourishes a source of insatiable creativity, full of sorrow and beauty, of which this roving and nostalgic Colombian is but one cipher more, singled out by fortune. Poets and beggars, musicians and prophets, warriors and scoundrels, all creatures of that unbridled reality, we have had to ask but little of imagination, for our crucial problem has been a lack of conventional means to render our lives believable. This, my friends, is the crux of our solitude.

And if these difficulties, whose essence we share, hinder us, it is understandable that the rational talents on this side of the world, exalted in the contemplation of their own cultures, should have found themselves without valid means to interpret us. It is only natural that they insist on measuring us with the yardstick that they use for themselves, forgetting that the ravages of life are not the same for all, and that the quest of our own identity is just as arduous and bloody for us as it was for them. The interpretation of our reality through patterns not our own, serves only to make us ever more unknown, ever less free, ever more solitary. Venerable Europe would perhaps be more perceptive if it tried to see us in its own past. If only it recalled that London took three hundred years to build its first city wall, and three hundred years more to acquire a bishop; that Rome labored in a gloom of uncertainty for twenty centuries, until an Etruscan King anchored it in history; and that the peaceful Swiss of today, who feast us with their mild cheeses and apathetic watches, bloodied Europe as soldiers of fortune, as late as the Sixteenth Century. Even at the height of the Renaissance, twelve thousand lansquenets in the pay of the imperial armies sacked and devastated Rome and put eight thousand of its inhabitants to the sword.

I do not mean to embody the illusions of Tonio Kröger, whose dreams of uniting a chaste north to a passionate south were exalted here, fifty-three years ago, by Thomas Mann. But I do believe that those clear-sighted Europeans who struggle, here as well, for a more just and humane homeland, could help us far better if they reconsidered their way of seeing us. Solidarity with our dreams will not make us feel less alone, as long as it is not translated into concrete acts of legitimate support for all the peoples that assume the illusion of having a life of their own in the distribution of the world.

Latin America neither wants, nor has any reason, to be a pawn without a will of its own; nor is it merely wishful thinking that its quest for independence and originality should become a Western aspiration. However, the navigational advances that have narrowed such distances between our Americas and Europe seem, conversely, to have accentuated our cultural remoteness. Why is the originality so readily granted us in literature so mistrustfully denied us in our difficult attempts at social change? Why think that the social justice sought by progressive Europeans for their own countries cannot also be a goal for Latin America, with different methods for dissimilar conditions? No: the immeasurable violence and pain of our history are the result of age-old inequities and untold bitterness, and not a conspiracy plotted three thousand leagues from our home. But many European leaders and thinkers have thought so, with the childishness of old-timers who have forgotten the fruitful excess of their youth as if it were impossible to find another destiny than to live at the mercy of the two great masters of the world. This, my friends, is the very scale of our solitude. In spite of this, to oppression, plundering and abandonment, we respond with life. Neither floods nor plagues, famines nor cataclysms, nor even the eternal wars of century upon century, have been able to subdue the persistent advantage of life over death. An advantage that grows and quickens: every year, there are seventy-four million more births than deaths, a sufficient number of new lives to multiply, each year, the population of New York sevenfold. Most of these births occur in the countries of least resources—including, of course, those of Latin America. Conversely, the most prosperous countries have succeeded in accumulating powers of destruction such as to annihilate, a hundred times over, not only all the human beings that have existed to this day, but also the totality of all living beings that have ever drawn breath on this planet of misfortune.

On a day like today, my master William Faulkner said, "I decline to accept the end of man." I would feel unworthy of standing in this place that was his, if I were not fully aware that the colossal tragedy he refused to recognize thirty-two years ago is now, for the first time since the beginning of humanity, nothing more than a simple scientific possibility. Faced with this awesome reality that must have seemed a mere utopia through all of human time, we, the inventors of tales, who will believe anything, feel entitled to believe that it is not yet too late to engage in the creation of the opposite utopia. A new and sweeping utopia of life, where no one will be able to decide for others how they die, where love will prove true and happiness be possible, and where the races condemned to one hundred years of solitude will have, at last and forever, a second opportunity on earth.

INTERVIEW WITH GARCÍA MÁRQUEZ

"Gabriel García Márquez on Love, Plagues and Politics," by Marlise Simons, who translated the interview (*New York Times*, 21 February 1988; © The New York Times)

Gabriel García Márquez is about to publish "Love in the Time of Cholera," a work he calls a novel of manners: the story of two people whose love, thwarted in their youth, finally flourishes when they are close to 80.

A Colombian by birth as well as by literary inspiration, he will soon be 60 and seems as busy, vigorous and playful as ever. After mediating in the early 1980s between the Colombian Government and leftist guerrillas, he has not returned to Colombia because of widespread violence there. These days, he and his wife, Mercedes, divide their time between Mexico City, their permanent home for the last 25 years, and Havana, where he is organizing and directing the Foundation of New Latin American Cinema. Film is an old love of this Nobel laureate, and the dramatic possibilities of television also fascinate him.

Though widely viewed as a political activist of the Left, to his friends he is simply unorthodox, a storyteller who objects to theorizing and generalizations and who likes to deal with life in the unexpected anecdotal way it comes. Over several afternoons in Mexico City recently, we talked about his interest in plagues, politics and cinema, as well as his latest book. I asked him to comment on his extraordinary productivity:

SIMONS: You have just finished a play and are writing film scripts and directing a film institute. Are you changing your life?

GARCÍA MÁRQUEZ: No, because I am writing a novel. And I am finishing this one so I can start another. But I have never had so many things going on at the same time. I think I have never before felt so fulfilled, so much in the prime of my life.

I'm writing. Six different stories are being filmed. I'm at the cinema foundation. And the play will be opening this year in Argentina and Brazil.

For a long time, of course, things did not work out for me—almost the first 40 years of my life. I had financial problems; I had work problems. I had not made it as a writer or as anything else. It was a difficult time emotionally and psychologically; I had the idea that I was like an extra, that I did not count anywhere. And then, with

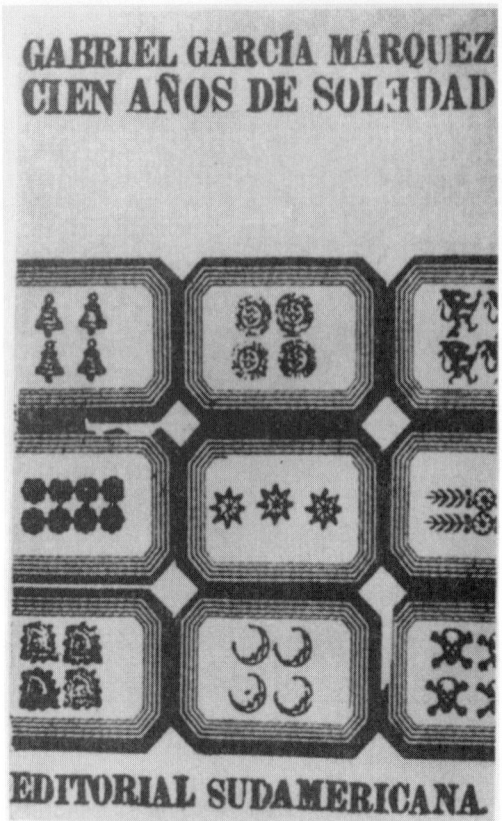

GABRIEL GARCÍA MÁRQUEZ
CIEN AÑOS DE SOLEDAD

EDITORIAL SUDAMERICANA

Dust jacket for the first edition of García
Márquez's breakthrough work, *One Hundred
Years of Solitude*

"One Hundred Years of Solitude," things
turned. Now all this is going on without my
being dependent on anyone. Still, I have to
do all sorts of things. I have to sit on a bicy-
cle in the morning. I am on an eternal diet.
Half my life I couldn't eat what I wanted
because I couldn't afford to, the other half
because I have to diet.

SIMONS: And now, in your latest book, "Love
in the Time of Cholera," the theme and style
seem very different. Why did you write a
love story?

GARCÍA MÁRQUEZ: I think aging has made
me realize that feelings and sentiments, what
happens in the heart, are ultimately the most
important. But in some way, all my books are
about love. In "One Hundred Years" there is
one love story after another. "Chronicle of
Death Foretold" is a terrible drama of love. I
think there is love everywhere. This time
love is more ardent. Because two loves join
and go on.

I think, though, that I could not
have written "Love in the Time of Cholera"
when I was younger. It has practically a lifetime's experience in it. And it includes many
experiences, my own and other peoples'.
Above all, there are points of view I didn't
have before. I'll be 60 this year. At that age,
one becomes more serene in everything.

SIMONS: Also more generous, perhaps. Because this is a tremendously
generous book.

GARCÍA MÁRQUEZ: A Chilean priest told me it was the most Christian
book he'd ever read.

SIMONS: And the style? Do you see this as a departure from your earlier
work?

GARCÍA MÁRQUEZ: In every book I try to take a different path and I
think I did here. One doesn't choose the style. You can investigate and

try to discover what the best style would be for a theme. But the style is determined by the subject, by the mood of the times. If you try to use something that is not suitable, it just won't work. Then the critics build theories around that and they see things I hadn't seen. I only respond to our way of life, the life of the Caribbean. You can take my books and I can tell you line for line what part of reality or what episode it came from.

SIMONS: There was an insomnia plague in "One Hundred Years of Solitude," and in one of your stories a plague killed all the birds. Now there is the "Time of Cholera." What is it that intrigues you so about plagues?

GARCÍA MÁRQUEZ: Cartagena really had a great plague at the end of the last century. And I've always been interested in plagues, beginning with "Oedipus Rex." I've read a lot about them. "A Journal of the Plague Year" by Daniel Defoe is one of my favorite books. Plagues are like imponderable dangers that surprise people. They seem to have a quality of destiny. It's the phenomenon of death on a mass scale. What I find curious is that the great plagues have always produced great excesses. They make people want to live more. It's that almost metaphysical dimension that interests me.

I have used other literary references. "The Plague" of Camus. There is a plague in "The Betrothed" of Alessandro Manzoni. I'm always looking up books that deal with a theme I'm dealing with. I do it to make sure that mine is not alike. Not precisely to copy from them but to have the use of them somehow. I think all writers do that. Behind every idea there is a thousand years of literature. I think you have to know as much as possible of that to know where you are and how you are taking it further.

SIMONS: What was the genesis of "Love in the Time of Cholera?"

GARCÍA MÁRQUEZ: It really sprang from two sources that came together. One was the love affair of my parents, which was identical to that of Fermina Daza and Florentino Ariza in their youth. My father was the telegraph operator of Aracataca [Colombia]. He played the violin. She was the pretty girl from a well-to-do family. Her father was opposed because the boy was poor and he was a liberal. All that part of the story was my parents'. . . . When she went to school, the letters, the poems, the violin serenades, her trip to the interior when her father tried to make her forget him, the way they communicated by telegram—all that is authentic. And when she returns, everyone thinks she has forgotten him. That too. It's exactly the way my parents told it. The only difference is they married. And, as soon as they were married, they were no longer interesting as literary figures.

SIMONS: And the other source?

GARCÍA MÁRQUEZ: Many years ago, in Mexico, I read a story in a newspaper about the death of two old Americans—a man and a woman—who would meet every year in Acapulco, always going to the same hotel, the same restaurants, following the same routine as they had done for 40 years. They were almost 80 years old and kept coming. Then one day they went out in a boat and, in order to rob them, the boatman murdered them with his oars. Through their death, the story of their secret romance became known. I was fascinated by them. They were each married to other people.

I always thought I would write my parents' story, but I didn't know how. One day, through one of those absolutely incomprehensible things that happen in literary creation, the two stories came together in my mind. I had all the love of the young people from my parents and from the old couple I took the love of old people.

SIMONS: You have said that your stories often come from a single image that strikes you.

GARCÍA MÁRQUEZ: Yes. In fact, I'm so fascinated by how to detect the birth of a story that I have a workshop at the cinema foundation called "How to Tell a Story." I bring together 10 students from different Latin American countries and we sit at a round table without interruption for four hours a day for six weeks and try to write a story from scratch. We start by going round and round. At first there are only differences. . . . The Venezuelan wants one thing, the Argentine another. Then suddenly and idea appears that grabs everyone and the story can be developed. We've done three so far. But, you know, we still don't know how the idea is born. It always catches us by surprise.

In my case, it always begins with an image, not an idea or a concept. With "Love in the Time of Cholera," the image was of two old people dancing on the deck of a boat, dancing a bolero. Once you have the image, then what happens? The image grows in my head until the whole story takes shape as it might in real life. The problem is that life isn't the same as literature, so then I have to ask myself the big question: How do I adapt this, what is the most appropriate structure for this book? I have always aspired to finding the perfect structure. One perfect structure in literature is that of Sophocles' "Oedipus Rex." Another story, "Monkey's Paw," by an English writer, William Jacobs.

When I have the story and the structure completely worked out, I can start—but only on condition that I find the right name for each character. If I don't have the name that exactly suits the character, it doesn't come alive. I don't see it.

Once I sit down to write, usually I no longer have any hesitations. I may take a few notes, a word or a phrase or something to help me the following morning, but I never work with a lot of notes. That's what I learned when I was young. I know writers who have books full of notes and they wind up thinking about their notes and never write books.

SIMONS: You've always said you still feel as much a journalist as a writer of fiction. Some writers think that in journalism the pleasure of discovery comes in the research, while in fiction the pleasure of discovery comes in the writing. Would you agree?

GARCÍA MÁRQUEZ: Certainly there are pleasures in both. To begin with, I consider journalism to be a literary genre. Intellectuals would not agree, but I believe it is. Without being fiction, it is a form, an instrument, for expressing reality.

The timing may be different but the experience is the same in literature and journalism. In fiction, if you feel you get a scoop, a scoop about life that fits into your writing, it's the same emotion as a journalist when he gets to the heart of a story. Those moments occur when you least expect them and they bring extraordinary happiness. Just as a journalist knows when he's got the story, a writer has a similar revelation. Of course, he still has to illustrate and enrich it, but he knows he's got it. It's almost an instinct. The journalist knows if he has news or not. The writer knows if it's literature or not, if it's poetry or not. After that, the writing is very much the same. Both use many of the same techniques.

SIMONS: But your journalism is not exactly orthodox.

GARCÍA MÁRQUEZ: Well, mine isn't informative, so I can follow my own preferences and look for the same veins I look for in literature. But my misfortune is that people don't believe my journalism. They think I make it all up. But I promise you, I invent nothing either in journalism or fiction. In fiction, you manipulate reality because that's what fiction is for. In journalism, I can pick the subjects that suit my character because I no longer have the demands of a job.

SIMONS: Do you remember any of your journalistic pieces with special affection?

GARCÍA MÁRQUEZ: There was one little one called "The Cemetery of Lost Letters," from the time I was working at *El Especdador*. I was sitting on a tram in Bogotá. And I saw a sign that said: "House of Lost Letters." I rang the bell. They told me that all the letters that could not be delivered—with wrong addresses, whatever—were sent to that house. There was an old man in it who dedicated his life entirely to finding their destination. Sometimes it took him days. If it couldn't be found, the letter was burned but never opened. There was one addressed "To the woman who goes to the Church de Las Armas every Wednesday at 5 P.M." So the old man went there and found seven women and questioned each of them. When he picked the right one, he needed a court order to open the letter to be sure. And he was right. I'll never forget that story. Journalism and literature were almost joined. I have never been able to completely separate them.

SIMONS: What are you trying to achieve at the cinema foundation?

GARCÍA MÁRQUEZ: I'd like to see filmmaking as an artistic expression in Latin America valued the same way as our literature is now. We have very fine literature, but it has taken a long time to be recognized. It has been a very hard struggle. And sometimes it is still difficult.

SIMONS: The literature now seems to have a life of its own.

GARCÍA MÁRQUEZ: You know, this really started to happen when we conquered our own readers at home. When they started to read us in Latin America. We had always thought the opposite was important. When we published a book, we didn't care if it was sold here as long as we could get it translated. And yet we knew what would happen. It would be translated and get a few obligatory critical notes from the specialists. The book would stay within the Spanish Studies ghettos of the universities and never get out. When we started to be read in Latin America, everything opened up.

The same is beginning to happen with film. There are now good films being made in Latin America. And this is being done not through great productions with a lot of capital. It is done within our own means and with our own methods. And the films are appearing at the international festivals and are being nominated for prizes. But they still have to conquer their own audience here. The problem lies with the big distributors. They need to spend a lot of money to promote unknown films and then they get no returns. The day our films make money, the whole focus will change. We saw it in literature; we will see it in films in the years ahead.

SIMONS: Politics is so important to you. But you don't use your books to promote your political ideas.

GARCÍA MÁRQUEZ: I don't think literature should be used as a firearm. But, even against your own will, your ideological positions are inevitably reflected in your writing and they influence readers. I think my books have had political impact in Latin America because they help to create a Latin America identity; they help Latin Americans to become more aware of their own culture.

ON LANGUAGE

"I never feel comfortable reading in another language, because the only language I really feel inside is Spanish. However, I speak Italian and French, and I know English well enough to have poisoned myself with *Time* magazine every week for twenty years."

García Márquez

From a 1981 interview with Peter Stone, "Gabriel García Márquez," in *Writers at Work: The Paris Review Interviews: Sixth Series,* edited by George Plimpton (New York: Viking, 1984), p. 333.

An American asked me the other day what was the real political intention behind the cinema foundation. I said the issue is not what is behind it but what lies ahead of it. The idea is to stimulate awareness of the Latin American cinema, and that is fundamentally a political objective. Of course, the project is strictly about filmmaking but the results will be political. People often think that politics are elections, that politics are what governments do. But literature, cinema, painting and music are all essential to forging Latin America's identity. And that's what I mean by politics.

SIMONS: Would you say that is different from placing artistic talent at the service of politics?

GARCÍA MÁRQUEZ: I would never do that. Well, let me be clearer. The arts are always at the service of politics, of some ideology, of the vision the writer or the artist has of the world. But the arts should never be at the service of a government.

SIMONS: What is your vision for Latin America?

GARCÍA MÁRQUEZ: I want to see a Latin America that is united, autonomous and democratic.

SIMONS: In the European sense?

García Márquez with Joan Mellen in 1986

GARCÍA MÁRQUEZ: In the sense that it should have common interests and approaches.

SIMONS: Is that the reason you are now writing about Simón Bolívar?

GARCÍA MÁRQUEZ: Not really. I picked the theme of Bolívar because I was interested in his personality. No one knows what he was really like because Bolívar became enshrined as a hero. I see him as a Caribbean, influenced and formed by Romanticism. Just imagine what an explosive combination. . . .

But the ideas of Bolívar are very topical. He imagined Latin America as an autonomous and unified alliance, an alliance that he thought could become the largest and most powerful in the world. He had a very nice phrase for it. He said: "We are like a small mankind of our own." He was an extraordinary man, yet he got badly beaten and was ultimately defeated. And he was defeated by the same forces that are at work today—the feudal interest and traditional local power groups that protect their interests and privileges. They closed ranks against him and finished him off. But his dream remains valid—to have a united and autonomous Latin America.

You see, I'm looking for different words. I really detest political-speak. Words like "the people," for example, have lost their meaning. We have to fight against fossilized language. Not only in the case of the Marxists, who have petrified the language most, but the liberals too. "Democracy" is another such word. The Soviets say they're democratic; the Americans say they're democratic; El Salvador does, and Mexico too. Everyone who can organize an election says he's democratic. "Independence" is another one. These are words that have come to mean very little. They're disconnected; they don't describe the reality they represent. I'm always looking for words that aren't exhausted. You know what my biggest failing in life has been? One that can no longer be remedied? It's not being able to speak English perfectly as a second language. If only I had spoken English . . .

SIMONS: Would you have written in English?

GARCÍA MÁRQUEZ: No, no. But after Latin America, my best audience is in the United States, and in the universities there. There's a vast readership that interests me. But I could never become their friend because I don't speak English. I have French and Italian. Of course, it's also their failing for not speaking Spanish. But I think I'm more interested than they are.

SIMONS: What was it like to write the play? Did that give you any trouble?

GARCÍA MÁRQUEZ: Well, it's really a monologue that I wrote for Graciela Duffau, the Argentine actress. It's called "Diatribe of Love Against a Seated Man." An angry woman is telling her husband everything that passes through her head. It goes on for two hours. He is sitting in a chair reading a newspaper and doesn't react at all. But a monologue isn't entirely a play. That is, there are many rules and laws of the theater that don't apply here.

SIMONS: And what is your next writing project?

GARCÍA MÁRQUEZ: I'm going to finish "Bolívar." I need a few more months. And I'm going to write my memoirs. Usually authors write their memoirs when they can no longer remember anything. I'm going to start slowly and write and write. They won't be normal memoirs. Every time I have 400 pages ready, I'll publish a volume and see. I could go up to six.

NOT HIS CUP OF CAFÉ

Gabriel García Márquez decided not to go to a meeting of Nobel Prize-winners in Paris last month. The reason:

"I try not to go to conferences. I don't know what to do there. And I found this one very intimidating. President Mitterrand—as you know he's a friend—personally invited me and I told him I would go. But then I looked at the agenda and at the 80 or so prize-winners and saw the French had drawn up subjects that were entirely abstract. 'Culture and Society,' for example. What would I do at a seminar with Claude Simon on culture and society? . . .

"I think a lot about culture, but about popular culture. And I'm the product of a culture of immediate and burning problems. The French move in the thoroughly glacial sphere of pure ideas. And they don't succumb easily. They are brought up and formed in academic tournaments. I don't like to theorize. I told Mitterrand that I considered myself culturally incompatible and that recognizing one's own limitations is a privilege of age. Mitterrand, who is a man of culture, understood this very well."

GARCÍA MÁRQUEZ AS STUDIED

OTHER AUTHORS FREQUENTLY STUDIED WITH GARCÍA MÁRQUEZ

"In a literary panorama dominated by Julio Cortazar's *Hopscotch*, Lezama Lima's *Paradiso*, Carlos Fuentes's *A Change of Skin*, and Guillermo Cabrera Infante's *Three Trapped Tigers*," critic Emir Rodriguez Monegal has written, "all experimental works to the limit of experimentation itself; all hard and demanding on their readers." García Márquez, in his *One Hundred Years of Solitude*, "with an Olympian indifference to alien technique, sets himself free to narrate, with an incredible speed and apparent innocence, an absolutely linear and chronological story . . . with its beginning, middle and end."[1]

These authors, Cortazar, José Lezama Lima, Fuentes, and Cabrera Infante, writing out of their shared Latin American experience, might be studied with García Márquez both because they all belong to the same literary movement, the Boom, and no less because they are all experimental writers in their choice of form. With other writers belonging to this "Boom," García Márquez shares the cultural geography of Latin America.

Adding Mario Vargas Llosa to the list, they share the experience of exile and a degree of cosmopolitanism. Although Jorge Luis Borges does not belong chronologically to this movement, he has influenced all these writers; the frequent metaphor of the labyrinth in the works of García Márquez may be traced to its appearance in the work of Borges. A course in twentieth-century Latin American fiction would include Borges, Cortazar, Juan Rulfo, Alejo Carpentier, Vargas Llosa, Fuentes, Cabrera Infante, Miguel Angel Asturias, Lezama Lima, and, of course, García Márquez.

García Márquez shares themes with the Guatemalan writer Asturias, who is also a Nobel laureate. Asturias wrote a trilogy on the banana boom and the United Fruit Company invasion of Latin America. In *El señor presidente* (1946; translated as *The President*, 1963), Asturias

García Márquez in the late 1960s

deals with the theme of dictatorship, and its main character is a composite of several Latin American dictators. There is, Asturias has said, an "intuition" possessed by these figures, "a sort of sense of smell or power of divination that dictators have, and which means that it's not everyone who can be one."[2]

Yet, because the two are so different in approach, with Asturias a politically committed realist, they would not necessarily be studied together. Other Latin American writers who have written on the subject of the indigenous dictatorships are Carpentier, the Cuban novelist, in *El recurso del método* (1974; translated as *Reasons of State,* 1976), and Augusto Roa Bastos in *Yo el Supremo* (I, the Supreme, 1975).

García Márquez has combined several genres. His work is biblical in tone and epic in scope, both genres working in *One Hundred Years of Solitude*. A study of biblical myth in the novel would certainly include this work.

He has written romance in *Love In The Time Of Cholera*, but in so speculative a manner that it is difficult to imagine another work with which it might be compared. He has written a family saga in *One Hundred Years of Solitude,* but because his work is so rooted in its setting, one cannot profitably study it alongside other family sagas, such as Thomas Mann's *Buddenbrooks* (1901).

One Hundred Years of Solitude, which creates an autonomous community and traces its founding, might be studied with William Faulkner's novel *Absalom, Absalom!* (1936) although the points of view are diametrically opposed. Faulkner locates savagery and barbaric injustice in the settling of his community, while García Márquez finds grace, justice, and compassion in the early days of Macondo.

Many critics have noticed that Faulkner's Yoknapatawpha County, the location in which several of his works are set, in its autonomy and cultural consistency bears some relation to Macondo, which is the background for several of the novels and stories of García Márquez. An entire course could be titled "William Faulkner and Gabriel García Márquez," especially since García Márquez has acknowledged Faulkner as a major influence on his work.

Mark Frisch has proposed teaching *One Hundred Years of Solitude* with *The Sound and The Fury,* "viewing Faulkner as a novelist in the New World."[3] García Márquez has himself remarked that "the Faulknerian method is very effective for relating Latin American reality."[4] He has also noted that Yoknapatawpha County in fact has banks on the Gulf of Mexico and thus the Caribbean, so that "in a way, Faulkner is a Latin American writer."[5]

One Hundred Years of Solitude might also be studied alongside the novel of fantasy, although this study would deemphasize the strong political context that runs through the entire novel. Yet, García Márquez could certainly be studied alongside writers who partake of the techniques of magic realism, even if they are from other cultures; these would include Toni Morrison and Salman Rushdie. An examination of early examples of the use of fantasy in the works of Edgar Allan Poe, Guy de Maupassant, and Henry James could lead to a discussion of García Márquez. Latin American examples of fantasy might include Asturias's *Hombres de maíz* (1949; translated as *Maize Men*, 1975), Carpentier's *El reino de este mundo* (1949; translated as *The Kingdom of This World*, 1957), and the short stories of Julio Cortázar.[6]

A course in "The Apocalyptic Vision in Contemporary American Fiction" might place García Márquez alongside Thomas Pynchon, Julio Cortazar, and John Barth. García Márquez could also be studied in a course on modernism that would place his work alongside works by Marcel Proust, Italo Calvino, and Robert Musil, as well as those of James Joyce and Virginia Woolf.

Chronicle Of A Death Foretold partakes of the genre of the detective story, but the differences so outweigh the similarities that it cannot be compared to examples of the detective novel, such as those written in the United States by Dashiell Hammett or Raymond Chandler. He has written an historical novel, but *The General In His Labyrinth* belongs so particularly to Latin America, that it should be studied alongside nonfiction works chronicling the life of Simón Bolívar, rather than works of fiction.

It seems, however, that *The Autumn of the Patriarch,* which uses a stream-of-consciousness technique, might be compared to the works of European modernists such as those of Joyce—particularly in his *Ulysses* (1922)—or Woolf. Equally, a course in the Latin American novel of the dictator could be organized, beginning with *Tirando Banderas* (1926; translated as *The Tyrant (Tirano Banderas): A Novel of Warm Lands*, 1929) by the Spanish author Ramon del Valle Inclan, and including *El señor presidente*, as well as *Reasons of State, I, the Supreme*, and *The Autumn of the Patriarch*.

More advanced students could study *One Hundred Years of Solitude* with lesser known works from other South American countries, such as Rigoberta Menchu's *Me Llamo Rigoberta Menchu y asi nacio mi con-*

cienca (1983; translated as *I . . . Rigoberta Men-chu: An Indian Woman in Guatemala*, 1984) and the Mexican American writer Rudolfo Anaya's *Bless Me, Ultima* (1972) which has a Mexican setting.[7]

So varied is the fiction of García Márquez that though he could be studied in a course on literary modernism as a movement, he might just as effectively appear in a course on postmodernism in fiction, which would draw on the work of Calvino, Don DeLillo, Cabrera Infante, Pynchon and other post-modernist writers. As a political novelist, García Márquez might be studied with authors such as Fyodor Dostoyevsky, Joseph Conrad, Ignazio Silone, and André Malraux. A course in the theme of brotherhood in the novel might include Conrad, Faulkner, García Márquez, and the cinema of Luis Buñuel.[8]

RECLAIMING HISTORY

"'Aquí no pasa nada.' 'Nothing happens here.' The obligatory pause in the conversation, the look that waits to see whether the listener knows the reference. The moment's pause to let the quotation marks sink in. I know the passage well. It's from the García Márquez classic, *One Hundred Years of Solitude.* The book that a former *Commandante Supremo* of the M-19 Revolutionary Movement—Alvaro Fayad—used to say was the only text where a Colombian could recover the history of his country, the only required reading for a Colombian revolutionary."

Anne Carrigan

From *The Palace of Justice: A Colombian Tragedy* (New York & London: Four Walls Eight Windows, 1993).

GABRIEL GARCÍA MÁRQUEZ AND THE INVENTION OF AMERICA

From Carlos Fuentes, *Gabriel García Márquez and the Invention of America,* E. Allison Peers Lectures, no. 2 (Liverpool: Liverpool University Press, 1987) © Carlos Fuentes. This lecture was delivered on 13 March 1987 in the Senate House of the University of Liverpool.

> This is a cow. She must be milked every morning so that she will produce milk, and the milk must be boiled in order to be mixed with coffee to make coffee and milk.

> I need only, to make them reappear, pronounce the *names:* Balbec, Venice, Florence, within whose syllables had gradually accumulated all the longing inspired in me by the places for which they stood.

> "How realities are to be learned or discovered is perhaps too great a question for you or me to determine, Cratylus; but it is worthwhile to have reached even this conclusion, that they are to be learned and sought for, not from *names* but much better through themselves than through names . . ."

> "That is clear, Socrates . . ."

The first of these three quotations is from a famous passage in *One Hundred Years of Solitude,* by Gabriel García Márquez, in which, after a plague of insomnia, the whole village of Macondo is affected by loss of memory, so that Aureliano Buendía devises a saving formula: he marks everything in the village with its name—*table, chair, clock, wall, bed, cow, goat, pig, hen.*

> At the beginning of the road into the swamp they put up a sign that said MACONDO and another larger one on the main street that said GOD EXISTS.

In the second quotation, from *Swann's Way,* the Narrator has just accomplished one of the greatest feats of modern fiction: the liberation of time, through the liberation of an instant from time that permits the human person to re-create himself or herself and his or her time. This splendid literary achievement, through which the novel becomes the ideal vehicle for the reintroduction of the human person into time and through time into himself or herself, his or her authenticity, has its fragile but luminescent origin in what is probably a handful of lies: just a few names, Balbec, Guermantes, Venice, Parma, in which the Narrator learns that names forever absorb the image of reality because they are the privileged meeting places of desire; and desire through names can substitute for time itself:

> Even in spring, to come in a book upon the name of Balbec sufficed to awaken in me the desire for storms at sea and for the Norman Gothic.

But Proust's novel, as Roland Barthes warns us, is a voyage of both learning and disillusionment: from an age of words when we think that we create what we name (Parma, Balbec, Guermantes), to an age when the original prestige of names is ruined by contact with the outer world ("So it was this! Madame de Guermantes was only this!") to the age of things, where words manifest themselves as something outside the speaker, as objects (Bloch's anti-Semitic speeches are a rejection of guilty passion in himself for another: it reveals the truth of the passion as it becomes a thing).

The third quotation is from Plato's *Cratylus,* perhaps the first book of literary theory of the Western world. In it, several attitudes toward names are debated by Socrates and his friends. To Cratylus, names are intrinsic to things: they are natural. To Hermongenes, they are purely conventional: whatever name you give to a thing is its right name. Socrates concedes that an onomastic legislator might give things their fixed or absolute or ideal name; but this substantialist demiurge is soon defeated by history. He makes names, but, alas, the dialectician uses them, and, says Socrates, simply by paying good coin to the Sophists, we will not learn the true name that we come to know dialectically, in its usage, but not originally, in its essence.

Plato, who does not hold the world of letters in high esteem, would not fall into any trap laid by the likes of Marcel Proust (or García Márquez). He makes Socrates reveal the deceit of Hermes, which is similar to that of Kafka's messengers: though he is identified with the power of speech, Hermes, the messenger of the word, the purported interpreter of the gods, cannot even give us the true names of the divinities, for it is clear that among themselves the gods address one another in a manner different from our own. They use their true names; we do not.

It is Hermes who is guilty. He circulates words as if they were money and robs them of their permanence, which is the same as their essence; he makes words have a double meaning, sometimes true, sometimes false, always worn thin.

Socrates would then have men of reason dispense with names and rather seek to know things directly, in themselves or through each other, in their relationships. The *Cratylus* is, of course, a polemic against Heraclitus and his philosophy of constant change. It defends a substantialist point of view: if things are always changing, there will always be no knowledge. Names are changing and changeable words, and they belong to the unstable and essential world where "all things are like leaky pots."

L O V E IN THE
T I M E OF
C H O L E R A

G a b r i e l
G a r c í a M á r q u e z

Dust jacket for the U.S. edition of *El amor en los tiempos del cólera* (1985), García Márquez's novel about the power of love that was inspired by his parents' romance

Cratylus is not convinced by Socrates; he prefers to think that Heraclitus's ideas are true. Socrates lets the argument rest. He bids Cratylus come back another time and teach him; and Cratylus leaves hoping that Socrates will also continue to think of these matters. So the dialogue ends on a civilized note of mutual tolerance.

This is America. It is a continent. It is big. It is a place discovered to make the world larger. In it live noble savages. Their time is the Golden Age. America was invented for people to be happy in. You cannot be unhappy in America. It is a sin to have tragedy in America. There is no need for unhappiness in America. America does not need to conquer anything. It is too vast. America is its own frontier. America is its own utopia.

And America is a name.

Gabriel García Márquez is the name of an American writer, a writer of the New World that stretches from pole to pole rather than from sea to shining sea.

America is a name. A name discovered. A name invented. A name desired.

In his classic book *The Invention of America,* the Mexican historian Edmundo O'Gorman maintains that America was invented rather than discovered. If this is true, we must believe that, first of all, it was desired and then imagined. O'Gorman speaks of Europeans who were prisoners of their world, prisoners who could not even call their jail their own.

Geocentrism and scholasticism: two centripetal and hierarchical visions of a perfect, archetypical universe, unchangeable—yet finite because it was the place of the Fall.

The response to this "feeling of enclosure and impotence" was a hunger for space that quickly became identified with a hunger for freedom. Some of the names of this hunger are Nicholas of Cusa and later Giordano Bruno, Luca Signorelli and Piero della Francesca, Ficino and Copernicus, Vasco da Gama and then Columbus. Some of the names of this freedom in its European and American incarnations are:

First, the freedom to act on what is. This is the freedom won by Machiavelli in Europe and acted on by Cortés in America. It is the freedom of an epic world made to the measure of the self-made man, not he who inherits power but he who is capable, with equal measures of will and virtue, of winning it. This is the world, in the Latin American novel, of the descendants of Machiavelli and Cortés in the jungles and plains of the American continent: the Ardavines, the ferocious political bosses of the Venezuelan *llanos* in Rómulo Gallegos; Pedro Páramo, the fissured Mexican *cacique* in Juan Rulfo; Facundo, Sarmiento's immortal portrait of the archetypical *caudillo.* And: Francia, Estrada Cabrera, Porfirio Díaz, Juan Vicente Gómez, Trujillo, and Somoza in the news; and in the novel, Asturias' El Señor Presidente, Carpentier's El Primer Magistrado, Roa Bastos' El Supremo, and, outliving them all, incorporating them all, García Márquez's ageless Patriarch:

"The only thing that gave us security in earth was the certainty that he was there, invulnerable to plague and hurricane . . . invulnerable to time."

The second is the freedom to act on what should be. This is the world of Thomas More in Europe and of Vasco de Quiroga in America. Discovered because invented because imagined because desired because named, America became the utopia of Europe. The American mission was to be the other version of a European history condemned as corrupt and hypocritical by the humanists of the time. On the contrary, Montaigne in France, Vives in Spain, and the Erasmists all over, saw in America the utopian promise of a New Golden Age, the only chance for Europe to recover, eventually, its moral health as it plunged into the bloody Wars of Religion.

Historically, Father Vasco de Quiroga, the Spanish reader of More's *Utopia,* lived in Mexico in the sixteenth century, arriving only a few years after the Conquest, and created communities totally faithful to the precepts of the English writer. Quiroga—venerated to this day by the Tarascan Indians as "Tata Vasco"—believed that only the utopian commonwealth would save the native inhabitants of America from violence and desperation.

He established the first utopian communities in Mexico City and Michoacán in 1535. That same year, Thomas More was beheaded by order of Henry VIII. So much, one would say, for utopia.

Yet utopia persisted as one of the central strains of the culture of the Americas. We were condemned to utopia by the Old World. What a heavy load! Who could live up to this promise, this demand, this contradiction: to be utopia where utopia was demolished, burned and branded and killed by those who wanted utopia: the epic actors of the Conquest, the awed band of soldiers who entered Tenochtitlán with Cortés in 1519 and discovered the America they had imagined and desired: a New World of enchantment and fantasy only read about, before, in the romances of chivalry. And who were then forced to destroy what they had named in their dreams as utopia.

So Carpentier's narrator in *The Lost Steps* follows the Orinoco River upstream, to its sources, to the Golden Age, to utopia, to

this living in the present, without possessions, without the chains of yesterday, without thinking of tomorrow . . .

And so the Buendías found a precarious Arcadia in the jungles of Colombia, where not only the virtues of the Golden Age of the past are acclaimed but also those of the coming Utopia of Progress. We realize in García Márquez that, since the Enlightenment, Europe is the utopia of Latin America: law and science and beauty and progress were now a Latin American albatross hung around the neck of Europe: we expected from the West the photograph that finally fixed our image for eternity; or the ice that burns as it cools. But this notion of progress—and the names that accompany it—is to prove illusory:

> "It's the largest diamond in the world."
> "No," the gypsy countered. "It's ice."

This gypsy leads us to the third aspect of freedom at the root of the name America: the freedom to preserve an ironical smile, a freedom not unlike that won by the first Spanish philosopher, the Stoic from Córdoba, Seneca, but even more rooted in the Renaissance reflection on the duality of truth and on the difference between the appearance and the reality of things. To deny any absolute, be it the absolute of faith before or of reason now; to season all things with the ironic praise of folly and thus appear a madman in the eyes of both Topos and U-Topos: this is the world of Erasmus in Europe and especially in Spain, where Erasmus became, more than a thinker, a banner, an attitude, a persistent intellectual disposition that lives to this day in Borges and Reyes, in Arreola and Paz and Cortázar.

Indeed, Erasmus is the writer of the samizdat of Spanish and Spanish-American literature, the underground courier of so many of our attitudes and words, he who failed externally in Spain only to be victorious eternally forever and ever: Erasmus the father of *Don Quixote*; the grandfather of Tristram Shandy and Jacques le Fataliste; the great-grandfather of Catherine Moreland and Emma Bovary; the great-uncle of Prince Myshkin; and the revered ancestor of the Nazarín of Pérez Galdós, the Pierre Ménared of Borges, and the Oliveira of Cortázar—but also of the Buendías, who incessantly decipher the signs of the world, those that are put on trees and cows so their names will not be forgotten, or their functions, those signs they have seen behind the world's appearances, those they have read in the chronicles of their own lives, feverishly naming things and people and then feverishly deciphering what they themselves have written. What they have discovered—invented—desired—named.

> Macondo . . . was built on the bank of a river of clear water that ran along a bed of polished stones, which were white and enormous, like prehistoric eggs. The world was so recent that many things lacked names and in order to indicate them it was necessary to point . . .

The invention of America is indistinguishable from the naming of America. Indeed, Carpentier gives priority to this function of the American writer: to baptize things that without him would be nameless. To discover is to invent is to name. No one dares stop and reflect whether the names being given to things real and imagined are intrinsical to the named, or merely conventional, certainly not substantial to them. The invention of America occurs in a pre-Socratic time, that time whose disappearance Nietzsche lamented; it happens in a mythical time magically arisen in the midst of the nascent Age of Reason, as if to warn it, in Erasmian terms, that reason that knows not its limits is a form of madness.

García Márquez begins his Nobel Lecture by recalling the fabulous things named by the navigator Antonio Pigafetta as he accompanied Magellan on the first circumnavigation of the globe:

> He had seen hogs with navels on their haunches, clawless birds whose hens laid eggs on the backs of their mates, and others still, resembling tongueless pelicans, with beaks like spoons. He wrote of having seen a misbegotten creature with the head and ears of a mule, a camel's body, the legs of a deer and the whinny of a horse. He described how the first native encountered in Patagonia was confronted with a mirror, whereupon that impassioned giant lost his senses to the terror of his own image.

This discovery of the marvellous because it is imagined and desired occurs in many other fantastic chroniclers of the invention of America; but even the more sober, one feels, had to invent in order to justify their discovery of, even their being in, the New World. The pragmatical Genoese, Christopher Columbus, thinks he can fool the Queen who sent him off at great expense, by inventing the existence of gold and spices where they do not exist. When at last he does find gold—in Haiti—he calls the island La Española, says that there all is "as in Castile," then "better than in Castile," and finally, since there is gold, the gold must be the size of beans, and the nights must be as beautiful as in Andalusia, and the women whiter than in Spain, and sexual relations much purer (to please the puritanical Queen and not frighten off further appropriations), but there are Amazons as well, and sirens, and a Golden Age, and a good, innocent savage (to please

"GABO" AND THE NOBEL

"'Gabo' is what García Márquez is called by nearly everyone in the Spanish-speaking world. That or el maestro, or, in Colombia, Nuestro Nobel, our Nobel Prize winner. One of his friends remarked to me that García Márquez is in many ways El Único Nobel, the only Nobel Laureate, which struck me as fundamentally true, at least in Latin America. Another friend, Enrique Santos Calderón, the editor-in-chief of El Tiempo, Colombia's leading daily newspaper, says that the Nobel Prize was a vindication of Colombian culture. 'In a country that's gone to shit, Gabo is a symbol of national pride.'"

Jon Lee Anderson

From "The Power of García Márquez," *The New Yorker* (27 September 1999): 58.

Colombian newspaper advertisement for García Márquez's 1985 novel, *Love in the Time of Cholera*

the Queen this time by amazing her). Then the good Genoese merchant reasserts himself: the forests of the Indies where he has landed can be turned into fleets of ships.

So we are still in the East. America has not been named, although its marvels have. Columbus has named what he was sent to find: gold, spices, Asia. His biggest invention is finding China and Japan in the New World. For Vespucci, however, the new thing about the New World is its newness. The Golden Age and the Good Savage are here, described and named by him in the New World, as a New Golden Age and a New Good Savage bereft of history, once more in Paradise, discovered before the Fall, untainted by the old. Indeed, we deserve Amerigo's name: he invented our imaginary newness.

For it is this sense of total newness, of primeval appearance, that gives its true tone to names and words in America. The urgency of naming and describing the New World—of naming and describing in effect, the most ancient trait of the New World. Suddenly, here, in the vast reaches of the Amazonian jungle, the Andean heights, or the Patagonian plains, we are again in the very emptiness of terror that Hölderlin spoke of: the terror that strikes us when we feel so close to nature that we fear we shall become one with her, devoured by her, deprived of speech and identity by her; yet equally terrified by our expulsion from nature, our orphanhood outside her warm maternal embrace. Our silence within. Our solitude without.

I will not go into a long discussion of the place of nature in the novel. But in my heart the European fiction of the nineteenth century takes place in cities and in rooms. Donald Fanger has given us a most brilliant discourse on the appearance of the city in Gogol, Balzac, Dickens, and Dostoevsky. Walter Benjamin has reminded us of the existence of nineteenth-century interiors as places where personal property is secure; when it is not, a new hero appears to protect it: the detective of Collins' *Moonstone*, of Poe's "Purloined Letter," of Conan Doyle's "Bruce-Partington Plans." And George Steiner has observed that only the literatures of Russia and the United States reclaim wide spaces—Tolstoy and Turgenev, Cooper and Melville—without sacrificing the counterpoint of some of the most suffocating enclosures of all fiction: Poe's nailed coffins and walled sepulchres, and Dostoevsky's tiny rooms and shadowy staircases, where Raskolnikov plots and Rogozhin awaits. But perhaps nowhere is the terror of being thrust outside history or into history as explicitly linked to the act of naming as in the literature of Latin America. Indeed, the immediacy of the voyages of discovery, written in our language, is a factor here; John Smith and the other original wetbacks at Plymouth Rock definitely did not see mermaids on the coast of Massachusetts.

But again, as I attempted to dramatize in my play *All Cats Are Grey* (1970), history is most explicitly linked to language in America. The passage of the language of the Aztec nation into a silence resembling death—or nature—and the passage of the Spanish language into a politically victorious yet culturally suspect and tainted condition not only is the foundation of the civilization of the New World: it perpetually questions it as it repeats a history that becomes a myth.

Moctezuma the Aztec emperor refuses to hear the voices of men; he will listen only to the language of the gods. Cortés the conqueror is only too ready to listen to the voices of men and turn the complaints against the centralist, patrimonial despot. He even takes on an interpreter, the Indian princess Marina (La Malinche), whom he calls *Mi Lengua*—my tongue—and who bears him a son: the first Mexican, the first *mestizo,* a Spanish-speaking native. The witness to all this is Hermes, the messenger, the writer, under the guise this time of Bernal Díaz del Castillo. This is his name: given yet intrinsic, essential yet secondhand, false yet evocative; changeable yet his destiny. Bernal Díaz del Castillo writes fifty years after the facts; he can name everything, down to the last horse and its owner; he can name because he can still desire, like Marcel Proust, and, like him, searches for lost time. He weeps over what he had to destroy, and so he is our first novelist, an epic writer who destroys the chance of utopia in genocide and is then conquered by the myth of the defeated hero who must now pay in words his debt to the city he enslaved.

More than four hundred years after the discovery and conquest of America, Rómulo Gallegos writes in his masterpiece, *Canaima*:

> Amanadoma, Yavita, Pimichin, el Casiquiare, el Atabapo, el Guainía: with these names these men did not describe the landscape, they did not reveal the total mystery (of the jungle and the river) into which they had entered; they were only mentioning the places where things happened to them—yet all the jungle, fascinating and terrible, was already throbbing in the power of the words . . .

For, behind these men, if they do not say, name, invent, imagine, discover, desire, lies the "immense mysterious regions where man had not yet penetrated: Venezuela of the unfinished discovery." And there, nameless, the individual may find himself "suddenly absent from himself, at the mercy of the jungle . . ."

Similarly, in Alejo Carpentier, the fascinating, at times even joyous, voyage of discovery up the Orinoco—the voyage to utopia in *The Lost Steps*—suddenly oversteps the limits of the word; in the "vast jungle filling with night terrors," the word splits open, answers itself, pleads, groans, howls:

> But then came the vibration of the tongue between the lips, the indrawn snoring, the panting contrapuntal to the rattle of the maraca . . . As it went on, this outcry over a corpse surrounded by silent dogs became horrible . . . Before the stubbornness of death, which refused to release its prey, the Word suddenly grew faint and disappeared. In the mouth of the Shaman, the Threne gasped and died away convulsively, blinding me with the realization that I had just witnessed the Birth of Music.

In this instant of Dionysiac joy and Proustian liberation Carpentier's Narrator would perhaps like to stand eternally: on the threshold between Music and Word. But the separations unleashed by history have not yet been totally discovered: he is sent spinning off to the very beginning of time, then to the world without word that existed before mankind. It is in this context, in this precarious balance between silence and the word, that the world of Gabriel García Márquez is poised.

Many thought in Latin America, when *One Hundred Years of Solitude* was first published and achieved its enormous and instantaneous success, that its popularity (comparable in the Hispanic world only to that of Cervantes and *Don Quixote*) was due to the element of immediate recognition present in the book. There is a joyous rediscovery of identity here, an instant reflex by which we are presented, in the genealogies of Macondo, to our grandmas, our sweethearts, our brothers and sisters, our nursemaids. Today, twenty years after the fact, we can see clearly that there was more than instant anagnorisis in the García Márquez phenomenon, that his novel, one of the most amusing ever written, does not exhaust its meanings in a first reading. This first reading (for amusement and for recognition) demands a second reading, which becomes, in effect, the real reading.

That is the secret of this mythical and simultaneous novel: *One Hundred Years of Solitude* presupposes two readings because it presupposes two writings. The first reading coincides with the writing we take as true: a novelist by the name of Gabriel García Márquez is retelling, chronologically, with biblical—indeed, Rabelaisian—hyperbole, the lineages of Macondo; Aureliano son of José Arcadio son of Aureliano son of José Arcadio. The second reading begins the moment the first one ends. The chronicle of Macondo had already been written; it is among the papers of a gypsy thaumaturge named Melquíades, whose appearance in the novel one hundred years before, when Macondo was founded, turns out to be identical to his revelation as the narrator, one hundred years later. In that instant, the book recommences, but this time the chronological history of Macondo has been revealed as a mythic and simultaneous historicity.

Historicity and myth: the second reading of *One Hundred Years of Solitude* conflates, both factually and fantastically, the order of what has happened (the chronicle) and the order of what might have happened (the imagination), with the result that the fatality of the former is liberated by the desire of the latter. Each historical act of the Buendías in Macondo is a sort of axis around which whirl all the possibilities unbeknown to the external chronicler but which, notwithstanding, are as real as the dreams, the fears, the madness, the imagination of the actors of the his- or her-story.

One way of seeing Latin American history, then, is as a pilgrimage from a founding utopia to a cruel epic that degrades utopia if the mythic imagination does not intervene so as to interrupt the onslaught of fatality and seek to recover the possibilities of freedom. One of the more extraordinary aspects of García Márquez's novel is that its structure corresponds to the profounder historicity of Latin America: the tension between utopia, epic, and myth. The founding of Macondo is the founding of utopia. José Arcadio Buendía and his family have wandered in the jungle, in circles, until they encounter precisely the place where they can found the New Arcadia, the promised land of origin:

> The men of the expedition felt overwhelmed by their most ancient memories in that paradise of dampness and silence, going back to before original sin, as their boots sank into pools of steaming oil and their machetes destroyed bloody lilies and golden salamanders.

Like More's Utopia, Macondo is an island of the imagination. José Arcadio discovers an enormous Spanish galleon anchored in the middle of the jungle, its hull fastened to a surface of stones, its insides occupied by a thick forest of flowers. He concludes that "Macondo is surrounded by water on all sides."

From this island, José Arcadio invents the world, points things out with his finger, then learns how to name things, and, finally, how to forget them, and so is forced to rename, rewrite, remember. But at the very same moment that the founding Buendía realizes "the infinite possibilities of forgetfulness," he must appeal for the first time to the otherwise infinite possibilities of writing. He hangs signs on objects; he discovers reflexive knowledge (he who, before, knew only through divination), and so he feels obliged to dominate the world of science: what he naturally knew before, now he will know only through the help of maps, magnets, and magnifiers.

The utopian founders were soothsayers. They knew how to recognize the language of the world, hidden but preestablished; they had no need to create a second language; they had only to open themselves to the language of what was. How to know this preexisting language that truly names things in their essence and in their true relationships is the Platonic problem, and José Arcadio Buendía, when he abandons divination in favour of science, when he migrates from sacred knowledge to the exercise of hypothesis, opens the doors to the novel's second part: the part that belongs to the epic, which is a historical process in which the utopian foundation of Macondo is denied by the active necessity of linear time. This part, significantly, happens between the thirty-two armed uprisings headed by Colonel Aureliano Buendía, the banana fever, and the final abandonment of Macondo—the founding utopia exploited, degraded, and in the end killed by the epic of activity, commerce, and crime.

The flood—the punishment—leaves behind it a Macondo forgotten even by the birds, where dust and heat have become so tenacious that it is hard to breath. Who remains there? The survivors, Aureliano and Amaranta Úrsula, hidden away by solitude and love (and by the solitude of love) in a house where it is almost impossible to sleep because of the

García Márquez (left) in Barcelona with fellow Latin American authors Mario Vargas Llosa, Julio Cortazar, and Carlos Barral, 1970

---

noise of the red ants. Then the third space of the book opens. This is the mythical space, whose simultaneous and renewable nature will not be understandable until the final paragraphs, when we find out that all this history was in fact already written by the gypsy Melquiades, the seer who accompanied Macondo in its foundation and who, in order to keep Macondo alive, must have recourse to the same trick used by José Arcadio: the trick of writing.

Comparable in this and many other aspects to Cervantes, García Márquez establishes the frontiers of reality within a book and the frontiers of a book within reality. The symbiosis is perfect, and once it takes place, we can begin the mythical reading of this beautiful, joyful, sad book about a town that proliferates, like the flowers inside the stranded Spanish galleon, with the richness of a South American Yoknapatawpha. As in his master William Faulkner, in García Márquez a novel is the fundamental act we call myth: the re-presentation of the founding act. At the mythical level, *One Hundred Years of Solitude* is an incessant interrogation: What does Macondo know of itself? That is, what does Macondo know of its own creation?

The novel is a response to this question. In order to know, Macondo must tell itself all the "real" history and all the "fictitious" history, all the proofs admitted by the court of justice, all the evidence certified by the public accountants, but also all the rumours, legends, gossip, pious lies, exaggerations, and fables that no one has written down, that old have told the young and the spinsters whispered to the priest: that the sorcerers have invoked in the centre of the night and the clowns have acted out in the centre of the square. The saga of Macondo and the Buendías thus includes the totality of the oral, legendary past, and with it we are told that we cannot feel satisfied with the official, documented history of the times: that history is also all the things that men and women have dreamed, imagined, desired, and named.

That it understands this is one of the great strengths of Latin American literature, because it reveals a profound perception of Latin American reality: a culture where the mythical constantly speaks through voices of dream and dance, of toy and song, but where nothing is real unless it is set down in writing—in the diaries of Columbus, in the letters of Cortés, in the memoirs of Bernal, in the laws of the Indies, in the constitutions of the independent republics. The struggle between the legal literature and the unwritten myths of Latin America is the struggle of our Roman tradition of statutory law, and of the Hapsburg and French traditions of centralism, with our undiscovered, inexhaustible, and, we hope, redeemable possibilities as free, unfinished human beings. Legitimacy in Latin America has always depended on who owns the written papers: Mexico's Porfirio Díaz, the ageing patriarch who justifies himself as the repository of the Liberal Constitution? Or Emiliano Zapata, who says he owns the original deeds to the land granted by the King of Spain? This is the struggle John Womack has staged superbly in his book on Mexico's agrarian revolution. The truth is that Zapata owns more than a piece of paper: he owns a poem, a dream, a myth.

García Márquez brings to his novels the same distinction and the same approach. The simultaneous nature of his world is inexorably linked to the total culture (dreams, habits, laws, facts, myths: culture in the sense understood by Vico) of Latin America. What is simultaneous in Macondo? First, as in all mythical memories, the recall of Macondo is creation and re-creation at the same time. García Márquez embodies this in an edenic couple, José Arcadio and Úrsula, pilgrims who have fled the original world of their sin and their fear to found a Second Paradise in Macondo. But the foundation—of a town or of its lineage—presupposes the repetition of the act of coupling, of exploitation, of the land or the flesh. In this sense, *One Hundred Years of Solitude* is a long metaphor which merely designates the instantaneous act of carnal love between the first man and the first woman, José Arcadio and Úrsula, who fornicate in fear that the fruit of their union shall be a child with the tail of a pig, but who must nevertheless procreate so that the world shall maintain itself.

Memory repeats the models of the origin, in the same way that over and over, Colonel Buendía makes golden fish that he then melts in order to make golden fish that he then melts to . . . to . . . to be constantly reborn, desired and desiring, discovering and discovered, inventive and invented, naming and named. *One Hundred Years of Solitude* is a true re-vision and re-creation of the utopias, the epics, and the myths of America. It shows us a group of men and women deciphering a world that might devour them: a surrounding magma. It tells us that nature has domains, but men and women have demons. Bedevilled, like the race of the Buendías, founders and usurpers, creators and destructors, Satoris and Snopes in one same breed.

But in order to achieve this simultaneity, the myth must have a precise time and a precise writing—or telling—or reading. A Spanish galleon is anchored in the mountain. A freight car full of peasants murdered by the banana company crosses the jungle and the bodies are thrown into the sea. A grandfather ties himself forever to an oak tree until he himself becomes an emblematic trunk, sculptured by storm, wind, and dust. Flowers rain down from the sky. Remedios the Beautiful ascends to this same sky as she spreads out her bedsheets to dry. In each of these acts of fiction, the linear time of the epic dies (this really happened), but the nostalgic time of utopia, past or future, also disappears (this should happen), and the absolute present time of the poetic myth is born (this is happening).

That is the precise time of García Márquez. And the precise writing is the second writing, which, in the second reading, makes us understand the full meaning of the acts of fiction, finally bracketed between the initial fact that one day José Arcadio Buendía decides that from then on it shall always be Monday and the final fact when Úrsula says: "It is as if time had been turning in circles and we had now come back to the beginning." She is wrong. Her time is an illusion; it is the reading that is right as it coincides with the writing. A universal writer, García Márquez is aware that, ever since Joyce, we cannot pretend that the writer isn't there; but also that, ever since Cervantes, we cannot pretend that the reader isn't there; and, moreover, that, ever since Homer, we cannot pretend that the listener isn't there.

We cannot renounce our consciousness of any of these great accomplishments of literature. García Márquez certainly does not give up as he finally integrates his American imagination and his universal imagination in the essential, the artificial, the conventional, the naturally named chronicle of Macondo. Deciphered by several members of the Buendía family, this chronicle is the story of their lives and the prediction that they would spend their lives trying to decipher the chronicle: the lives: the world. Reading and living thus become coexistent; by the same token, so do listening and writing. Aureliano Babilonia, the last male heir of the Buendías, deciphers the instant he is living; he deciphers as he lives it; he prophesies himself in the act of deciphering the last page of the manuscript: as if he were seeing himself in a talking mirror.

> This is a novel. A novel is something that is written. A novel is something that is read. A novel is something that is heard. We must do this so that reality can be remembered. The names in a novel are times and places in the present. There is no other way of truly knowing the relationship between things. The alternative is silence. The alternative is death.

NOTES

1. Rita Guibert, "Gabriel Garcia Marquez," in *Seven Voices: Seven Latin American Writers Talk to Rita Guibert* (New York: Knopf, 1973), p. 306.

2. Morton P. Levitt, "The Meticulous Modernist Fictions Of García Márquez," in *Gabriel Garcia Márquez,* edited by Harold Bloom (New York: Chelsea House, 1989), p. 237.

3. Mark Frisch, "Teaching *One Hundred Years Of Solitude* with *The Sound and the Fury,*" online document. http://www2.semo.edu/cfs/frisch.html

4. Ibid.

5. Guibert, *Seven Voices,* p. 327.

6. See Amaryll Chanady, "A Narratological Approach," in *Approaches to Teaching García Márquez's One Hundred Years Of Solitude,* edited by Maria Elena de Valdes and Mario J. Valdes. New York: Modern Language Association of America, 1990), pp. 127–136.

7. See Walter D. Mignolo, "One Hundred Years of Solitude in Latin American Literature Courses," in *Approaches to Teaching García Márquez's One Hundred Years Of Solitude,* p. 69.

8. Guibert, "Interview with Julio Cortazar," in *Seven Voices,* p. 301.

RESOURCES FOR
GARCÍA MÁRQUEZ STUDY

Study Questions *157*

Glossary of Terms *161*

Bibliography *163*

STUDY QUESTIONS

1. What themes and motifs are shared by William Faulkner's imaginary world, Yoknapatawpha County, and García Márquez's Macondo? Compare the historical origins of these two communities, within the ethical context created by the author.

2. In what ways does the imaginary Caribbean village in *Chronicle of a Death Foretold* become a microcosm of Colombia, its laws, morality, religion, politics, sexuality, and superstitions?

3. Discuss how the moments of magic realism in García Márquez's novels intersect with his "realistic" depictions of people and society.

4. What does the recurring figure of Colonel Aureliano Buendía, the hero of *One Hundred Years of Solitude,* represent in the works of García Márquez?

5. Locate the quintessential García Márquez images and metaphors, from the almond trees to the leaf storm, and discuss how they serve in the development of his themes.

6. What does García Márquez mean by "solitude," and how does it figure in his work from *Leaf Storm* to *One Hundred Years of Solitude*?

7. What forces conspire in the works of García Márquez against the exercise of human will?

8. How does García Márquez treat the theme of the irrationality of human experience?

9. What role does coincidence play in his work?

10 What purpose is revealed in the fact that several of the works of García Márquez (*In Evil Hour, The Autumn of the Patriarch, Chronicle of a Death Foretold*) begin with either a death or a funeral?

11. How in the works of García Márquez does magic realism work in conjunction with:

    a. flashback versus linear narrative?

    b. the theme of memory?

    c. exaggeration?

12. In what ways in the novels of García Márquez is time a theme? In what ways is time a character?

13. How does García Márquez handle point of view in his novels? Describe the characteristics of his omniscient narrators. From whence do they gain their authority? Locate the moments in the novels of García Márquez where the omniscient narrator lapses into the first person? Why does García Márquez employ this technique?

14. What effect does the uniqueness of García Márquez's descriptions have on our attitude toward the narrative voice?

15. How does the technique of the "catalogue" or "list" function in the fiction of García Márquez?

16. Discuss the role of the citizen-narrator in *Chronicle of a Death Foretold* and *Love in the Time of Cholera*.

17. How does the worldview of García Márquez emerge from the moments of magic realism in his novels?

18. How are flashbacks, foreshadowing, and flash-forwards connected to the frequent humor in García Márquez's novels?

19. What effect do digressions have on the themes of the novels of García Márquez?

20. Discuss the treatment of animals that figure prominently in García Márquez's fiction, such as the dogs in *The Autumn of the Patriarch* or the birds in *Love in the Time of Cholera*. In *Love in the Time of Cholera*, for example, Jeremiah de Saint-Amour is buried with his dog, who has chosen to die with him.

21. What place does García Márquez grant romantic love in his universe? Compare his exploration of love in *Love in the Time of Cholera* with that in *One Hundred Years of Solitude*.

22. Examine the reiteration of motifs in his fiction, from black or green vomit to the "bitter scent of almonds" that matches Florentino's "almond-shaped eyes" in *Love in the Time of Cholera.*

23. Discuss the themes of politics and war in the novels of García Márquez, beginning with the sequence of civil wars between Liberals and Conservatives. Show how he combines these civil wars with La Violencia, the period in Colombian history from 1948 to 1964. Does García Márquez favor the Liberals, to whose party Colonel Aureliano Buendía belongs?

24. What degree of sympathy does the author express toward the figure of Simón Bolívar in *The General in His Labyrinth?*

25. What is the purpose behind García Márquez's frequent use of specific time cues? For example, in *Love in the Time of Cholera* he makes a point of telling us that the dignitaries arrive at precisely three o'clock in the afternoon.

26. Discuss the treatment of women in *One Hundred Years of Solitude,* from Ursula to Amaranta to Rebeca to Remedios to Meme to Amaranta Ursula.

27. How much plot is there in the novels of García Márquez, and in what unconventional ways does he handle plot? For example, Dr. Urbino is about to leave *Love in the Time of Cholera* after the first chapter, yet García Márquez takes the time to include a flashback to twenty years earlier to describe a day when he and his wife Fermina Daza argue about whether there was soap in the bathroom.

28. In what ways do autobiographical elements enter into the novels of García Márquez, and how are they connected to his themes?

29. Compare in the work of García Márquez the culture and setting of the Caribbean coast with that of the foggy, cold, colonial culture of Bogotá and its environs.

30. Compare the treatment of magic realism in García Márquez with that in other authors, such as José Donoso, Salman Rushdie, Toni Morrison, and Isabel Allende.

31. What techniques does García Márquez share with his modernist predecessors such as James Joyce, Virginia Woolf, Thomas Mann, and Franz Kafka?

32. Compare García Márquez's characterization of Simón Bolívar with the facts known about the life of the historical Bolívar.

33. Show evidence of García Márquez's use of magic realism in his journalistic work *News of a Kidnapping*.

34. Apply the deconstructionist views of Jacques Derrida and Jacques Lacan to *One Hundred Years of Solitude*.

35. What does Carlos Fuentes mean when he argues that in the case of *One Hundred Years of Solitude*, "all 'fictional' history coexists with 'real' history, what is dreamed with what is documented. . . ."?

36. Discuss, as Regina Janes argues in *García Márquez: Revolutions in Wonderland*, how *One Hundred Years of Solitude* is a "total novel" that treats Latin America "socially, historically, politically, mythically and epically."

GLOSSARY OF TERMS

El Bogotázo: period of rioting following the murder of Jorge Eliécer Gaitán in 1948.

The Boom: the resurgence of Latin American novelists and poets in the 1960s and 1970s. These writers include García Márquez, Carlos Fuentes, Mario Vargas Llosa, Julio Cortázar, and others.

Cachacos: term for the people of Bogotá and the interior of Colombia.

Coda: an endnote, or final word, in which the author elucidates what has come before. A coda might also reveal what happened to the characters after the close of the novel proper.

Coincidence: a novelist's dependence on the fortuitous to move along the plot of the story. Events that happen by chance instead of being motivated by the psychology of a character or the demands of history.

Conceit: an extended metaphor, a figure of speech that establishes an elaborate parallel between unlike things ordinarily not connected to each other. The comparison between love and cholera, which runs through *Love in the Time of Cholera,* is an example of a conceit.

Costeños: term for people of the Caribbean coast of Colombia.

Epic: a story that chronicles the daring exploits of heroes and equally the fate of the society and community in the background.

Epiphany: a physical image—appealing to one or more of the five senses—that produces a sudden insight or illumination spiritual in content. An epiphany usually grants to the character in the story understanding of his entire life situation.

Episodic: a work that is structured loosely according to the random accumulation of scenes and events and rejects the classic Aristotelian model of a beginning, middle, and an end in which there is an exposition, rising action, climax, and resolution of the action.

Imagery: the use of figurative language, connecting emotional, political, or psychological themes with sensory comparisons. The scent of bitter almond and almond trees form persistent images in the work of García Márquez, particularly in *One Hundred Years of Solitude* and *Love in the Time of Cholera.*

Intertexuality: references in the text of a work to other writing by the same author, or references to the work of other authors that reflect similar themes or images.

Interior Monologue: a text comprised of the random thoughts of a character organized according to the free association of ideas.

Irony: a technique frequently employed by García Márquez. *Verbal irony* means saying one thing and meaning another. *Dramatic irony* is produced when the reader knows more about events or individuals than do characters; *situational irony* results when events prove contradictory to what had been expected.

Magic Realism: fiction in which no distinction is made between realistic and nonrealistic events; Cuban novelist Alejo Carpentier is usually considered the first to apply the term to literature, believing that a type of storytelling in which the distinction between fantasy and reality is blurred was typical of Carribean authors. García Márquez argues that the rationalism of European readers tends to prevent them from accepting that magic realism is inspired by everyday life in Latin America in which reality is full of extraordinary things.

Mestizo: a person of mixed Spanish and Indian blood.

Narrator: a novel or story may be told either by a first-person narrator, usually a character in the story, or by a third-person narrator, who is most often omniscient, or all-knowing, and sees into the motives of all the characters. An omniscient narrator may intrude into the narrative to comment on the action or the characters. García Márquez uses a quasi-omniscient narrator, who surprises the reader by using the first person, "I" or "We" or "Our," and so defining himself as a member of the community about which he is writing.

Naturalism: a form of realism, but with particular attention to the raw physical details of life. It views its characters as creatures of nature, animal in their needs and desires.

Picaresque: an episodic novel that chronicles a series of adventures and daring escapades of a roguish character known as a picaro, or knave, who is generally mischievous, sly, crafty, and a rascal. Both of the Spanish novels addressed by García Márquez, *Lazarillo de Tormes* and *Don Quixote,* are picaresque novels.

Plot: the sequence of events in a story, linked, usually but not always, through causal connections. The action of a novel, or, what happens.

Realism: the major tradition in the novel that began as a form of entertainment for the middle classes. It demands verisimilitude of the action, a resemblance to everyday life as the reader knows it; the behavior of the characters in a realist work is causally connected, and action in the present can be traced to causes in the past. Realism minimizes the use of coincidence or accident.

Setting: the background of the story or novel, not only the room or the weather or the streets, but the historical and cultural context of the work of fiction. The setting of García Márquez's novels figures importantly in both plot and characterization, and even becomes a character in its own right, particularly in *Chronicle of a Death Foretold* and *Love in the Time of Cholera,* where by the end the river takes over the foreground of the narrative. Most often García Márquez sets his stories on the Caribbean coast of Colombia, the region of his birth.

Verisimilitude: the credibility of a story, its similarity to life as we know it.

La Violencia: literally, "the violence"; the period of political violence that wracked Colombia from the early 1940s to the middle of the 1960s.

Zambos: people of mixed African and Indian descent.

BIBLIOGRAPHY

Adams, Robert M. "Big Little Book," *New York Review of Books,* 14 April 1983, p. 3.

Barnard, Timothy, and Peter Rist, eds. *South American Cinema: A Critical Filmography, 1915–1994.* Austin: University of Texas Press, 1996.

Barroa, Rei. *Literature of the Americas.* College Park: University of Maryland Press, 1990.

Bell, Michael. *Gabriel García Márquez: Solitude and Solidarity.* New York: St. Martin's Press, 1993.

Bell-Villada, Gene H. *García Márquez: The Man And His Work.* Chapel Hill & London: University of North Carolina Press, 1990. A comprehensive and illuminating introduction to García Márquez with many quotations from interviews and a strong biographical approach.

Bloom, Harold, ed. *Gabriel García Márquez.* New York: Chelsea House, 1989. This is a good collection of eighteen essays. Two deal with the influence of William Faulkner on García Márquez. Colombian politics is discussed in Regina Janes's essay, "Liberals, Conservatives, and Bananas: Colombian Politics in the Fictions of García Márquez," as well as in "The Autumn of the Patriarch," by the superb critic Raymond Williams. Begin, as Bloom does, with "García Márquez: From Aracataca to Macondo" by Mario Vargas Llosa.

Brink, Andre. "Making and Unmaking: Gabriel García Márquez: One Hundred Years of Solitude," in *The Novel: Language and Narrative from Cervantes to Calvino.* New York: New York University Press, 1998. A South African novelist, Brink has used many of the techniques of magic realism in his own work, particularly in the novels *Imaginings of Sand* (1997) and *Devil's Valley* (1999).

Brotherson, Gordon. *The Emergence of the Latin American Novel.* Cambridge: Cambridge University Press, 1979.

Buford, Bill. "Haughty Falconry and Collective Guilt," *TLS: The Times Literary Supplement* (London), 10 September 1982, p. 965.

Butt, John. "The Liberator in Defeat," *TLS: The Times Literary Supplement,* 14–20 July 1989, p. 781.

Clemons, Walter. "A Dictator's Debris," *Newsweek,* 88 (8 November 1976): 105.

Conversations with Latin American Writers: Gabriel García Márquez, interviewed by Silvia Lemus, 44 minutes, Films For The Humanities & Sciences, 1998, video. Lemus, the interviewer, is the wife of Mexican novelist Carlos Fuentes. She interviews García Márquez in Cartagena, the setting for *Love In The Time Of Cholera.* The discussion ranges from autobiographical sources of the novel to García Márquez's reflections on the art of fiction.

Dolan, Sean. *Gabriel García Márquez*. New York: Chelsea House, 1994.

Donoso, José. *The Boom in Spanish American Literature,* translated by Gregory Kolvakos. New York: Columbia University Press/Center for Inter-American Relations, 1977. This superb and personal book chronicling Donoso's own career places García Márquez in the literature of the era and of his continent. There are personal glimpses of García Márquez and other writers such as Carlos Fuentes and of course Donoso himself.

Dreifus, Claudia. "*Playboy* Interview: Gabriel García Márquez," *Playboy,* 30, no. 3 (February 1983): 65–77, 172–78. The political naiveté of the interviewer mars this interview. When García Márquez asks her playfully whether, like other North American journalists, she is going to ask him whether he is a communist, she becomes flustered, and lacking any knowledge of Colombian politics, goes ahead and does it.

Fau, Margaret Eustella. *Gabriel García Márquez: An Annotated Bibliography, 1947–1979,* Westport, Conn.: Greenwood Press, 1980.

Fau and Nelly Sfeir de González. *Bibliographic Guide to Gabriel García Márquez, 1979–1985,* Westport, Conn.: Greenwood Press, 1986.

Foster, David William. *Handbook of Latin American Literature.* New York: Garland, 1987.

Frisch, Mark. "Teaching *One Hundred Years Of Solitude* with *The Sound and the Fury.*" on-line document. http://www.2.semo.edu/cfs/frisch.html.

Gabriel García Márquez: Magic and Reality, written, directed, and produced by Ana Cristina Navarro, 60 minutes, Films For the Humanities & Sciences, 1981, video. Available in both Spanish and English, this documentary offers interviews with the author as well as several of his friends and critics, among them Alfonso Fuenmayor, who appears as a character in *One Hundred Years of Solitude*. Especially interesting is the footage of the Bogotázo, of the riots following the assassination of Liberal leader Jorge Eliecer Gaitan, and of old photographs and rare footage as well of the Santa Marta railroad built by the banana company, and the strike described in *One Hundred Years of Solitude*; survivors of the massacre are interviewed.

Gallagher, D. P. *Modern Latin American Literature.* New York: Oxford University Press, 1973.

Gonzalez, Nelly Sfeir de. *Bibliographic Guide to Gabriel García Márquez, 1986–1992.* Westport, Conn.: Greenwood Press, 1994.

Guibert, Rita. *Seven Voices: Seven Latin American Writers Talk to Rita Guibert.* New York: Knopf, 1973. This book is an excellent introduction to García Márquez and easily the most comprehensive interview with this author. He discusses his work process and his techniques fully. See also in this volume a rare interview with Guillermo Cabrera Infante, who offers some remarks about García Márquez.

Gullon, Ricardo. "Gabriel García Márquez and the Lost Art of Storytelling." *Diacritics.* (1971): 27–32.

Guzman Campos, Gérman. *Camilo Torres.* New York: Sheed & Ward, 1969.

Guzman Campos, Orlando Fals Borda, and Eduardo Umana Luna. *La Violencia en Colombia: Estudio de un Proceso Social,* volume 1, Bogota: Ediciones Tercer Mundo, 1963. This book, although only available in Spanish, is indispensable for any understanding of Colombia and the historical culture from which García Márquez emerged.

Harss, Luis, and Barbara Dohmann. *Into the Mainstream: Conversations with Latin American Writers*. New York: Harper & Row, 1967.

Janes, Regina, *Gabriel García Márquez: Revolutions in Wonderland*. Columbia: University of Missouri Press, 1981.

Janes. *One Hundred Years of Solitude: Modes of Reading*. Boston: Twayne, 1991.

Kakutani, Michiko. "García Márquez Novel Covers Love and Time," *New York Times*, 6 April 1988, p. C21.

Kennedy, William. "All of Life, Sense and Nonsense, fills an an Argentine's Daring Fable," *National Observer*, 9 (20 April 1970): 23.

Kennedy. "The Yellow Trolley Car in Barcelona and Other Visions: A Profile of Gabriel García Márquez." *Atlantic*, 231, no. 1 (January 1973): 50–58. Republished in *Riding the Yellow Trolley Car: Selected Nonfiction*. New York: Viking, 1993, pp. 243–267. Despite Kennedy's knowledge of Spanish, and the generous offering of his time by García Márquez, this interview adds too little to the existing literature. This was the first biographical interview widely available to readers in the United States and England.

Luis, William, ed. *Dictionary of Literary Biography*, volume 113: *Modern Latin-American Writers*. Detroit: Gale, 1992.

"Magic, Matter, and Money: Pioneers Who Have Explored Four Aspects of Reality," *Time*, 120 (1 November 1982): 88–89.

Mano, D. Keith. "A Death Foretold," *National Review* (10 June 1983): 699–700.

McGuirk, Bernard, and Richard Cardwell, eds. *Gabriel García Márquez: New Readings*. Cambridge: Cambridge University Press, 1987. This anthology is superior to Bloom's and more scholarly in approach. There are twelve essays, including Robin Fiddian's "A Prospective Post-script: Apropos of *Love in the Time of Cholera*," which offers a somewhat dissenting view regarding the treatment of women in the works of García Márquez. "On 'Magical' and Social Realism in García Márquez" by Gerald Martin is particularly helpful.

McMurray, George R. *Gabriel García Márquez*. New York: Ungar, 1983.

Mead, Robert G. Jr. "*One Hundred Years of Solitude*," *Saturday Review*, 7 (March 1970): 34–35.

Müller-Bergh, Klaus. "*Relato de un náufrago*: García Márquez's Tale of Shipwreck and Survival at Sea," *Books Abroad*, 47, no. 3 (Summer 1973), pp. 460–466.

Oberhelman, Harley D. "The Presence of Faulkner in the Writings of García Márquez," *Graduate Studies Texas Tech University*, 22 (August 1980): 1–43.

O'Hara, J. D. "Sick, Simpering Tyrant," *Washington Post Book World*, 14 November 1976, p. 14.

Pynchon, Thomas. "The Heart's Eternal Vow," *New York Times Book Review*, 10 April 1988, pp. 48–49.

Riding, Alan. "Revolution and the Intellectual in Latin America," *New York Times*, 13 March 1983.

Rodman, Selden. "Gabriel García Márquez," in *Tongues of Fallen Angels: Conversations*. New York: New Directions, 1974.

Sheppard, R. Z. "Love Among the Ruins," *Time*, 145 (22 May 1995): 73.

Simons, Marlise. "The Best Years of His Life: An Interview with Gabriel

García Márquez." *New York Times Book Review*, 10 April 1988. Simons is a journalist and not a scholar, but there are some interesting moments here.

Simons. "Love and Age: A Talk with García Márquez." *New York Times Book Review*, 7 April 1985. This interview appeared at the time of the publication of *Love in the Time Of Cholera* and is excellent.

Simons. "A Talk With Gabriel García Márquez." *New York Times Book Review*, 5 December 1982.

Stone, Peter. "Gabriel García Márquez," in *Writers At Work: The Paris Review Interviews—Sixth Series*, edited by George Plimpton. New York: Viking, 1984, pp. 313–339.

Streitfield, David. "The Intricate Solitude of Gabriel García Márquez," *Washington Post*, 10 April 1994, pp. F1, F4.

Valdes, Maria Elena de and Mario J. Valdes, eds. *Approaches to Teaching García Márquez's One Hundred Years Of Solitude*. New York: Modern Language Association of America, 1990.

Vargas, Gérman. "Autor de una obra que hará ruido," *Encuentra liberal* (Bogotá), 29 April 1967.

Vargas Llosa, Mario. *García Márquez: Historia de un Deicidio*. Barcelona: Breve Biblioteca de Respuesta: Barral Editores, 1971. Written at a time when Vargas Llosa and García Márquez were still friends, this book is an affectionate and comprehensive critical biography. Especially useful are the discussions of the youth of García Márquez as a *costeño*. See the Bloom anthology for a piece by Vargas Llosa in English: "García Márquez: From Aracataca to Macondo," pp. 5–19.

Wood, Michael. *Gabriel García Márquez: One Hundred Years of Solitude*. Cambridge & New York: Cam-

bridge University Press, 1990. This personal, yet brilliant and accessible, study of García Márquez is the most measured piece of writing about this author. The chronology is particularly useful and includes historical material as well as the details of the life of García Márquez.

Zamora, Lois Parkinson and Wendy B. Faris, eds. *Magical Realism: Theory, History, Community*. Durham: Duke University Press, 1995. This comprehensive volume is a must for penetrating the nuances of "magical realism" from its beginnings to the present and including its use by other authors.

WEB SITES

www.rpg.net/quail/labyrinth/gabo
Created and maintained by A. Ruch, "Macondo" is a complete and quite reliable site. There are special features, such as news about García Márquez, recent articles, information about new books in the works, and the latest on new motion-picture adaptations. "Macondo" includes an impressive section titled "Biography" that includes a time line with the dates of his major works and the events that helped shape his writing; "Bibliography," which includes works available only in Spanish; "Criticism"; "Audio: Books on Tape"; "Images," which is an online gallery of García Márquez images, photographs, paintings and book covers; "Papers," containing links to essays; "Film," a link to a directory of films based on García Márquez's works; his Nobel Prize lecture; links to other resources; and "Bookstore," linked to Amazon.com for easy ordering. This web site is not only comprehensive, but it is also charming, thought-provoking, and obviously created with considerable affection for the subject. No other web site

about García Márquez comes close to "Macondo" in its professionalism, enthusiasm, and passion.

www.levity.com/corduroy/marquez.htm

Also a García Márquez site, with quotations from his novels, news articles, home pages, biographies, and a link to the web site "Macondo." Several of the links may be nonoperational, however, and one, a review of *The General In His Labyrinth,* written for "The Tech," was not particularly illumi-nating. The "New Readings" link led, not very helpfully, to the "Cambridge On Line Catalog."

http://lanic.utexas.edu/la/colombia/

Several links relevant to Colombian culture and politics are available through the Latin American Information Center maintained at the University of Texas website, including a link to a general overview of Colombian history maintained by the Library of Congress: http://lcweb2.loc.gov/frd/cs/cotoc.html.

MASTER INDEX

A

Absalom, Absalom! (Faulkner) 137
Acosta, Walter 116
Adams, Robert M. 50
"El ahogado más hermoso del mundo"
    (García Márquez) 91
Alberto, Eiseo 104–105
Alcoriza, Luis 104
Alea, Tomas Gutierrez 105
All Cats Are Grey (Fuentes) 147
Allende, Salvador 9
Alternativa 9
El amor en los tiempos del cólera (García
    Márquez). See *Love in the Time of Chol-
    era*
Anaya, Rudolfo 139
Antigone (Sophocles) 14
Argentina 125
Ariel 52
"Artificial Roses" (García Márquez) 86
*El asalto: El operativo con que el FSLN se
    lanzó al mundo: Un relato* (García
    Márquez) 95
Asturias, Miguel Angel 135, 137
The Autumn of the Patriarch (García
    Márquez) 7, 19, 29–30, 33, 36, 40, 47–
    48, 51, 56, 65, 72, 91–92, 106, 110,
    112, 114, 117, 138
*La aventura de Miguel Littín, clandestino en
    Chile* (García Márquez). See *Clandestine
    in Chile: The Adventures of Miguel Littín*

B

"Balthazar's Marvelous Afternoon" (García
    Márquez) 86
Balzac, Honoré de 52
Bargas, Marcelle 52

Barral, Carlos 151
Barrera, Olegario 104
Barth, John 138
Barthes, Roland 140
Batista y Zaldívar, Fulgencio 71, 113
Bell-Villada, Gene H. 52, 106, 112
Bernstein, J. S. 84, 86
Betancur, Belisario 21
"The Betrothed" (Manzoni) 127
"Big Mama's Funeral" (García Márquez)
    28, 79, 86–87, 91
"Big Mama's Funeral: Tuesday Siesta"
    (García Márquez) 86
Birri, Fernando 116
"Bitterness for Three Sleepwalkers"
    (García Márquez) 94
"Blacamán el bueno vendedor de mila-
    gros" (García Márquez) 91
Blades, Ruben 117
Blanco, Jesus Sosa 113
Bless Me, Ultima (Anaya) 139
Bloom, Harold 106
"Bolívar" (García Márquez) 133
Bolívar, Simon 34, 38, 40, 52, 63, 73–74,
    78–79, 99
"Bon voyage, Mr. President" (García
    Márquez) 101
Bon Voyage, Mr. President and Other Stories
    (García Márquez) 101
Bonaparte, Napoleon 63
Books Abroad 49
The Boom in Spanish American Literature
    (Donoso) 72, 108
Borda, Eduardo Zalamea 13
Borda, Orlando Fals 108
Borges, Jorge Luis 106, 135
Brazil 125
"Bruce-Partington Plans" (Conan Doyle)
    147
Buddenbrooks (Mann) 137

"Buen viaje, señor presidente" (García Márquez). *See* "Bon voyage, Mr. President"

Buendía, Aureliano 63, 81

Buford, Bill 50

Buñuel, Luis 106, 139

Butt, John 52

C

Cabrera Infante, Guillermo 135, 139

Calvino, Italo 138

Camargo, Lleras 70

Campos, Germán Guzman 108

Camus, Albert 77

Canaima (Gallegos) 148

Cardwell, Richard 106

Carpentier, Alejo 135, 137–138, 142–144, 148

Castaño, Fabio Vásquez 71

Castro, Fidel 9, 18, 71, 78

El cataclismo de Damocles/The Doom of Damocles (García Márquez) 99

Catán, Daniel 117

Cato, Susana 105

"The Cemetery of Lost Letters" (García Márquez) 130

Cervantes, Miguel de 49, 53, 106, 148

A Change of Skin (Fuentes) 135

Chavarri, Jaime 105

Chicago Tribune 52

Chile 122

Chile, el golpe y los gringos (García Márquez) 91

Chronicle of a Death Foretold (García Márquez) 7, 17, 29, 32–33, 40–41, 50–51, 62, 64, 76, 80, 94–95, 104, 106, 108, 113–114, 116, 126, 138

Cien años de soledad (García Márquez). *See One Hundred Years of Solitude*

Clandestine in Chile: The Adventures of Miguel Littín (García Márquez) 96

Clemons, Walter 51

Collins, Wilkie 147

The Colombia Country Report on Human Rights Practices for 1998 75

"Colombian Literature: A Fraud on the Nation" (García Márquez) 77

Conan Doyle, Arthur 147

Conrad, Joseph 114, 139

Contigo en la distancia 105

Coronation (Donoso) 26

El coronel no tiene quien le escriba (García Márquez). *See No One Writes to the Colonel*

Cortázar, Julio 138, 151

Cratylus (Plato) 140

Cronaca di una morte annunciata (motion picture) 115

Crónica de una muerte anunciada (García Márquez). *See Chronicle of a Death Foretold*

Crónica de una muerte anunciada (play) 116

Crónicas y reportajes (García Márquez) 94

Cuando era feliz e indocumentado (García Márquez) 91

Cuatro cuento (García Márquez) 91

D

De Europe y America (1955-1960) (García Márquez) 94

De viaje por los paises socialists: 90 dias en la "Cortina de Hierro" (García Márquez) 94

"Death Constant Beyond Love" (García Márquez) 94

Death in Venice (Mann) 114

The Death of Artemio Cruz (Fuentes) 108

Defoe, Daniel 111, 127

DeLillo, Don 139

"Dialogue with the Mirror" (García Márquez) 94

Diatriba de amor contra un hombre sentado (García Márquez) 102

"Diatribe of Love Against a Seated Man" (García Márquez) 133

Díaz, Porfirio 152

"Diecisiete ingleses envenenados" (García Márquez). *See* "Seventeen Poisoned Englishmen"

Doce cuentos peregrinos (García Márquez). *See Strange Pilgrims: Twelve Stories*

Un Domingo feliz 104

Don Quixote (Cervantes) 49, 106, 114, 148

Donoso, José 26–27, 49, 72, 108

Dorris, Michael 52

Dostoyevsky, Fyodor 139

Drake, Sir Francis 12

Dreifus, Claudia 20

Duffau, Graciela 133

Duque Naranjo, Lisandro 104–105

E

Ecuador 121

Edipo alcalde 53, 105

Ejército de Liberación Nacional. *See* ELN
   (Army of National Liberation)

"El avión de la bella durmiente" (García
   Márquez). *See* "Sleeping Beauty and the
   Airplane"

El Espectador 24, 90–91, 109, 117

El Salvador 121–122

Elite 101

ELN (Army of National Liberation) 18, 71,
   74–76

"En este pueblo no hay ladrones" (García
   Márquez). *See* "There Are No Thieves in
   this Town"

Encyclopedia Britannica 40

Entre Cachacos I (García Márquez) 94

Entre Cachacos II (García Márquez) 94

Erasmus 144

Eréndira 115

Escobar, Pablo 73, 75

"Espantos de agosto" (García Márquez).
   See "The Ghosts of August"

El Espectador 13–16, 69

"Eva Is Inside Her Cat" (García Márquez)
   94

"Eyes of a Blue Dog" (García Márquez) 94

Eyes of a Blue Dog (motion picture) 116

F

Fable of the Beautiful Pigeon Fancier 104

Fabula de la Bella Palomera 104

Fanger, Donald 147

Far Apart 105

FARC (Revolutionary Armed Forces of
   Colombia) 71, 74–76

Faulkner, William 14, 33, 47–48, 106,
   114, 124, 137–139, 151

Fiddian, Robin 53

Florencia en el Amazona 117

Flores, Arturo 116

"For The Sake Of A Country Within Reach
   of the Children" (García Márquez) 79

Foundation of New Latin American Cinema 125

The Four Hundred Blows 14

The Fragrance of Guava (García Márquez)
   95

Franco, Francisco 19, 92, 113

Frente Unido (United Front) 18

Fuentes, Carlos 49, 104, 108, 117, 135,
   139

Fuentes-Berain, Marcela 117

Fuerzas Armadas Revolucionarias de
   Colombia. *See* FARC (Revolutionary
   Armed Forces of Colombia)

"Los funerales de la Mamá Grande". *See*
   "Big Mama's Funeral"

Los funerales de la Mamá Grande
   (García Márquez) 20, 24, 47, 85–86,
   94

G

*Gabriel García Márquez and the Invention of
   America* (Fuentes) 139–154

"Gabriel García Márquez on Love, Plagues
   and Politics" (Simons) 125–134

Gabriel García Márquez: New Readings
   (McGuirk & Cardwell) 106

*Gabriel García Márquez: One Hundred Years
   of Solitude* (Wood) 30, 106

*Gabriel García Márquez: Revolutions in
   Wonderland* (Janes) 49

*Gabriel García Márquez: The Man And His
   Work* (Bell-Villada) 106

Gaitán, Jorge Eliécer 13, 67–68, 71

Galán Sarmiento, Luis Carlos 73

Gallegos, Rómulo 148

Garcia Agraz, Carlos 105

Garcia Agraz, Jose Luis 105

García Márquez, Gabriel
   Awards and Recognition 20–21
   Childhood and Biographical
      Glimpses 10–20
   critical reception 49–56
   getting established 24–27
   on cinema 130
   on journalism 129
   on language 131
   on "Love in the Time of Cholera" 126
   on plague themes 126–127
   on politics 133
   parents 127–128
   techniques 28–49

García Márquez, Mercedes Barcha 16–17,
   24, 26–27, 48, 94, 96, 108–109, 112,
   125

"García Márquez: From Aracataca to
   Macondo" (Vargas Llosa) 107

García Márquez: Historia de un Deicidio (Vargas Llosa) 19, 107

García Moreno, Gabriel 121

García, Gabriel Eligio 10, 107, 127–128

García, Luis Cova 52

Garrido, Consuelo 105

El general en su laberinto (García Márquez). See *The General in His Labyrinth*

The General in His Labyrinth (García Márquez) 8, 12, 34, 38, 40, 52, 60, 99, 114–115

Gentile, Cayetano 113

"The Ghosts of August" (García Márquez) 101

Globe and Mail 52

Gómez Castro, Laureano 68–69

Gómez, Juan Vicente 113

González, Ofelia 116

Griffin, Clive 106

Grossman, Edith 96, 99, 101–103

Guatemala 122

Guerra, Ruy 104, 115

Guerra, Tonino 115

Guibert, Rita 31, 52–53

H

Harss, Luis 54

Havana, Cuba 125

Heart of Darkness (Conrad) 114

Hellman, Lillian 53

Hemingway, Ernest 14, 47–48

El Heraldo 14

Hermosillo, Jaime Humberto 115–116

Hernández Martínez, Maximiliano 121

Hogan, Randolph 90

La hojarasca (García Márquez). See *Leaf Storm*

"Un hombre muy viejo con unas alas enormes" (García Márquez) 91

Hombres de maíz (Asturias). See *Maize Men* 138

Hoogesteijn, Solveig 115

"How to Tell a Story" (García Márquez) 128

"The Humor of *One Hundred Years of Solitude*" (Griffin) 106

I

"'I only came to use the phone'" (García Márquez) 101

"I Sell My Dreams" (García Márquez) 101

I, the Supreme (Roa Bastos) 138

Iguarán Cotes, Tranquilina 11, 31, 76

In Evil Hour (García Márquez) 20, 24, 47, 71, 85

"The Incredible and Sad Tale of Innocent Eréndira and Her Heartless Grandmother" (García Márquez) 30–31, 41, 62, 91, 94, 96, 102, 115, 117

"La increíble y triste historia de la cándida Eréndira y de su abuela desalmada" (García Márquez). See "The Incredible and Sad Tale of Innocent Eréndira and Her Heartless Grandmother"

"La increíble y triste historia de la cándida Eréndira y de su abuela desalmada" (García Márquez) 91

La increíble y triste historia de la cándida Eréndira y de su abuela desalmada (García Márquez) 91, 94, 115

Infante, Cabrera 135

Innocent Eréndira and her Heartless Grandmother (play) 116

Innocent Eréndira and Other Stories (García Márquez) 94

The Invention of America (O'Gorman) 142

Isaacs, Jorge 105

Isabel viendo llover en Macondo (García Márquez) 87

J

Jacobs, William 129

James, Henry 138

Janes, Regina 49, 60, 67, 107

Jaramillo, Rogelio 116

John Paul II 78

Journal of the Plague Year (Defoe) 111, 127

Joyce, James 13–14, 106, 114, 138

Juego peligroso 104

K

Kafka, Franz 13, 114

Kakutani, Michiko 51

Kennedy, William 49

The Kingdom of This World (Carpentier) 138

Kröger, Tonio 123

L

"La santa" (García Márquez). *See* "The Saint"

La langosta azul 103

Lazarillo de Tormes 13, 43

Leaf Storm (García Márquez) 14, 24, 31, 47, 65, 85, 112

Leaf Storm and Other Stories (García Márquez) 14, 83

León, María Andrea de 116

"Liberals, Conservatives and Bananas: Colombian Politics in the Fictions of Gabriel García Márquez" (Janes) 107

Life 55

"Light Is like Water" (García Márquez) 102

"Light is like Water" (García Márquez) 38

Lima, Lezama 135

Littín, Miguel 96, 115

López de Santana, Antonio 121

Lorenz, Günther 52

The Lost Steps (Carpentier) 143, 148

Love in the Time of Cholera (García Márquez) 7, 12, 17, 20, 28–29, 31–34, 36, 38–40, 46, 48, 50, 52, 54, 96, 106, 109, 113–115, 117, 127–128, 137

Luna, Eduardo Umana 108

"La luz es como el agua" (García Márquez). *See* "Light Is like Water"

M

M-19 (19th of April Movement) 10, 73–74, 78

Macondo 149, 152

Maddock, Melvin 55

Magellan 120

Magic and Reality 62

Maize Men (Asturias) 138

La mala hora (García Márquez). See *In Evil Hour*

Malagon, Stella 105

Malraux, André 139

Mann, Thomas 106, 114, 123

Mann,Thomas 137

Mano, D. Keith 51

Manzoni, Alessandro 127

"El mar del tiempo perdido" (García Márquez) 91, 115

El mar del tiempo perdido (motion picture) 115

Maria (Isaacs) 105

Maria de mi corazon 115

"María dos Prazeres" (García Márquez) 41, 43, 102

Márquez Iguarán, Luisa Santiago 10, 107, 127–128

Márquez Iguarán, Nicolás 11, 62, 64, 66, 76, 112

Martin, Gerald 109

Martinez Pardo, Hernando 103

Massetti, Jorge 18

Maupassant, Guy de 138

McGuirk, Bernard 106

"Me alquilo para soñar" (García Márquez). *See* "I Sell My Dreams"

Me Llamo Rigoberta Menchu y asi nacio mi concienca (I . . . *Rigoberta Menchu: An Indian Woman in Guatemala*)) (Menchu) 138

Mead, Robert G. Jr. 50

Melo, José María 64

Melville, Herman 7

Menchu, Rigoberta 138

Mendoza, Plinio Apuleyo 95, 111

The Metamorphosis (Kafka) 13, 114

Mexico 128

Mexico City, Mexico 125

Milagro en Roma 104

"Miss Forbes's Summer of Happiness" (García Márquez) 102

Mito 84

Mitterand, François 21

MNL (New Liberalism Movement) 73

Moby-Dick; or, The Whale (Melville) 7

Modern Critical Views: Gabriel García Márquez 106

Momento 16, 91

"The Monkey's Paw" (Jacobs) 129

"Monólogo de Isabel viendo llover en Macando" (García Márquez) 91

"Montiel's Widow" (García Márquez) 86

Moonstone (Collins) 147

More, Thomas 143

Morón, Victor Medina 71

Morrison, Toni 138

Movimiento 19 de Abril. *See* M-19 (19th of April Movement)

Movimiento Nuevo Liberalismo. *See* MNL (New Liberalism Movement)

Mrs. Dalloway (Woolf) 14, 36

"Muerte constante más allá del amor" (García Márquez) 91

Mujer que llegaba a las seis 116

Müller-Bergh, Klaus 49

Musil, Robert 138
Mutis, Álvaro 24, 26

N

"Nabo, el negro que hizo esperar a los ángeles" (García Márquez) 91
Nariño, Antonio 63
National Observer 49
National Review 51
El Negro que hizo esperar a los ángeles (García Márquez) 91
Neruda, Pablo 49, 122
New York Review of Books 50
New York Times 51
New York Times Book Review 50
News of a Kidnapping (García Márquez) 73, 103
Newsweek 51
Nicaragua 122
"The Night of the Curlews" (García Márquez) 94
No One Writes to the Colonel (García Márquez) 20, 24, 26–27, 31, 47, 67, 71, 84–86, 112, 116
No One Writes to the Colonel (play) 116
No One Writes to the Colonel and Other Stories (García Márquez) 20, 84, 86
Nobel Prize Lecture *See* "The Solitude of Latin America"
Notas de prensa, 1980–1984 (García Márquez) 101
Noticia de un secuestro (García Márquez). See *News of a Kidnapping*
La novela en América Latina: Diálogo (García Márquez) 90

O

O'Gorman, Edmundo 142
O'Hara, J. D. 51
Obra periodistica (García Márquez) 94
The Obscene Bird of Night (Donoso) 26
Oedipus Rex (Sophocles) 14, 53, 105, 127, 129
Of Love And Other Demons (García Márquez) 51
Ohana, Claudia 115

Ojos de perro azul (García Márquez) 91, 94
El olor de la guayaba: Conversaciones con Plinio Apuleyo Mendoza (García Márquez). See *The Fragrance of Guava*
"One Day After Saturday" (García Márquez) 20, 31, 86–87, 110
One Hundred Years of Solitude (García Márquez) 7–8, 11–12, 19–20, 27–33, 36, 39–40, 46–50, 52–53, 55–56, 60, 64, 67–68, 72, 78, 81, 87, 89, 92–93, 106–107, 109, 114, 117, 126–127, 135, 137–139, 148–153
"One of These Days" (García Márquez) 85–86, 91
Operacion Carlota (García Márquez) 94
"The Other Side of Death" (García Márquez) 94
El otoño del patriarca (García Márquez). See *The Autumn of the Patriarch*

P

Pachón, Maruja 73–74, 103
Padilla, Herberto 9
Palencia, Cayetano 113
Papas, Irene 115
Paradiso (Lima) 135
Paris Review 10, 38
Pastrana, Andrés 75–76
Periodismo militante (García Márquez) 94
Perón, Juan Domingo 69
Persecución y muerte de minorías: dos perspectivas polémicas (García Márquez & Nolasco-Juarez) 96
The Philosopher's Stone (Balzac) 52
Pigafetta, Antonio 120
Pinilla, Rojas 15, 90
The Plague (Camus) 77, 127
Plato 140
Playboy 20
Poe, Edgar Allan 138
Porrua, Paco 27
Prensa Latina 8, 18
The President (Asturias) 135, 137
Primeros Reportajes (García Márquez) 101
"La prodigiosa tarde de Baltazar". *See* "Balthazar's Marvelous Afternoon"
Proust, Marcel 138, 140
"Purloined Letter" (Poe) 147
Pynchon, Thomas 50, 138–139

Q

Quiroga, Vasco de 143

R

Rabassa, Gregory 83, 85, 87, 91, 94
La Raison 16
"El rastro de tu sangre en la nieve" (García
  Márquez). *See* "The Trail of Your Blood
  in the Snow"
*El rastro de tu sangre en la nieve; El verano
  feliz de la Señora Forbes* (García
  Márquez) 95
Reasons of State (Carpentier) 137–138
La Recherche d'absolu (Balzac). See *The
  Philosopher's Stone*
El recurso del método (Carpentier). See
  Reasons of State
El reino de este mundo (Carpentier). See
  The Kingdom of this World 138
Relato de un naúfrago (García Márquez).
  See *The Story of a Shipwrecked Sailor*
Revista de Bellas Artes 104
Ripstein, Arturo 104
Roa Bastos, Augusto 137
Rojas Pinilla, Gustavo 69
Roosevelt, Theodore 72
"Rosas artificiales" (García Márquez). *See*
  "Artificial Roses"
Rosi, Francesco 115
Rulfo, Juan 26, 135
Rushdie, Salman 138

S

Sabato, Ernesto 26
"The Saint" (García Márquez) 101
Santander, Francisco de Paula 63
Saturday Night Thief 105
Saturday Review 50
"The Sea of Lost Time" (García Márquez)
  94
El secuestro: Relato cinematográfico (García
  Márquez) 95
Senna, Orlando 105
"Un señor muy viejo con unas alas
  enormes" (García Márquez) 91, 116
Un señor muy viejo con unas alas enormes
  (motion picture) 116

El señor presidente (Asturias). See *The Pres-
  ident*
"Seventeen Poisoned Englishmen" (García
  Márquez) 102
Sheppard, R. Z. 51
A Short History of the World (Wells) 16
"La siesta del martes" (García Márquez).
  See "Big Mama's Funeral: Tuesday
  Siesta"
Simon, Claude 134
Simons, Marlise 125
"Sleeping Beauty and the Airplane"
  (García Márquez) 101
Socrates 141
"The Solitude of Latin America" (García
  Márquez) 120–124
"'Sólo vine a hablar por teléfono'" (García
  Márquez). *See* "'I only came to use the
  phone'"
"Someone Has Been Disarranging These
  Roses" (García Márquez) 94
Sophocles 14, 53, 105
The Sound and The Fury (Faulkner) 137
Stalin, Joseph 92
Steiner, George 147
Stone, Peter 38
The Story of a Shipwrecked Sailor (García
  Márquez) 15, 27, 90–91, 117
Strange Pilgrims: Twelve Stories (García
  Márquez) 38, 41, 101
Streitfield, David 50
Sturrock, John 50
Swann's Way (Proust) 140
Swedish Academy of Letters 123

T

Tavora, Salvador 116
Tebar, Juan 105
Textos consteños (García Márquez) 94
"There Are No Thieves in this Town"
  (García Márquez) 86
"The Third Resignation" (García Márquez)
  13, 94
Three Trapped Tigers (Cabrera Infante) 135
Tiempo de morir 104
Time 49, 51
Tirando Banderas (Valle Inclan). See *The
  Tyrant (Tirano Banderas): A Novel of
  Warm Lands* 138
TLS: The Times Literary Supplement 50, 52

Todos los cuentos de Gabriel García Márquez, 1947-1972 (García Márquez) 93

Torres Restrepo, Camilo 16–18, 71, 83, 108

Torrijos, Omar 9, 110

"The Trail of Your Blood in the Snow" (García Márquez) 102

"Tramontana" (García Márquez) 102

Triana, Jorge Ali 104–105

Truffaut, François 14

The Two Way Mirror 105

The Tyrant (Tirano Banderas): A Novel of Warm Lands (Valle Inclan) 138

Vargas, Germán 14

Velasco, Luis Alejandro 14, 27, 90

El verano de la señora Forbes 116

"El verano feliz de la señora Forbes" (García Márquez). *See* "Miss Forbes's Summer of Happiness"

Village Voice 117

Vinyes, Ramon 14, 111

La Violencia en Colombia: Estudio de un Proceso Social 108

"La viuda de Montiel". *See* "Montiel's Widow"

La viuda de Montiel (motion picture) 115

Viva Sandino (García Márquez) 95

U

"El último viaje del buque fantasma" (García Márquez) 91

Ulysses (Joyce) 13, 138

"Un día de estos" (García Márquez). *See* "One of These Days"

"Un día después del sábado". *See* "One Day after Saturday"

United Fruit Company 10, 66–67, 72, 83, 88, 110, 135

United States 122

El Universal 14

Urdaneta, Rafael 64

Uribe, Rafael Uribe 76, 112

Utopia (More) 143

W

Washington Post 50

Washington Post Book World 51

Wells, H. G. 16

"The Woman Who Came at Six O'clock" (García Márquez) 94

Wood, Michael 30, 65, 106

Woolf, Virginia 13–14, 36, 106, 138

Wright, Ann 95

Wright, Ronald 52

Y

Yo el Supremo (Roa Bastos) 137

Yo soy el que tu buscas 105

V

Valencia, Guillermo León 70

Valle Inclan, Ramon del 138

Vargas Llosa, Mario 8, 19, 26, 50, 90, 105, 107–108, 135, 151

Vargas, Cortés 67

Z

Zapata, Emiliano 152

Zatz, Asa 96